Another to you
for us' gift.

Happy Mother's Day!

Love,

Gretchen

May 1981

THE LORD GOD
MADE THEM ALL

THE LORD GOD MADE THEM ALL

By James Herriot

ST. MARTIN'S PRESS · NEW YORK

Copyright © 1981 by James Herriot
For information, write: St. Martin's Press,
175 Fifth Avenue, New York, N.Y. 10010
Manufactured in the United States of America
Library of Congress Cataloging in Publication Data
Herriot, James.
The Lord God made them all.
1. Herriot, James 2. Veterinarians—England
—Biography. I. Title.
SF613.H44A34   636.089'092'4 [B]   80-29097
ISBN 0-312-49834-2

Design by Nancy Dale Muldoon
10 9 8 7 6 5 4 3 2 1
First Edition

TO ZOE
latest beautiful grandchild

All things bright and beautiful,
All creatures great and small,
All things wise and wonderful,
The Lord God made them all.
—Cecil Frances Alexander, 1818–1895

THE LORD GOD
MADE THEM ALL

Chapter
1

When the gate fell on top of me I knew I was really back home.

My mind drifted effortlessly back to the days before my spell in the R.A.F., and I recalled the last time I had visited the Ripleys. It was to "nip some calves," as Mr. Ripley said over the phone, or more correctly to emasculate them by means of the Burdizzo bloodless castrator, and with his summons I realised that a large part of my morning had gone.

It was always something of a safari to visit Anson Hall, because the old house lay at the end of a ridged and rutted track that twisted across the fields through no fewer than seven gates.

Gates are one of the curses of a country vet's life and in the Yorkshire Dales, before the coming of cattle grids, we suffered more than most. We were resigned to opening two or three on many farms but seven was a bit much. And at the Ripleys' it wasn't just the number but the character.

The first one, which led off the narrow road, was reasonably normal—an ancient thing of rusty iron—but when unlatched it, it did at least swing round, groaning on its hinges. It was the only one that swung; the others were of wood and of the type known in the Dales as "shoulder gates." I could see how they got their name as I hoisted each one up, balanced the top spar on my shoulder and dragged it round. These had no hinges but were tied at one end with binder twine, top and bottom.

Even with an ordinary gate there is a fair amount of work involved. You have to stop the car, get out, open the gate, drive through, stop the car again, dismount and close the thing behind you. But the road to Anson Hall was hard labour. The gates deteriorated progressively as I approached the farm, and I was puffing with my efforts as I bumped and rattled my way up to number seven.

This was the last and the most formidable—a malignant entity with a personality of its own. Over decades it had been patched and repaired with so many old timbers that probably none of the original structure remained. But it was dangerous.

I got out of the car and advanced a few steps. We were old foes, this gate and I, and we faced each other for some moments in the silence. We had fought several brisk rounds in the past and there was no doubt the gate was ahead on points.

The difficulty was that, apart from its wobbly, loosely nailed eccentricity, it had only one string hinge, halfway down. This enabled it to pivot on its frail axis with deadly effect.

With the utmost care I approached the right-hand side and began to unfasten the binder twine. The string, I noted bitterly, like all the others was neatly tied in a bow, and as it fell clear I grabbed hastily at the top spar. But I was too late. Like a live thing the bottom rail swung in and rapped me cruelly on the shins, and as I tried to correct the balance the top bashed my chest.

It was the same as all the other times. As I hauled it round an inch at a time, the gate buffeted me high and low. I was no match for it.

It was no help to see Mr. Ripley watching me benevolently from the farmhouse doorway. While I wrestled the gate open, contented puffs rose from the farmer's pipe and he did not stir from his position until I had hobbled over the last stretch of grass and stood before him.

"Now then, Mr. Herriot, you've come to nip me a few calves?" A smile of unaffected friendship creased the stubbled cheeks. Mr.

Ripley shaved once a week— on market day— considering, with some logic, that since only his wife and his cattle saw him on the other six days there was no point in scraping away at his face every morning with a razor.

I bent and massaged my bruised ankles. "Mr. Ripley, that gate! It's a menace! Do you remember that last time I was here you promised me faithfully you'd have it mended? In fact you said you'd get a new one—it's about time, isn't it?"

"Aye, you're right, young man," Mr. Ripley said, nodding his head in profound agreement. "Ah did say that, but tha knaws, it's one o' them little jobs which never seem to get done." He chuckled ruefully, but his expression altered to concern when I wound up my trouser leg and revealed a long abrasion on my shin.

"Eee, that's a shame; that's settled it. There'll be a new gate on there by next week. Ah'll guarantee it."

"But Mr. Ripley, that's exactly what you said last time when you saw the blood running down my knee. Those were your very words. You said you'd guarantee it."

"Aye, I knaw, I knaw." The farmer tamped down the tobacco with his thumb and got his pipe going again to his satisfaction. "Me missus is allus on to me about me bad memory, but don't worry, Mr. Herriot, I've had me lesson today. I'm right sorry about your leg, and that gate'll never bother ye again. Ah guarantee it."

"Okay, okay," I said and limped over to the car for the Burdizzo. "Where are the calves, anyway?"

Mr. Ripley crossed the farmyard unhurriedly and opened the half door on a loose box. "They're in there."

For a moment I stood transfixed as a row of huge, shaggy heads regarded me impassively over the timbers, then I extended a trembling finger. "Do you mean those?"

The farmer nodded happily. "Aye, them's them."

I went forward and looked into the box. There were eight strapping yearlings in there, some of them returning my stare with mild interest, others cavorting and kicking up their heels among the straw. I turned to the farmer. "You've done it again, haven't you?"

"Eh?"

"You asked me to come and nip some calves. Those aren't calves, they're bulls! And it was the same last time. Remember those monsters you had in the same box? I nearly ruptured myself closing the nippers, and you said you'd get them done at three months old in future. In fact you said you'd guarantee it."

The farmer nodded solemnly in agreement. He always agreed one hundred percent with everything I said. "That's correct, Mr. Herriot. That's what ah said."

"But these animals are at least a year old!"

Mr. Ripley shrugged and gave me a world-weary smile. "Aye, well, time gets on, doesn't it? Fairly races by."

I returned to the car for the local anaesthetic. "All right," I grunted as I filled the syringe. "If you can catch them I'll see what I can do." The farmer lifted a rope halter from a hook on the wall and approached one of the big beasts, murmuring encouragingly. He snared the nose with surprising ease, dropping the loops over nose and horn with perfect timing as the animal tried to plunge past him. Then he passed the rope through a ring on the wall and pulled it tight.

"There y'are, Mr. Herriot. That wasn't much trouble was it?"

I didn't say anything. I was the one who was going to have the trouble. I was working at the wrong end, nicely in range of the hooves which would surely start flying if my patients didn't appreciate having a needle stuck into their testicles.

Anyway, it had to be done. One by one I infiltrated the scrotal area with the local, taking the blows on my arms and legs as they came. Then I started the actual process of castration, the bloodless crushing of the spermatic cord without breaking the skin. There was no doubt this was a big advance on the old method of incising the scrotum with a knife and in little calves it was a trifling business lasting only a few seconds.

[4]

But it was altogether different with these vast creatures. It was necessary to open the arms of the Burdizzo beyond right angles to grip the great fleshy scrotum, and then they had to be closed again. That was when the fun started.

Thanks to my injection the beast could feel little or nothing, but as I squeezed desperately it seemed that I was attempting the impossible. However, it is amazing what the human frame can accomplish when pushed to the utmost, and as the sweat trickled down my nose and I gasped and strained, the metal arms inched closer until the jaws finally clicked together.

I always nipped each side twice, and I took a rest before repeating the process lower down the cord. When I had done the same with the other testicle I flopped back against the wall, panting and trying not to think of the other seven beasts still to do.

It was a long, long time before I got to the last one and I was wrestling away, pop-eyed and open-mouthed, when the idea came to me.

I straightened up and came along the side of the animal. "Mr. Ripley," I said breathlessly, "why don't you have a go?"

"Eh?" The farmer had been watching me with equanimity, blowing out slow clouds of blue smoke, but it was plain that I had jolted him out of his composure. "What d'ye mean?"

"Well, this is the last one, and I want you to understand what I've been talking about. I'd like to see you close those nippers."

He thought the matter over for a moment or two. "Aye, but who's goin' to hold t'beast?"

"That's all right," I said. "We'll tie him up short to the ring and I'll set everything up for you, then we'll see how you get on."

He looked a little doubtful but I was determined to make my point and ushered him gently to the rear end of the animal. I enclosed the scrotum in the Burdizzo and placed Mr. Ripley's fingers round the handles.

"Right," I said. "Off you go."

The farmer took a long breath, braced himself and began to exert pressure on the metal arms. Nothing happened.

I stood there for several minutes as his face turned red, then purple, his eyes protruded even further than mine and the veins on his forehead stood out in livid ridges. Finally he gave a groan and dropped to his knees.

"Nay, lad, nay, it's no good, I can't do it."

He got to his feet slowly and mopped his brow.

"But Mr. Ripley." I put a hand on his shoulder and smiled kindly at him. "You expect me to do it."

He nodded dumbly.

"Ah well, never mind," I said. "You understand now what I've been talking about. This is an easy little job made difficult by leaving it until the beasts are as big as this. If you'd called me out when they were calves of three months, I'd have been on and off your place in a few minutes, wouldn't I?"

"Aye, you would, Mr. Herriot, you're right. I've been daft, and I'll see it doesn't happen again."

I felt really clever. I don't often have moments of inspiration, but the conviction swelled in me that one of them had come to me today. I had finally got through to Mr. Ripley.

The feeling of exhilaration gave me added strength and I finished the job effortlessly. As I walked to the car I positively glowed, and my self-satisfaction deepened when the farmer bent to the window as I started the engine.

"Well, thank ye, Mr. Herriot," he said. "You've taught me summat this mornin. Next time ye come I'll have a nice new gate for ye and I'll never ask ye to nip big beasts like that again. Ah guarantee it."

All that had happened a long time ago, before the R.A.F., and I was now in the process of reinserting myself into civilian life, tasting the old things I had almost forgotten. But at the moment when the phone rang I was tasting something very near to my heart—Helen's cooking.

It was Sunday lunchtime, when the traditional roast beef and Yorkshire pudding were served. My wife had just dropped a slab of the pudding on my plate and was pouring gravy over it, a rich, brown flood with the soul of the meat in it and an aroma to dream of. I was starving, after a typical country vet's Sunday morning of rushing round the farms and I was thinking, as I often did, that if I had some foreign gourmet to impress with the choicest sample of our British food, then this is what I would give him.

A great chunk of Yorkshire pud and gravy was the expedient of the thrifty farmers to fill their families' stomachs before the real meal started—"Them as eats most puddin' gets most meat," was the wily encouragement—but it was heaven. And as I chewed my first forkful I was happy in the knowledge that when I had cleared my plate Helen would fill it again with the beef itself and with potatoes, peas and runner beans gathered from our garden that morning.

The shrilling phone cut cruelly into my reverie, but I told myself that nothing was going to spoil this meal. The most urgent job in veterinary practice could wait until I had finished.

But my hand shook as I lifted the receiver, and a mixture of anxiety and disbelief flowed through me as I heard the voice at the other end. It was Mr. Ripley. Oh please, no, not that long, long trek to Anson Hall on a Sunday.

The farmer's voice thundered in my ear. He was one of the many who still thought you had to bawl lustily to cover the miles between.

"Is that vitnery?"

"Yes, Herriot speaking."

"Oh, you're back from t'war, then?"

"Yes, that's right."

"Well, ah want ye out here right away. One of me cows is right bad."

"What's the trouble? Is it urgent?"

"Aye, it is! I think she's maybe broke 'er leg!"

I held the ear piece away from me. Mr. Ripley had increased his volume, and my head was beginning to ring. "What makes you think that?" I asked, suddenly dry-mouthed.

"Well, she's on three legs," the farmer blasted back at me. "And t'other's sort of hangin', like."

Oh God, that sounded horribly significant. I looked sadly across the room at my loaded plate. "All right, Mr. Ripley, I'll be along."

"You'll come straight away, won't ye? Right now?" The voice was an importunate roar.

"Yes, I'll come straight away." I put down the receiver, rubbed my ear and turned to my wife.

Helen looked up from the table with the stricken face of a woman who can visualise her Yorkshire pudding sagging into lifeless ruin. "Oh surely you don't have to go this minute?"

"I'm sorry, Helen, this is one of those things I can't leave." I could picture only too easily the injured animal plunging around in her agony, perhaps compounding the fracture. "And the man sounds desperate. I've just got to go."

My wife's lips trembled. "All right, I'll put it in the oven till you come back."

As I left I saw her carrying the plate away. We both knew it was the end. No Yorkshire pud could survive a visit to Anson Hall.

I increased my speed as I drove through Darrowby. The cobbled market place, sleeping in the sunshine, breathed its Sunday peace and emptiness with all the inhabitants of the little town eating busily behind closed doors. Out in the country the dry stone walls flashed by as I kept my foot on the boards, and when I finally arrived at the beginning of the farm track I had a sense of shock.

It was the first time I had been there since I had left the service, and I suppose I had been expecting to find something different. But the old iron gate was just the same, except that it was even more rusty than before. With a growing feeling of doom I fought my way through the other gates, untying the strings and shouldering the top spars round till finally I came to number seven.

This last and most terrible of the gates was still there, and unchanged. It couldn't be true, I told myself as I almost tiptoed towards it. All sorts of things had happened to me since I had last

[8]

seen it. I had been away in a different world of marching and drilling and learning navigation and finally flying an aeroplane, while this rickety structure stood there unheeding.

I eyed it closely. The loose-nailed wobbly timbers were as before, as was the single string hinge—probably the same piece of string. It was unbelievable. And then I noticed something different. Mr. Ripley, apparently worried lest his livestock might rub against and damage the ancient bastion, had festooned the thing with barbed wire.

Maybe it had mellowed with time. It couldn't be as vicious as before. Gingerly I loosened the bottom string on the right-hand side, then with infinite care I untied the bow at the top. I was just thinking that it was going to be easy when the binder twine fell away and the gate swung with all its old venom on the left-hand string.

It got me on the chest first, then whacked against my legs, and this time the steel barbs bit through my trousers. Frantically I tried to throw the thing away from me, but it pounded me high and low and when I leaned back to protect my chest, my legs slid from under me and I fell on my back. And as my shoulders hit the track, the gate, with a soft woody crunch, fell on top of me.

I had been nearly underneath this gate several times in the past and had got clear at the last moment, but this time it had really happened. I tried to wriggle out, but the barbed wire had my clothing in its iron grip. I was trapped.

I craned desperately over the timbers. The farm was only fifty yards away, but there was not a soul in sight. And that was a funny thing. Where was the anxious farmer? I had expected to find him pacing up and down the yard, wringing his hands, but the place seemed deserted.

I dallied with the idea of shouting for help, but that would have been just too absurd. There was nothing else for it. I seized the top rail in both hands and pushed upwards, trying to close my ears to the tearing sounds from my garments, then, very slowly, I eased my way to safety.

I left the gate lying where it was. Normally I meticulously close all gates behind me but there were no cattle in the fields and anyway, I had had enough of this one.

I rapped sharply at the farmhouse door and Mrs. Ripley answered.

"Now then, Mr. Herriot, it's grand weather," she said. Her carefree smile reminded me of her husband's as she wiped at a dinner plate and adjusted the apron around her ample midriff.

"Yes . . . yes . . . it is. I've called to see your cow. Is your husband in?"

She shook her head. "Nay, 'e hasn't got back from t'Fox and Hounds yet."

"What!" I stared at her. "That's the pub at Diverton, isn't it? I thought he had an urgent case for me to see."

"Aye, well, he had to go across there to ring ye up. We haven't no telephone here, ye know." Her smile widened.

"But—but that was nearly an hour since. He should have been back here long ago."

"That's right," she said, nodding with perfect understanding. "But he'll 'ave met some of his pals up there. They all get into t'Fox and Hounds on a Sunday mornin'."

I churned my hair around. "Mrs. Ripley, I've left my meal lying on the table so that I could get here immediately!"

"Oh, we've 'ad ours," she replied, as though the words would be a comfort to me. And she didn't have to tell me. The rich scent drifting from the kitchen was unmistakably roast beef, and there was no doubt at all it would have been preceded by Yorkshire pudding.

I didn't say anything for a few moments, then I took a deep breath. "Well, maybe I can see the cow. Where is she, please?"

Mrs. Ripley pointed to a box at the far end of the yard.

"She's in there." As I set off across the cobbles she called after me. "You can be lookin' at her till 'e gets back. He won't be many minutes."

I flinched as though a lash had fallen across my shoulders.

[10]

Those were dreadful words. "Not many minutes" was a common phrase in Yorkshire and could mean anything up to two hours.

I opened the half-door and looked into the box at the cow. She was very lame, but when I approached her she hopped around in the straw, dotting the injured limb on the ground.

Well, she hadn't a broken leg. She couldn't take her weight on it, but there was none of the typical dangling of the limb. I felt a surge of relief. In a big animal a fracture usually meant the humane killer because no number of plaster bandages could take the strain. The trouble seemed to be in her foot but I couldn't catch her to find out. I'd have to wait for Mr. Ripley.

I went out into the afternoon sunshine and gazed over the gently rising fields to the church tower of Diverton pushing from the trees. There was no sign of the farmer and I walked wearily beyond the buildings onto the grass to await his coming.

I looked back at the house, and even through my exasperation I felt a sense of peace. Like many of the older farms, Anson Hall had once been a noble manor. Hundreds of years ago some person of title had built his dwelling in a beautiful place. The roof looked ready to fall in and one of the tall chimney stacks leaned drunkenly to one side, but the mullioned windows, the graceful arched doorway and the stately proportions of the building were a delight, with the pastures beyond stretching towards the green fells.

And that garden wall. In its former glory the sun-warmed stones would have enclosed a cropped lawn with bright flowers, but now there were only nettles. Those nettles fascinated me; a waist-high jungle filling every inch of space between wall and house. Farmers are notoriously bad gardeners but Mr. Ripley was in a class by himself.

My reverie was interrupted by a cry from the lady of the house. "He's comin', Mr. Herriot. I've just spotted 'im through the window." She came round to the front and pointed towards Diverton.

Her husband was indeed on his way, a black dot moving unhurriedly down through the fields and we watched him together for about fifteen minutes until at last he squeezed himself through a gap in a wall and came up to us, the smoke from his pipe rising around his ears.

I went straight into the attack. "Mr. Ripley, I've been waiting a long time! You asked me to come straight away!"

"Aye, ah knaw, ah knaw, but I couldn't very well ask to use t'phone without havin' a pint, could I?" He put his head on one side and beamed at me, secure in his unanswerable logic.

I was about to speak when he went on. "And then Dick Henderson bought me one, so I had to buy 'im one back, and then I was just leavin' when Bobby Talbot started on about them pigs he got from me last week."

His wife chipped in with bright curiosity. "Eee, that Bobby Talbot! Was he there this mornin', too? He's never away from t'pub, that feller. I don't know how his missus puts up with it."

"Aye, Bobby was there, all right. He allus is." Mr. Ripley smiled gently, knocked his pipe out against his heel and began to refill it. "And ah'll tell you who else ah saw—Dan Thompson. Haven't seen 'im since his operation. By gaw, it has fleeced him —he's lost a bit o' ground. Looks as though a few pints would do 'im good."

"Dan, eh?" Mrs. Ripley said eagerly. "That's good news, any road. From what I heard they thought he'd never come out of t'hospital."

"Excuse me," I broke in.

"Nay, nay, that was just talk," Mr. Ripley continued. "It was nobbut a stone in t'kidney. Dan'll be all right. He was tellin' me . . ."

I held up a hand. "Mr. Ripley, can I please see this cow? I haven't had my lunch yet. My wife put it back in the oven when you phoned."

"Oh, I 'ad mine afore I went up there." He gave me a reassuring smile and his wife nodded and laughed to put my mind fully at rest.

"Well, that's splendid," I said frigidly. "I'm glad to hear that."

[12]

But I could see that they took me at my word. The sarcasm was lost on them.

In the loose box Mr. Ripley haltered the cow and I lifted the foot. Cradling it on my knee I scraped away the caked muck with a hoof knife and there, glinting dully as the sunshine slanted in at the door, was the cause of the trouble. I seized the metal stud with forceps, dragged it from the foot and held it up.

The farmer blinked at it for a few seconds, then his shoulders began to shake gently. "One of me own hobnails. Heh, heh, heh. Well, that's a rum un. Ah must've knocked it out on t'cobbles; they're right slippery over there. Once or twice I've nearly gone arse over tip. I was sayin' to t'missus just t'other day . . ."

"I really must get on, Mr. Ripley," I interposed. "Remember, I still haven't had my lunch. I'll just slip out to the car for an antitetanus injection for the cow."

I gave her the shot, dropped the syringe into my pocket and was on my way across the yard when the farmer called after me.

"Have ye got your nippers with ye, Mr. Herriot?"

"Nippers . . .?" I halted and looked back at him. I couldn't believe this. "Well, yes, I have, but surely you don't want to start castrating calves now?"

The farmer flicked an ancient brass lighter and applied a long sheet of flame to the bowl of his pipe. "There's nobbut one, Mr. Herriot. Won't take a minute."

Ah, well, I thought, as I opened the boot and fished out the Burdizzo from its resting place on my calving overall. It didn't really matter now. My Yorkshire pudding was a write-off, a dried-up husk by now, and the beef and those gorgeous fresh vegetables would be almost cremated. All was lost, and nipping a calf wasn't going to make any difference.

As I turned back, a pair of double doors at the end of the yard burst open and an enormous black animal galloped out and stood looking around him warily in the bright sunshine, pawing the ground and swishing his tail bad-temperedly. I stared at the spreading horns, the great hump of muscle on the shoulder and

[13]

the coldly glittering eyes. It only needed a blast on a trumpet and sand instead of cobbles and I was in the Plaza de Toros in Madrid.

"Is that the calf?" I asked.

The farmer nodded cheerfully. "Aye, that's 'im. I thowt I'd better run 'im over to the cow house so we could tie 'im up by the neck."

A wave of rage swept over me and for a moment I thought I was going to start shouting at the man, then, strangely, I felt only a great weariness.

I walked over to him, put my face close to his and spoke quietly. "Mr. Ripley, it's a long time since we met, and you've had plenty of opportunities to keep the promise you made me then. Remember? About getting your calves nipped when they were little and about replacing that gate? Now look at that great bull and see what your gate has done to my clothes."

The farmer gazed with genuine concern at the snags and tears in my trousers and reached out to touch a gaping rent in my sleeve.

"Eee, I'm right sorry about that." He glanced at the bull. "And I reckon 'e is a bit big."

I didn't say anything and after a few moments the farmer threw up his head and looked me in the eye, a picture of resolution.

"Aye, it's not right," he said. "But ah'll tell ye summat. Just nip this 'un today, and I'll see nowt of this ever happens again."

I wagged a finger at him. "But you've said that before. Do you really mean it this time?"

He nodded vigorously. "Ah'll guarantee it."

Strangely, the familiar hollow promise did not irk me as I might have expected. Perhaps it was because I'd been away from Yorkshire so long, seeing a world changing faster than I sometimes liked, but this homely sign of immutability tickled me. I chuckled. And then I began to laugh. "A-ha," I bubbled, "a-ha-ha-ha!" Soon Mrs. Ripley got caught up with it. "Hee!" she agreed. "Hee-hee! Hee-hee!" And Mr. Ripley took his pipe from his mouth with great deliberation and said, "Heh. Heh-heh. Heh-

heh-heh." And the three of us stood there, bawling away a Sunday afternoon together.

Just then the bull snorted derisively.

"Aye, it's true," Mr. Ripley stammered through his laughter, wiping his eyes. "If ah was in your place, I wouldn't be laughing either."

Chapter
2

"Oooh . . . ooh-hoo-hooo!" The broken-hearted sobbing jerked me into full wakefulness. It was 1 A.M., and after the familiar jangling of the bedside phone I expected the gruff voice of a farmer with a calving cow. Instead, there was this terrible sound.

"Who is this?" I asked a little breathlessly. "What on earth is the trouble?"

I heard a gulping at the other end and then a man's voice pleading between sobs, "It's Humphrey Cobb. For God's sake, come out and see Myrtle. I think she's dyin'."

"Myrtle?"

"Aye, me poor little dog. She's in a 'ell of a state! Oooh-hooo!"

The receiver trembled in my grasp. "What is she doing?"

"Oh, pantin' and gaspin'. I think it's nearly all over with 'er. Come quick!"

"Where do you live?"

"Cedar House. End of Hill Street."

"I know it. I'll be there very soon."

"Oh, thank ye, thank ye. Myrtle hasn't got long. Hurry, hurry!"

I leaped from the bed and rushed at my clothes, draped over a chair against the wall. In my haste, in the darkness, I got both feet down one leg of my working corduroys and crashed full length on the floor.

Helen was used to nocturnal calls and often she only half

awoke. For my part, I always tried to avoid disturbing her by dressing without switching on the light, using the glow from the night light we kept burning on the landing for young Jimmy.

However, the system broke down this time. The thud of my falling body brought her into a sitting position.

"What is it, Jim? What's happening?"

I struggled to my feet. "It's all right, Helen, I just tripped over." I snatched my shirt from the chair back.

"But what are you dashing about for?"

"Desperately urgent case. I have to hurry."

"All right, Jim, but you won't get there any sooner by going on like this. Just calm down."

My wife was right, of course. I have always envied those vets who can stay relaxed under pressure. But I wasn't made that way.

I galloped down the stairs and through the long back garden to the garage. Cedar House was only a mile away and I didn't have much time to think about the case, but by the time I arrived I had pretty well decided that an acute dyspnoea like this would probably be caused by a heart attack or some sudden allergy.

In answer to my ring the porch light flashed on, and Humphrey Cobb stood before me. He was a little round man in his sixties, and his humpty-dumpty appearance was accentuated by his gleaming bald head.

"Oh, Mr. Herriot, come in, come in," he cried brokenly as the tears streamed down his cheeks. "Thank ye for gettin' out of your bed to help me poor little Myrtle."

As he spoke, the blast of whisky fumes almost made my head spin and I noticed that as he preceded me across the hall he staggered slightly.

My patient was lying in a basket by the side of an Aga cooker in a large, well-appointed kitchen. I felt a warm surge when I saw that she was a beagle like my own dog, Sam. I knelt down and looked at her closely. Her mouth was open and her tongue lolled, but she did not seem to be in acute distress. In fact, as I patted her head her tail flapped against the blanket.

[17]

A heart-rending wail sounded in my ear. "What d'ye make of her, Mr. Herriot? It's her heart, isn't it? Oh, Myrtle, Myrtle!" The little man crouched over his pet, and the tears flowed unchecked.

"You know, Mr. Cobb," I said. "She doesn't seem all that bad to me, so don't upset yourself too much. Just give me a chance to examine her."

I placed my stethoscope over the ribs and listened to the steady thudding of a superbly strong heart. The temperature was normal, and I was palpating the abdomen when Mr. Cobb broke in again.

"The trouble is," he gasped, "I neglect this poor little animal."

"What do you mean?"

"Well, ah've been all day at Catterick at the races, gamblin' and drinkin', with never a thought for me dog."

"You left her alone all that time in the house?"

"Nay, nay, t'missus has been with her."

"Well, then." I felt I was getting out of my depth. "She would feed Myrtle and let her out in the garden?"

"Oh aye," he said, wringing his hands. "But I shouldn't leave 'er. She thinks such a lot about me."

As he spoke, I could feel one side of my face tingling with heat. My problem was suddenly solved.

"You've got her too near the Aga," I said. "She's panting because she's uncomfortably hot."

He looked at me doubtfully. "We just shifted 'er basket today. We've been gettin' some new tiles put down on the floor."

"Right," I said. "Shift it back again and she'll be fine."

"But Mr. Herriot." His lips began to tremble again. "It's more than that. She's sufferin'. Look at her eyes."

Myrtle had the lovely big liquid eyes of her breed and she knew how to use them. Many people think the spaniel is number one when it comes to looking soulful, but I personally plump for the beagle. And Myrtle was an expert.

"Oh, I shouldn't worry about that, Mr. Cobb," I said. "Believe me, she'll be all right."

He still seemed unhappy. "But aren't ye going to do something?"

It was one of the great questions in veterinary practice. If you didn't "do something," they were not satisfied. And in this case, Mr. Cobb was in greater need of treatment than his pet. Still, I wasn't going to stick a needle into Myrtle just to please him so I produced a vitamin tablet from my bag and pushed it over the back of the little animal's tongue.

"There you are," I said. "I'm sure that will do her good." And after all, I thought, I wasn't a complete charlatan—it wouldn't do her any harm.

Mr. Cobb relaxed visibly. "Eee, that's champion. You've set me mind at rest." He led the way into a luxurious drawing room and tacked unsteadily towards a cocktail cabinet. "You'll 'ave a drink before you go?"

"No, really, thanks," I said. "I'd rather not, if you don't mind."

"Well, I'll 'ave a drop. Just to steady me nerves. I was that upset." He tipped a lavish measure of whisky into a glass and waved me to a chair.

My bed was calling me, but I sat down and watched as he drank. He told me that he was a retired bookmaker from the West Riding and that he had come to Darrowby only a month ago. Although no longer directly connected with horse racing, he still loved the sport and never missed a meeting in the north of England.

"I allus get a taxi to take me and I have a right good day." His face was radiant as he recalled the happy times, then for a moment his cheeks quivered and his woebegone expression returned. "But I neglect me dog. I leave her at home."

"Oh nonsense," I said. "I've seen you out in the fields with Myrtle. You give her plenty of exercise, don't you?"

"Oh aye, lots of walks every day."

"Well, then she really has a good life. This is just a silly little notion you've got."

He beamed at me and sloshed out another few fingers of

whisky. "Eee, you're a good lad. Come on, you'll just have one before you go."

"Oh, all right, just a small one, then."

As we drank he became more and more benign until he was gazing at me with something like devotion.

"James Herriot," he slurred. "I suppose it'll be Jim, eh?"

"Well, yes."

"I'll call you Jim, then, and you can call me Humphrey."

"Okay, Humphrey," I said, and swallowed the last of my whisky. "But I really must go now."

Out in the street he put a hand on my arm and his face became serious again. "Thank ye, Jim. Myrtle was right bad tonight and I'm grateful."

Driving away, I realised that I had failed to convince him that there was nothing wrong with his dog. He was sure I had saved her life. It had been an unusual visit and as my 2 A.M. whisky burned in my stomach I decided that Humphrey Cobb was a very funny little man. But I liked him.

After that night I saw him quite frequently, exercising Myrtle in the fields. With his almost spherical build he seemed to bounce over the grass, but his manner was always self-contained and rational, except that he kept thanking me for pulling his dog back from the jaws of death.

Then quite suddenly I was back at the beginning again. It was shortly after midnight and as I lifted the bedside phone, I could hear the distraught weeping before the receiver touched my ear.

"Oooh . . . oooh . . . Jim, Jim. Myrtle's in a terrible bad way. Will ye come?"

"What . . . what is it this time?"

"She's twitchin'."

"Twitching?"

"Aye, twitchin' summat terrible. Oh, come on, Jim, lad, don't keep me waiting. I'm worried to death. I'm sure she's got distemper." He broke down again.

[20]

My head began to reel. "She can't have distemper, Humphrey. Not in a flash, like that."

"I'm beggin' you, Jim," he went on as though he hadn't heard. "Be a pal. Come and see Myrtle."

"All right," I said wearily. "I'll be there in a few minutes."

"Oh, you're a good lad, Jim, you're a good lad. . . ." The voice trailed away as I replaced the phone.

I dressed at normal speed with none of the panic of the first time. It sounded like a repetition, but why after midnight again? On my way to Cedar House I decided it must be another false alarm—but you never knew.

The same dizzying wave of whisky fumes enveloped me in the porch. Humphrey, sniffling and moaning, fell against me once or twice as he ushered me into the kitchen. He pointed to the basket in the corner.

"There she is," he said, wiping his eyes. "I've just got back from Ripon and found 'er like this."

"Racing again, eh?"

"Aye, gamblin' on them 'osses and drinkin' and leavin' me poor dog pinin' at home. I'm a rotter, Jim, that's what I am."

"Rubbish, Humphrey! I've told you before. You're not doing her any harm by having a day out. Anyway, how about this twitching? She looks all right now."

"Yes, she's stopped doing it, but when I came in her back leg was goin' like this." He made a jerking movement with his hand.

I groaned inwardly. "But she could have been scratching or flicking away a fly."

"Nay, there's summat more than that. I can tell she's sufferin'. Just look at them eyes."

I could see what he meant. Myrtle's beagle eyes were pools of emotion, and it was easy to read melting reproach in their depths.

With a feeling of futility I examined her. I knew what I would find—nothing. But when I tried to explain to the little man that his pet was normal, he wouldn't have it.

[21]

"Oh, you'll give her one of them wonderful tablets," he pleaded. "It cured her last time."

I felt I had to pacify him, so Myrtle received another installment of vitamins.

Humphrey was immensely relieved and weaved his way to the drawing room and the whisky bottle.

"I need a little pick-me-up after that shock," he said. "You'll 'ave one, too, won't you, Jim, lad?"

This pantomime was enacted frequently over the next few months, always after race meetings and always between midnight and 1 A.M. I had ample opportunity to analyse the situation, and I came to a fairly obvious conclusion.

Most of the time Humphrey was a normal conscientious pet owner, but after a large intake of alcohol his affectionate feelings degenerated into glutinous sentimentality and guilt. I invariably went out when he called me because I knew that he would be deeply distressed if I refused. I was treating Humphrey, not Myrtle.

It amused me that not once did he accept my protestations that my visit was unnecessary. Each time he was sure that my magic tablets had saved his dog's life.

Mind you, I did not discount the possibility that Myrtle was deliberately working on him with those eyes. The canine mind is quite capable of disapproval. I took my own dog almost everywhere with me, but if I left him at home to take Helen to the cinema he would lie under our bed, sulking, and, when he emerged, would studiously ignore us for an hour or two.

I quailed when Humphrey told me he had decided to have Myrtle mated because I knew that the ensuing pregnancy would be laden with harassment for me.

That was how it turned out. The little man flew into a series of alcoholic panics, all of them unfounded, and he discovered imaginary symptoms in Myrtle at regular intervals throughout the nine weeks.

I was vastly relieved when she gave birth to five healthy pups. Now, I thought, I would get some peace. The fact was that I was just about tired of Humphrey's nocturnal nonsense. I have always made a point of never refusing to turn out at night, but Humphrey had stretched this principle to breaking point. One of these times he would have to be told.

The crunch came when the pups were a few weeks old. I had had a terrible day, starting with a prolapsed uterus in a cow at 5 A.M. and progressing through hours of road slogging, missed meals and a late-night wrestle with ministry forms, some of which I suspected I had filled up wrongly.

My clerical incompetence has always infuriated me and when I crawled, dog-tired, into bed, my mind was still buzzing with frustration. I lay for a long time, trying to put those forms away from me, and it was well after midnight when I fell asleep.

I have always had a silly fancy that our practice knew when I desperately wanted a full night's sleep. It knew and gleefully stepped in. When the phone exploded in my ear, I wasn't really surprised.

As I stretched a weary hand to the receiver, the luminous dial of the alarm clock read 1:15 A.M.

"Hello," I grunted.

"Oooh . . . oooh . . . oooh!" The reply was only too familiar.

I clenched my teeth. This was just what I needed. "Humphrey! What is it this time?"

"Oh, Jim, Myrtle's really dyin', I know she is. Come quick, lad, come quick!"

"Dying?" I took a couple of rasping breaths. "How do you make that out?"

"Well . . . she's stretched out on 'er side, tremblin'."

"Anything else?"

"Aye, t'missus said Myrtle's been lookin' worried and walkin' stiff when she let her out in the garden this afternoon. I'm not long back from Redcar, ye see."

"So you've been to the races, eh?"

"That's right . . . neglectin' me dog. I'm a scamp, nothin' but a scamp."

I closed my eyes in the darkness. There was no end to Humphrey's imaginary symptoms. Trembling, this time, looking worried, walking stiff. We'd had panting and twitching and head nodding and ear shaking—what would it be next?

But enough was enough. "Look, Humphrey," I said. "There's nothing wrong with your dog. I've told you again and again . . ."

"Oh, Jim, lad, don't be long. Oooh-hooo!"

"I'm not coming, Humphrey."

"Nay, nay, don't say that! She's goin' fast, I tell ye!"

"I really mean it. It's just wasting my time and your money, so go to bed. Myrtle will be fine."

As I lay quivering between the sheets, I realised that refusing to go out was an exhausting business. There was no doubt in my mind that it would have taken less out of me to get up and attend another charade at Cedar House than to say no for the first time in my life. But this couldn't go on. I had to make a stand.

I was still tormented by remorse when I fell into an uneasy slumber, and it is a good thing that the subconscious mind works on during sleep because with the alarm clock reading 2:30 A.M. I came suddenly wide awake.

"My God!" I cried, staring at the dark ceiling. "Myrtle's got eclampsia!"

I scrambled from the bed and began to throw on my clothes. I must have made some commotion because I heard Helen's sleepy voice.

"What is it? What's the matter?"

"Humphrey Cobb!" I gasped, tying a shoe lace.

"Humphrey . . . but you said there was never any hurry . . ."

"There is this time. His dog's dying." I glared again at the clock. "In fact, she could be dead now." I lifted my tie, then hurled it back on the chair. "Damn it! I don't need that!" I fled from the room.

Down the long garden and into the car with my brain spelling out the concise case history which Humphrey had given me. Small bitch nursing five puppies, signs of anxiety and stiff gait this afternoon, and now prostrate and trembling. Classical puerperal eclampsia. Rapidly fatal without treatment. And it was nearly an hour and a half since he had phoned. I couldn't bear to think about it.

Humphrey was still up. He had obviously been consoling himself with the bottle because he could barely stand.

"You've come, Jim, lad," he mumbled, blinking at me.

"Yes, how is she?"

"Just t'same . . ."

Clutching my calcium and my intravenous syringe, I rushed past him into the kitchen.

Myrtle's sleek body was extended in a tetanic spasm. She was gasping for breath, quivering violently, and bubbles of saliva dripped from her mouth. Those eyes had lost their softness and were fixed in a frantic stare. She looked terrible, but she was alive . . . she was alive.

I lifted the squealing pups onto a rug nearby and quickly clipped and swabbed the area over the radial vein. I inserted the needle into the blood vessel and began to depress the plunger with infinite care and very slowly. Calcium was the cure for this condition but a quick blast would surely kill the patient.

I took several minutes to empty the syringe, then sat back on my heels and watched. Some of these cases needed narcotics as well as calcium, and I had nembutal and morphine ready to hand. But as the time passed, Myrtle's breathing slowed down and the rigid muscles began to relax. When she started to swallow her saliva and look round at me, I knew she would live.

I was waiting for the last tremors to disappear from her limbs when I felt a tap on my shoulder. Humphrey was standing there with the whisky bottle in his hand.

"You'll 'ave one, won't you, Jim?"

I didn't need much persuading. The knowledge that I had almost been responsible for Myrtle's death had thrown me into a mild degree of shock.

My hand was still shaking as I raised the glass, and I had barely taken the first sip when the little animal got up from the basket and walked over to inspect her pups. Some eclampsias were slow to respond but others were spectacularly quick, and I was grateful for the sake of my nervous system that this was one of the quick ones.

In fact the recovery was almost uncanny because, after sniffing her family over, Myrtle walked across the table to greet me. Her eyes brimmed with friendliness and her tail waved high in the true beagle fashion.

I was stroking her ears when Humphrey broke into a throaty giggle. "You know, Jim, I've learned summat tonight." His voice was a slow drawl but he was still in possession of his wits.

"What's that, Humphrey?"

"I've learned . . . hee-hee-hee . . . I've learned what a silly feller I've been all these months."

"How do you mean?"

He raised a forefinger and wagged it sagely. "Well, you've allus been tellin' me that I got you out of your bed for nothin' and I was imaginin' things when I thought me dog was ill."

"Yes," I said. "That's right."

"And I never believed you, did I? I wouldn't be told. Well, now I know you were right all the time. I've been nobbut a fool, and I'm right sorry for botherin' you all those nights."

"Oh, I shouldn't worry about that, Humphrey."

"Aye, but it's not right." He waved a hand towards his bright-faced, tail-wagging little dog. "Just look at her. Anybody can see there was never anythin' wrong with Myrtle tonight."

[26]

Chapter
3

The high moorland road was unfenced, and my car wheels ran easily from the strip of tarmac onto the turf, cropped to a velvet closeness by the sheep. I stopped the engine, got out and looked around me.

The road cut cleanly through the grass and heather before dipping into the valley beyond. This was one of the good places where I could see into two dales, the one I had left and the one in front. The whole land was spread beneath me; the soft fields in the valley floors, the grazing cattle, the rivers pebbled at their edges in places, thickly fringed with trees at others.

The brilliant green of the walled pastures pushed up the sides of the fells until the heather and the harsh moor grass began, and only the endless pattern of walls was left, climbing to the mottled summits, disappearing over the bare ridges that marked the beginning of the wild country.

I leaned back against the car and the wind blew the cold sweet air around me. I had been back in civilian life only a few weeks, and during my time in R.A.F. blue I had thought constantly of Yorkshire, but I had forgotten how beautiful it was. Just thinking from afar could not evoke the peace, the solitude, the sense of the nearness of the wild that makes the Dales thrilling and comforting at the same time. Among the crowds of men and the drabness and stale air of the towns, my imagination could not sufficiently conjure up a place where I could be quite alone on the wide green roof of England where every breath was filled with the grass scent.

I had had a disturbing morning. Everywhere I had gone I was reminded that I had come back to a world of change, and I did not like change. One old farmer saying, "It's all t'needle now, Mr. Herriot," as I injected his cow had made me look down almost with surprise at the syringe in my hand, realising suddenly that this was what I was doing most of the time now.

I knew what he meant. Only a few years ago I would more likely have "drenched" his cow. Grabbed it by the nose and poured a pint of medicine down its throat.

We still carried a special drenching bottle around with us—an empty wine bottle because it had no shoulders and allowed the liquid to run more easily. Often we would mix the medicine with black treacle from the barrel that stood in the corner of most cow byres.

All this was disappearing, and the farmer's remark about "all t'needle" brought it home to me once more that things were never going to be the same again.

A revolution had begun in agriculture and in veterinary practice. Farming had become more scientific, and concepts cherished for generations were being abandoned, while in the veterinary world the first rivulets of the flood of new advances were being felt.

Previously undreamed-of surgical procedures were being carried out, the sulpha drugs were going full blast and, most exciting of all, the war, with its urgent need for better treatment of wounds, had given a tremendous impetus to the development of Sir Alexander Fleming's discovery of penicillin. This, the first of the antibiotics, was not yet in the hands of the profession except in the form of intramammary tubes for the treatment of mastitis, but it was the advance guard of the therapeutic army that was to sweep our old treatments into oblivion.

There were signs, too, that the small farmer was on the way out. These men, some with only six cows, a few pigs and poultry, still made up most of our practice and they were the truly rich characters, but they were beginning to wonder if they could make a living on this scale, and one or two had sold out to the bigger men. In our practice now, in the eighties, there are virtually no small farmers left. I can think of only a handful — old men doggedly doing the things they have always done for the sole reason that they have always done it. They are the last remnants of the men I cherished, living by the ancient values, speaking the old Yorkshire dialect that television and radio have swamped.

I took a last long breath and got into my car. The uncomfortable feeling of change was still with me but I looked through the window at the great fells thrusting their bald summits into the clouds, tier upon tier of them, timeless, indestructible, towering over the glories beneath, and I felt better immediately. The Dales had not changed at all.

I did one more call, then drove back to Skeldale House to see if there were any more visits before lunch.

All was new here, too. My partner, Siegfried, had married and was living a few miles outside Darrowby, and Helen and I with our little son, Jimmy, were installed in the practice headquarters. When I got out of the car I gazed up at the ivy climbing over the mellow brick to the little rooms that looked out from under the tiles to the hills. Helen and I had started our married life in those rooms but now we had the run of the whole house. It was too big for us, of course, but we were happy to be there because we both loved the old place, with its spaciousness and its Georgian elegance.

The house looked much the same as when I had first seen it those years ago. The only difference was that they had taken the iron railings away for scrap metal during the war, and our plates were now hanging on the wall.

Helen and I slept in the big room which I had occupied in my bachelor days, and Jimmy was in the dressing room where Siegfried's student brother, Tristan, used to rest his head. Tristan, alas, had left us. When the war ended, he was Captain Farnon of the Royal Army veterinary corps. He married and joined the Ministry of Agriculture as an infertility investigation officer. He left a sad gap in our lives, but fortunately we still saw him and his wife regularly.

I opened the front door and in the passage, the fragrance of *pulv aromat* was strong. It was the aromatic powder we mixed with our medicaments, and it had an excitement for me. It always seemed to be hanging about the house. It was the smell of our trade.

Halfway along the passage I passed the doorway to the long high-walled garden and turned into the dispensary. This was a room whose significance was already on the wane. The rows of beautifully shaped glass bottles with their Latin titles engraved on them looked down at me—*spiritus Aetheris Nitrosi, Liquor Ammonii Acetatis Fortis, Potassii Nitras, Sodii Salicylas.* Noble names. My head was stuffed with hundreds of them, their properties, actions and uses, and their dosage in horse, ox, sheep, pig, dog and cat. But soon I would have to forget them all and concern myself only with how much of the latest antibiotic or steroid to administer.

Some years were to pass before the steroids arrived on the scene, but they, too, would bring another little revolution in their wake.

As I left the dispensary I almost bumped into Siegfried. He was storming along the passage and he grabbed my arm in an agitated manner.

"Ah, James, just the man I was looking for! I've had the most ghastly time this morning. I knocked the exhaust off my car going up that bloody awful track to High Liston, and now I'm without transport. They've sent for a new exhaust, but until it arrives and they get it fitted I'm stuck. It's maddening!"

"That's all right, Siegfried. I'll do your calls."

"No, no, James, it's kind of you, but don't you see, this sort of thing is going to happen again and again. That's what I wanted to talk to you about. We need a spare car."

[30]

"A spare?"

"That's right. Doesn't have to be a Rolls Royce. Just something to fall back upon at a time like this. As a matter of fact, I rang Hammond at the garage to bring round something suitable for us to look at. I think I can hear him outside now."

My partner was always one for instant action, and I followed him to the front door. Mr. Hammond was there with the vehicle for our inspection. It was a 1933 Morris Oxford, and Siegfried trotted down the steps towards it.

"A hundred pounds, you said, eh, Mr. Hammond?" He walked around the car a couple of times, picking pieces of rust from the black paintwork, opening the doors and peering at the upholstery. "Ah, well, it's seen better days, but the appearance doesn't matter as long as it goes all right."

"It's a sound little job, Mr. Farnon," the garage proprietor said. "Re-bored two thousand miles ago and don't use hardly any oil. New battery and a good bit o' tread on the tyres." He adjusted the spectacles on his long nose, drew his thin frame upright and adopted a businesslike expression.

"Mmmm." Siegfried shook the rear bumper with his foot, and the old springs groaned. "How about the brakes? Important in this hilly country."

"They're champion, Mr. Farnon. First-rate."

My colleague nodded slowly. "Good, good. You don't mind if I drive her round the block, do you?"

"Nay, nay, of course not," Mr. Hammond replied. "Give 'er any trial you like." He was a man who prided himself on his imperturbability, and he dropped confidently into the passenger seat as Siegfried took the wheel.

"Hop in the back, James!" my partner cried. I opened the rear door and took my place behind Mr. Hammond in the musty interior.

Siegfried took off abruptly with a roaring and creaking from the old vehicle, and despite the garage man's outward calm I saw the back of his shirt collar rise a couple of inches above his blue serge jacket as we shot along Trengate.

The collar subsided a little when Siegfried slowed down at the church to make a left turn but reappeared spasmodically as we negotiated a series of sharp and narrow bends at top speed.

When we reached the long straight lane that runs parallel to Trengate Mr. Hammond appeared to relax, but when Siegfried put his foot on the boards and sent the birds squawking from the overhanging branches as he thundered beneath them, I saw the collar again.

When we reached the end of the lane, Siegfried came almost to a halt as he turned left.

"I think we'll test the brakes, Mr. Hammond," he said cheerfully and hurled the car suddenly along the home straight for Trengate. He really meant to carry out a thorough test. The roar of the ancient engine rose to a scream, and as the street approached with frightening rapidity the collar reappeared, then the shirt.

When Siegfried stood on the brakes, the car slewed violently to the right, and as we catapulted crabwise into Trengate, Mr. Hammond's head was jammed against the roof and his entire shirt back was exposed. When we came to a halt, he slid slowly back into his seat, and the jacket took over again. At no time had he spoken or, apart from his up-and-down movements, shown any emotion.

At the front door of the surgery we got out, and my colleague rubbed his chin doubtfully. "She does pull a little to the right on braking, Mr. Hammond. I think we'd need to have that rectified. Or perhaps you have another vehicle available?"

The garage man did not answer for a few moments. His spectacles were askew, and he was very pale. "Aye . . . aye . . ." he said shakily. "I 'ave another little job over there. It might suit you."

"Capital!" Siegfried rubbed his hands. "Perhaps you'd bring it along after lunch, and we can have a spin round to try it."

Mr. Hammond's eyes widened, and he swallowed a few times.

"Right . . . right, Mr. Farnon. But I'm goin' to be busy this afternoon. I'll send one of me men."

We bade him goodbye and went back into the house. Walking along the passage, my partner put an arm across my shoulders. "Well, James, another step towards increasing the efficiency of the practice. Anyway," he smiled and whistled a few cheerful bars, "I rather enjoy these little interludes."

Suddenly I began to feel good. So many things were new and different, but the Dales hadn't changed, and Siegfried hadn't changed either.

Chapter
4

"A voyage to Russia!" I stared at John Crooks.

Siegfried and I worked alone in the practice during the immediate postwar years, and this book is about that period. In 1951 John Crooks came to us as assistant and three years later left to set up his own practice in Beverley. Before he departed he paid us the charming compliment of "filling" a bottle with the air from Skeldale House, to be released in his new surgery with the object of transferring some of our atmosphere. Sometime in the future I shall write about John's spell in Darrowby, but at the moment I should like to jump forward in time to 1961 in order to interpolate some extracts from the journal I kept of my Russian adventure.

John was behind it. Although he no longer worked for us, he came back often as a friend and he had been describing some of his experiences in exporting animals from Hull. He often sailed with these animals as veterinary attendant, but it was the Russian thing that caught my imagination.

"That must have been very interesting," I said.

John smiled. "Oh yes, fascinating. I've been out there several times now and it's the real Russia, with the lid off, not a tour of the showplaces they want you to see. You get a glimpse of the country through the eyes of a seaman, and you meet the ordinary Russians, the commercial people, the workers."

"Sounds great!"

"And you get paid for it, too," John went on. "That makes it even better."

I sighed. "You're a lucky beggar. And these jobs come up pretty regularly?"

"Yes, they do." He looked at me closely, and I suppose my expression must have been wistful. "Would you like to have a go sometime?"

"Do you mean it?"

"Of course," he said. "Just say the word and you can sail on the next one. That'll be sometime around the end of October."

I thumped my fist into my palm. "Book me in, John. It's really kind of you. Country vetting is fine but sometimes I feel I'm sliding into a rut. A trip to Russia is just what I need."

"Well, that's grand." John stood up and prepared to leave. "I'll let you know the details later, but I believe you'll be sailing with a cargo of valuable sheep—breeding animals. The insurance company is bound to insist on veterinary supervision."

For a few weeks I went around in a fever of anticipation, but there were many people who didn't share my enthusiasm.

One cowman cocked an eye at me. "Ah wouldn't go there for a bloody big clock," he said. "One wrong word and you'll find yourself in t'nick for a long, long time."

He had a definite point. East-West relations were at one of their lowest ebbs at that time and I grew used to my clients making it clear that Russia was one place they would avoid. In fact, when I told Colonel Smallwood about it when I was tuberculin-testing his cattle a few days before I left, he raised his eyebrows and gave me a cold stare.

"Nice to have known you," he murmured.

But I have seafarers' blood in my veins going back several generations, and I felt only happy expectation.

October 28, 1961

The first day has come and gone. When I walked onto the

[35]

quayside at Hull, I saw our ship right in front of me. She is Danish, the *Iris Clausen* of 300 tons, and my first sensation is of mild shock that she is so small. I had cherished a mental picture of a substantial vessel for such a voyage.

When I first saw her at the dockside, only the bows and a portion of deck were visible. This part looked tiny, and a high superstructure obscured what I surmised must be the greater part of the ship. I walked along past this superstructure and experienced a moment of disquiet. I found that the ship ends right there. There just isn't any more.

To my untutored eyes, the *Iris Clausen* looked like a toy oil tanker, and it was difficult to imagine her crossing an ocean or weathering a storm.

The cargo of sheep had just been loaded and the decks were littered with straw. When I went into the little mess room I saw the captain, who was called Rasmussen, sitting at the head of the table around which were grouped representatives of the export company and two Russian veterinary surgeons who had been inspecting the sheep.

The table itself was heavily laden with a wonderful variety of Danish open sandwiches, beer, whisky, schnapps and other drinks, and with mountains of forms which everybody was furiously signing.

One of the Russians, a bespectacled little man, apparently realised who I was, because he came up and with a smile said, "Veterinary surgeon," and shook my hand warmly. His colleague, tall and gaunt, was painstakingly going through the forms and saying nothing.

The chief man from the export people informed me that not only am I to be the medical attendant to the 383 pedigree Romney Marsh and Lincoln sheep we are carrying, but I have also to deal with the Russians at our port of destination, Klaipeda. I have to bring back five acceptance forms signed by the Russians and myself, otherwise the company will not get paid.

"How much are the sheep worth?" I asked.

[36]

The export man's mouth twitched up at one corner. "Twenty thousand pounds."

My stomach lurched. It was a fortune. This was a responsibility I hadn't foreseen.

When the crowd had cleared, Captain Rasmussen and I were left alone in the room. He introduced himself charmingly and I was immediately attracted by his gentle manner. He is smallish, silver-haired and speaks excellent English.

He waved me to the chair by his side. "Sit down, Mr. Herriot, and let us talk."

We spoke about our families, then about the job in hand.

"This is a motor ship," said the captain. "Built for the sole purpose of transporting animals. There are two decks below with pens for the sheep. Perhaps you would like to see your charges?"

As we left the mess room I noticed that the captain was limping slightly. He smiled as he saw me looking down at his feet.

"Yes, I broke my ankle a few months ago. Fell down the steps from the bridge to my cabin during a storm. Silly of me."

I wondered if I would be doing any falling about over the next week or so. We walked around the sheep. Beautiful animals, all of them, and they were very comfortable, well bedded in straw and with lots of sweet hay to eat. The ventilation was just right and the atmosphere pleasantly warm.

When I left the captain, I was agreeably surprised at the first sight of my cabin. No doubt those on passenger liners are more sumptuous, but there is a bunk with spotless sheets and pillows, a desk, armchair and sofa, a wash basin, fitted wardrobe, two cupboards and a lot of drawers. The whole place is done out in shining light oak. I am very impressed with my temporary home.

I opened my suitcase. Only a tiny part of it was taken up by my personal effects; the rest was filled with the things I thought I might need. My black P.V.C. working coat, bottles of calcium, antibiotics and steroids, scalpel, scissors, suture materials, bandages, cotton wool and syringes.

I looked down thoughtfully at the limited array. Would I find it too meagre or would I not need any of it? The following days would tell me.

We took on the pilot at 8 P.M., and at 9 P.M. I heard some activity outside my window. I looked out and saw two of the crew winching up the anchor.

I went up on deck to watch our departure. The night was very dark, and the dockside was deserted. A cat scurried through the light thrown by a single street lamp but nothing else stirred. Then our siren gave a loud blast and I could see we were moving very slowly away from the quay. We glided through the narrow outlet of the dock, then began to head quite swiftly towards the mouth of the Humber, two miles away.

As I stood on the deck I could see several other ships sailing out on the evening tide, some quite close, cleaving through the water abreast of us only a few hundred yards away, a graceful and thrilling sight.

Away behind, the lights of Hull receded rapidly, and I was looking at their faint glitter beyond the stretch of dark water when I felt a touch on my arm.

It was a young sailor, and he grinned cheerfully as I turned round. "Doctor," he said. "You show me how to feed the sheeps?"

I must have looked puzzled because his grin widened as he explained. "Many times I sail with cattles and pigs but never with sheeps."

I understood and motioned him to lead on. Like all the crew, he was a Dane, big, fair-haired, typically Nordic, and I followed his broad back down to the animals' pens. He listened intently as I gave him the information about feeding and watering, especially about how much concentrates to give. I was particularly pleased to see that as well as the fine-quality hay, there was an abundance of a top-class brand of sheep nuts in big paper sacks.

While he got on with his work, I looked around at the animals which would be under my care. Most of them were Romney Marsh, and as the engines throbbed and the deck vibrated under my feet I marvelled again at their attractiveness. They had great woolly heads like teddy bears, and their eyes, soft and incurious, looked back at me as they lay in the straw or nibbled at their food.

Before coming down here to my cabin, I had an irresistible urge to return to the upper deck and look around. I have sea captains among my uncles and a great grandfather who was a ship's pilot and the sea has always had a pull for me. In the darkness I walked around the deck. This wasn't easy because there is only a narrow strip, twenty-five yards long, on either side.

The moon had come out, casting a cold white brilliance on the water of the river estuary. Far on the starboard side, a long row of lights glimmers—probably Grimsby. On the port side, about three hundred yards away, a ship sped silently through the night, keeping pace exactly with us. I watched her for a long time, but her position never varied and she was still there when I came down.

My cabin is now a place of shakes and shudders, of indefinable bumps, rattles and groans. As I write, I know for sure that we are now well out to sea because I am very aware of the rolling of the ship.

I have had an experimental lie in my bunk, and this is where the rolling is most noticeable. From side to side it goes, side to side, over and over again. At one time there was some talk of Helen coming with me on this trip, and I smile to myself at the thought. This wouldn't suit her at all—she soon becomes queasy sitting in the back of a car. But to me the gentle motion is like the rocking of a cradle. I know I shall sleep well.

Chapter
5

"Hello! Hello!" I bellowed.

"Hello! Hello!" little Jimmy piped just behind me.

I turned and looked at my son. He was four years old now and had been coming on my rounds with me for over a year. It was clear that he considered himself a veteran of the farmyards, an old hand versed in all aspects of agricultural lore.

This shouting was a common habit of mine. When a vet arrived on a farm, it was often surprisingly difficult to find the farmer. He might be a dot on a tractor half a mile across the fields; on rare occasions he might be in the house, but I always hoped to find him among the buildings, and I relied on a few brisk shouts to locate him.

Certain farms in our practice were for no apparent reason distinctive in that you could never find anybody around. The house door would be locked, and we would scour the barns, cow-houses and fold yards while our cries echoed back at us from the unheeding walls. Siegfried and I used to call them the "no-finding" places and they were responsible for a lot of wasted time.

Jimmy had caught on to the problem quite early, and there was no doubt he enjoyed the opportunity to exercise his lungs a bit. I watched him now as he strutted importantly over the cobbles, giving tongue every few seconds. He was also making an unnecessary amount of noise by clattering on the rough stones with his new boots.

Those boots were his pride, the final recognition of his status as veterinary assistant. When I first began to take him round with me, his initial reaction was the simple joy of a child at being able to see animals of all kinds, particularly the young ones—the lambs, foals, piglets, calves—and the thrill of discovery when he came upon a huddle of kittens in the straw or found a bitch with pups in a loose box.

Before long, however, he began to enlarge his horizons. He wanted to get into the action. The contents of my car boot were soon as familiar to him as his toy box at home, and he delighted in handing out the tins of stomach powder, the electuaries and red blisters, the white lotion and the still-revered long cartons of Universal Cattle Medicine. Finally he began to forestall me by rushing back to the car for the calcium and flutter valve as soon as he saw a recumbent cow. He had become a diagnostician as well.

I think the thing he enjoyed most was accompanying me on an evening call, if Helen would allow him to postpone his bedtime. He was in heaven driving into the country in the darkness, training my torch on a cow's teat while I stitched it.

The farmers were kind, as they always are with young people. Even the most uncommunicative would grunt, "Ah see you've got t'apprentice with ye," as we got out of the car.

But those farmers had something Jimmy coveted: their big hob-nailed boots. He had a great admiration for farmers in general; strong hardy men who spent their lives in the open and who pushed fearlessly among plunging packs of cattle and slapped the rumps of massive cart horses. I could see he was deeply impressed as he watched them—quite often small and stringy—mounting granary steps with twelve or sixteen stone stacks on their shoulders, or hanging on effortlessly to the noses of huge bullocks, their boots slithering over the floor, a laconic cigarette hanging from their lips.

It was those boots that got under Jimmy's skin most of all. Sturdy and unyielding, they seemed to symbolise for him the character of the men who wore them.

Matters came to a head one day when we were conversing in the car. Or, rather, my son was doing the conversing in the form of a barrage of questions which I did my best to fend off while trying to think about my cases. These questions went on pretty well nonstop every day, and they followed a well-tried formula.

"What is the fastest train—the Blue Peter or the Flying Scotsman?"

"Well now . . . I really don't know. I should say the Blue Peter."

Then, getting into deeper water, "Is a giant train faster than a phantom racing car?"

"That's a difficult one. Let's see, now . . . maybe the phantom racer."

Jimmy changed his tack suddenly. "That was a big man at the last farm wasn't he?"

"He certainly was."

"Was he bigger than Mr. Robinson?"

We were launching into his favourite "big man" game, and I knew how it would end, but I played my part. "Oh yes, he was."

"Was he bigger than Mr. Leeming?"

"Certainly."

"Was he bigger than Mr. Kirkley?"

"Without a doubt."

Jimmy gave me a sidelong glance, and I knew he was about to play his two trump cards. "Was he bigger than the gas man?"

The towering gentleman who came to read the gas meters at Skeldale House had always fascinated my son, and I had to think very carefully about my reply.

"Well, you know, I really think he was."

"Ah, but . . ." The corner of Jimmy's mouth twitched up craftily. "Was he bigger than Mr. Thackray?"

[42]

That was the killer punch. Nobody was bigger than Mr. Thackray, who looked down on the other inhabitants of Darrowby from six feet seven inches.

I shrugged my shoulders in defeat. "No, I have to admit it. He wasn't as big as Mr. Thackray."

Jimmy smiled and nodded, well satisfied, then he began to hum a little tune, drumming his fingers on the dashboard at the same time. Soon I could see he was having trouble. He couldn't remember how it went. Patience was not his strong point, and as he tried and stopped again and again, it was plain that he was rapidly becoming exasperated.

Finally, as we drove down a steep hill into a village and another abortive session of tum-te-tum-te-tum came to an abrupt halt, he rounded on me aggressively.

"You know," he exploded, "I'm getting just about fed up of this!"

"I'm sorry to hear that, old lad." I thought for a moment. "I think it's *Lilliburlero* you're trying to get." I gave a swift rendering.

"Yes, that's it!" He slapped his knee and bawled out the melody at the top of his voice several times in triumph. This put him in such high good humour that he broached something that must have been on his mind for some time.

"Daddy," he said. "Can I have some boots?"

"Boots? But you've got some already, haven't you?" I pointed down at the little Wellingtons in which Helen always rigged him before he set out for the farms.

He gazed at his feet sadly before replying. "Yes, I know, but I want proper boots like the farmers."

This was a facer. I didn't know what to say. "But, Jim, little boys like you don't have boots like that. Maybe when you're bigger . . ."

"Oh, I want them now," he moaned in anguished tones. "I want proper boots."

At first I thought it was a passing whim, but he kept up his

[43]

campaign for several days, reinforcing it with disgusted looks as Helen drew on the Wellingtons each morning and a listless slouching to convey the message that his footwear was entirely unsuitable for a man like him.

Finally Helen and I talked it over one night after he had gone to bed.

"They surely don't have farm boots his size, do they?" I asked.

Helen shook her head. "I wouldn't have thought so, but I'll look around in any case."

And it seemed that Jimmy wasn't the only little boy to have this idea because within a week my wife returned, flushed with success and bearing the smallest pair of farm boots I had ever seen.

I couldn't help laughing. They were so tiny, yet so perfect— thick hob-nailed soles, chunky uppers and a long row of lace-holes with metal loops at the top.

Jimmy didn't laugh when he saw them. He handled them almost with awe and once he had got them on, his demeanour changed. He was naturally square-set and jaunty, but to see him striding round a farmyard in corduroy leggings and those boots you would think he owned the place. He clumped and stamped, held himself very upright and his cries of "Hello! Hello!" took on a new authority.

He was never what I would call naughty—certainly never destructive or cruel—but he had that bit of devil which I suppose all boys need to have. He liked to assert himself, and, perhaps unconsciously, he liked to tease me. If I said, "Don't touch that," he would keep clear of the object in question but later would give it the merest brush with his finger, which could not be construed as disobedience but nevertheless served to establish his influence in the household.

Also, he was not above taking advantage of me in awkward situations. There was one afternoon when Mr. Garrett brought his sheepdog in. The animal was very lame and as I hoisted him onto the table in the consulting room, a small head appeared for a moment at the window that overlooked the sunlit garden.

I didn't mind that. Jimmy often watched me dealing with our small animal patients, and I half expected him to come into the room for a closer look.

It is often difficult to locate the source of a dog's lameness, but in this case I found it immediately. When I gently squeezed the outside pad on his left foot he winced, and a tiny bead of serum appeared on the black surface.

"He's got something in there, Mr. Garrett," I said. "Probably a thorn. I'll have to give him a shot of local anaesthetic and open up his pad."

It was when I was filling the syringe that a knee came into view at the corner of the window. I felt a pang of annoyance. Jimmy surely couldn't be climbing up the wistaria. It was dangerous, and I had expressly forbidden it. The branches of the beautiful creeper curled all over the back of the house, and though they were as thick as a man's leg near ground level, they became quite slender as they made their way up past the bathroom window to the tiles of the roof.

No, I decided that I was mistaken and began to infiltrate the pad. These modern anaesthetics worked very quickly and within a minute or two I could squeeze the area quite hard without causing pain.

I reached for the scalpel. "Hold his leg up and keep it as steady as you can," I said.

Mr. Garrett nodded and pursed his lips. He was a serious-faced man at any time and obviously deeply concerned about his dog. His eyes narrowed in apprehension as I poised my knife over the telltale drop of moisture.

For me it was an absorbing moment. If I could find and remove this foreign body, the dog would be instantly rid of his pain. I had dealt with many of these cases in the past, and they were so easy, so satisfying.

[45]

With the point of my blade I made a careful nick in the tough tissue of the pad, and at that moment a shadow crossed the window. I glanced up. It was Jimmy, all right, this time at the other side, just his head grinning through the glass from halfway up.

The little blighter *was* on the wistaria, but there was nothing I could do about it then, except to give him a quick glare. I cut a little deeper and squeezed, but still nothing showed in the wound. I didn't want to make a big hole, but it was clear that I had to make a cruciate incision to see further down. I was drawing the scalpel across at right angles to my first cut when, from the corner of my eye, I spotted two feet dangling just below the top of the window. I tried to concentrate on my job but the feet swung and kicked repeatedly, obviously for my benefit. At last they disappeared, which could only mean that their owner was ascending to the dangerous regions. I dug down a little deeper and swabbed with cotton wool.

Ah yes, I could see something now, but it was very deep, probably the tip of a thorn which had broken off well below the surface. I felt the thrill of the hunter as I reached for forceps, and just then the head showed itself again, upside down this time.

My God, he was hanging by his feet from the branches, and the face was positively leering. In deference to my client, I had been trying to ignore the by-play from outside, but this was too much. I leaped at the glass and shook my fist violently. My fury must have startled the performer, because the face vanished instantly and I could hear faint sounds of feet scrambling upwards.

That was not much comfort, either. Those top branches might not support a boy's weight. I forced myself back to my task.

"Sorry, Mr. Garrett," I said. "Will you hold the leg up again, please?"

He replied with a thin smile, and I pushed my forceps into the depths. They grated on something hard. I gripped, pulled gently and—oh, lovely, lovely—out came the pointed, glistening head of a thorn. I had done it.

It was one of the tiny triumphs that lighten vet's lives and I was beaming at my client and patting his dog's head when I heard the crack from above. It was followed by a long howl of terror, then a small form hurtled past the window and thudded with horrid force into the garden.

I threw down the forceps and shot out of the room, along the passage and through the side door into the garden. Jimmy was already sitting up among the wallflowers, and I was too relieved to be angry.

"Have you hurt yourself?" I gasped, and he shook his head.

I lifted him to his feet and he seemed to be able to stand all right. I felt him over carefully. There appeared to be no damage.

I led him back into the house. "Go along and see Mummy," I said and returned to the consulting room.

I must have been deathly pale when I entered because Mr. Garrett looked startled. "Is he all right?" he asked.

"Yes, yes, I think so. But I do apologise for rushing out like that. It was really too bad of me to . . ."

Mr. Garrett laid his hand on my shoulder. "Say no more, Mr. Herriot, I have children of my own." And then he spoke the words that have become engraven on my heart. "You need nerves of steel to be a parent."

Later at tea I watched my son demolishing a poached egg on toast, then he started to slap plum jam on a slice of bread. Thank heaven he was no worse for his fall, but still I had to remonstrate with him.

"Look, young man," I said. "That was a very naughty thing you did out there. I've told you again and again not to climb the wistaria."

Jimmy bit into his bread and jam and regarded me impassively. I have a big streak of old hen in my nature and down through the years, even to this day, he and later my daughter, Rosie, have recognised this and developed a disconcerting habit of making irreverent clucking noises at my over-fussiness. At this moment

I could see that whatever I was going to say he wasn't going to take too seriously.

"If you're going to behave like this," I went on, "I'm not going to take you round the farms with me. I'll just have to find another little boy to help me with my cases."

His chewing slowed down, and I looked for some reaction in this morsel of humanity who was later to become a far better veterinary surgeon than I could ever be, in fact, to quote thirty years later a dry Scottish colleague who had been through college with me and didn't mince words, "A helluva improvement on his old man."

Jimmy dropped the bread on his plate. "Another little boy?" he enquired.

"That's right. I can't have naughty boys with me. I'll have to find somebody else."

Jimmy thought this over for a minute or so, then he shrugged and appeared to accept the situation philosophically. He started again on the bread and jam.

Then in a flash his *sang froid* evaporated. He stopped in mid-chew and looked up at me in wide-eyed alarm.

His voice came out in a high quaver. "Would he have my boots?"

Chapter
6

"By gaw, it's Doctor Fu Manchu!"

The farmer dropped the buttered scone onto his plate and stared, horror-struck, through the kitchen window.

I was drinking a cup of tea with him and I almost choked in mid-sip as I followed his gaze.

Beyond the glass an enormous Oriental was standing. Slit eyes regarded us menacingly from a pock-marked face whose left cheek was hideously scarred from ear to chin, but the most arresting feature was the one-sided mustachio, black and greasy, with its single end dangling several inches from the upper lip. A robe of exotic colouring flowed from the man's shoulders and his hands, held across his body, were tucked deeply into the sleeves.

The farmer's wife screamed and jumped from the table, but I sat transfixed. I couldn't believe this apparition, framed as it was against the buildings and pastures of a Yorkshire farm.

The wife's rising screams were bordering on hysteria when suddenly she stopped and advanced slowly to the window. As she came close the big man's mouth relaxed into a friendly leer, then he withdrew a hand from the sleeve and waggled the fingers at her in Oliver Hardy fashion.

"It's Igor!" she gasped and swung round on her husband. "And that's me good house coat he's got on. You rotten devil, you put him up to this!"

The farmer rolled about in his chair, laughing helplessly. He couldn't have asked for a better response to his little joke.

Igor was one of a batch of prisoners of war who had recently arrived to work on the farm. There were hundreds of these men employed on the land at the end of the war and it was a happy arrangement all round. The farmers had a windfall in the shape of abundant labour, and the prisoners were content to spend their pre-repatriation time in the open air with ample farm meals to sustain them in a world of food rationing. I personally had a respite from one of my constant problems—the lack of help in my job. I found now that there were always willing hands to assist me in the rough-and-tumble of large-animal practice.

The prisoners were, of course, mainly German, but there were a number of Italians and, strangely, Russians. It baffled me at first when I saw hundreds of men who looked like Chinese in German uniforms disembarking at Darrowby railway station. I learned later that they were Mongolian Russians who had been pressed into fighting for the Germans and later were captured by the British. Igor was one of these.

I know of farming families who to this day spend their holidays at the homes of the Germans and Italians whom they befriended at this time.

I was still laughing after the Igor incident and the farmer was still receiving a tongue lashing from his wife when I climbed into my car and consulted the list of calls.

"Preston, Scarth Lodge, lame cow," I read. It was twenty minutes' drive away and, as always, I idly turned over the possibilities in my mind. Probably foul, maybe pus in the foot, which would entail some hacking with my hoof knife. Or it could be a strain. I'd soon see.

Hal Preston was bringing my patient in from the field as I arrived, and I didn't even have to get out of the car to make my diagnosis. It was one which gave me no joy.

The cow was hobbling slowly, her right hind foot barely touching the ground. The limb was shortened and carried underneath the body, while a bulge in the pelvic region showed where the great trochanter of the femur pushed against the skin. Upward displacement. Absolutely typical.

"Just happened this mornin'," the farmer said. "She was as right as rain last night. Ah can't think . . ."

"Say no more, Mr. Preston," I said. "I know what it is. She's got a dislocated hip."

"Is that serious?"

"Yes, it is. You see, it takes tremendous force to pull the head of the displaced bone back into its socket. Even in a dog it is a difficult job, but in cattle it's sometimes impossible."

The farmer looked glum. "That's a beggar. This is a right good cow, smashin' milker. What 'appens if you can't get it back?"

"I'm afraid she'd always be a bit of a cripple," I replied. "Dogs usually form a very good false joint, but it's different with a cow. In fact, many farmers decide to slaughter the animal."

"Oh, 'ell, I don't want that!" Hal Preston rubbed his chin vigorously. "We'll have to have a go."

"Good, that's what I want." I turned towards my car. "I'm going back to the surgery for the chloroform muzzle, and, in the meantime, will you go round your neighbours and get a few strong chaps? We'll need all the manpower we can find."

The farmer looked round the rolling green miles with not another dwelling in sight. "Me neighbours are a long way away, but I don't need 'em today. Look 'ere."

He led the way into the farm kitchen where the savoury aroma of roast bacon was heavy in the air. Four burly Germans were seated at the table. In front of each lay a plate mounded high with potatoes, cabbage, bacon and sausage.

"They've sent me these fellers to help with haytime," Mr. Preston explained. "I reckon they look pretty useful."

"They do indeed." I smiled at the men and waved my hand in greeting. They jumped to their feet and bowed. "Right," I said to the farmer, "you can be having your dinners while I'm gone. I'll be back in about half an hour."

When I returned, we led the cow to a patch of soft grass. Her progress was painfully slow as she trailed her almost useless hind leg.

I buckled the muzzle to her head and dribbled the chloroform onto the sponge. As she inhaled the strange vapour her eyes widened in surprise, then she stumbled forward and sank to the turf.

I slipped a round stake into the animal's groin and stationed the two biggest men at either end of it, then I fastened a rope above the fetlock and gave the other end to Mr. Preston and the remaining two Germans.

The stage was set. I crouched over the pelvis and placed both hands on the bulging head of the femur. Would it stay obstinately still or would I feel it riding up the side of the acetabulum on the way to its proper home?

Anyway, this was the moment, and I took a deep breath. "Pull!" I shouted, and the three men on the rope hauled away, while the brown corded arms on each side of me took the strain on the stake.

No doubt an unedifying spectacle, this tug of war with the sleeping animal in the middle. Not much science in evidence, but country practice is often like that.

However, I had no time for theorising—all my mind was concentrated on that jutting bone under my hands. "Pull!" I yelled again, and fresh grunts of effort came back in reply.

I clenched my teeth. The thing wasn't moving. I couldn't believe it could resist the terrific traction, but it was like a rock.

Then, when the feeling of defeat was rising, I felt a stirring beneath my fingers. It all happened in seconds after that—the lifting of the femoral head as I pushed frantically at it and the loud click as it flopped into its socket. We had won.

I waved my arms in delight. "All right, let go!" I crawled to the cow's head and whipped off the muzzle.

We heaved her onto her chest, and she lay there, blinking and shaking her head as consciousness returned. I could hardly wait for what is one of the most rewarding moments in veterinary practice, and it came when the cow rose to her feet and strolled over the grass without the trace of a limp. The five faces, sweating in the hot sunshine, watched in happy amazement, and though I had seen it all before, I felt the warm flush of triumph that is always new.

I handed cigarettes round the prisoners, and before I left I drew on my scanty store of German.

"*Danke schoen!*" I said fervently, and I really meant it.

"*Bitte! Bitte!*" they cried, all smiles. They had enjoyed the whole thing, and I had the feeling that this would be one of the tales they would tell when they returned to their homes.

A few days later, Siegfried and I alighted at Village Farm, Harford. We had come together because we had been told that our patient, a Red Poll bullock, was of an uncooperative disposition, and we thought that a combined operation was indicated.

The farmer led us to the fold yard where about twenty cattle were eating turnips. "That's the one," he said, pointing to an enormously fat beast, "and that's the thing I was tellin' ye about." He indicated a growth as big as a football dangling from the animal's belly.

Siegfried gave him a hard look. "Really, Mr. Harrison, you should have called us out to this long ago. Why did you let it get so big?"

The farmer took off his hat and scratched his balding head ruminatively. "Aye, well, you know how it is. Ah kept meanin' to give you a ring, but it slipped me mind and time went on."

"It's a hell of a size now," Siegfried grunted.

"Ah know, ah know. I allus had the hope that it might drop off because he's a right wild sod. You can't do much with 'im."

"All right, then." Siegfried shrugged. "Bring a halter, and we'll drive him into that box over there."

The farmer left, and my partner turned to me. "You know, James, that tumour isn't as fearsome as it looks. It's beautifully

[53]

pedunculated, and if we can get a shot of local into that narrow neck we can ligate it and have it off in no time."

The farmer returned with the halter, and he was accompanied by a dark little man in denims.

"This is Luigi," he said. "Italian prisoner. Don't speak no English, but 'e's very handy at all sorts o' jobs."

I could imagine Luigi being handy. He was short in stature, but his wide spread of shoulder and muscular arms suggested great strength.

We said hello, and the Italian returned our greetings with an inclination of his head and a grave smile. He carried an aura of dignity and self-assurance.

After a bit of galloping round the fold yard, we managed to get our patient into the box, but we soon realised that our troubles were only beginning.

Red Polls are big cattle, and an ill-natured one can be a problem. This fat creature had a mean look in his eyes, and all our attempts to halter him were unavailing. He either whipped away from the rope or shook his head threateningly at us. Once, as he thundered past me I got my fingers into his nose, but he brushed me off like a fly and lashed out with a hind leg, catching me a glancing blow on the thigh.

"He's like an elephant," I gasped. "God only knows how we're going to catch him."

The sedative injections for such animals and the metal crushes to restrain them were still years in the future, and Siegfried and I were looking gloomily at the bullock when Luigi stepped forward.

He held up a hand and loosed off a burst of Italian at us. None of us could understand him, but we took his point as he ushered us back against the wall with great ceremony. Plainly he was going to do something, but what?

He advanced stealthily on the bullock, then with a lightning movement he seized one of the ears in both hands. The animal took off immediately but without its previous abandon. Luigi was screwing the ear round on its long axis, and it seemed to act as a brake because the beast slowed to a halt and stood there, head on one side, glancing almost plaintively up at the little man.

I was reminded irresistibly of pictures of Billy Bunter being held by a Greyfriars prefect, and I almost expected the bullock to cry, "Ouch! Yaroo! Leggo my ear!"

But I didn't have much time for musing because Luigi, in full command of the situation, jerked his head towards the hanging tumour.

Siegfried and I leaped forward. We had never seen anybody catch a beast by the ear before, but we weren't going to discuss it. This was our chance.

I cradled the growth in my hands while Siegfried injected the local into the neck. As the needle entered the skin the hairy leg twitched, and under ordinary circumstances we would have been kicked out of the box, but Luigi took another half-turn on the ear and rapped out a colourful reprimand. The animal subsided immediately and stood motionless as we worked.

Siegfried applied a strong ligature and severed the neck of the growth bloodlessly with an ecraseur. The tumour thudded onto the straw. The operation was over.

Luigi released the ear and received our congratulations with a half-smile and a gracious nod of his head. He really was a man of enormous presence.

Now, more than thirty years later, Siegfried and I still talk about him. We have both tried to catch large cattle by the ears without the slightest success; so was Luigi just an amateur with wrists of steel or was he a farmer, and do they do it that way in Italy after a lifetime of practice? We still don't know.

One still summer evening I was returning from a call when I heard the sound of singing. It was a rich, swelling chorus of many voices, and it seemed to come from nowhere. I stopped the car and wound down the window. The fells rose around me, their summits glinting in the last sunshine, but the only living creatures were the cattle and sheep grazing on the walled slopes.

Then I saw Knowle Manor perched on a plateau high above, and I remembered that hundreds of Russian prisoners were billeted there.

These men were singing the songs of their homeland, but the sound drifting from the windows of the big house was not that of a casual party. There was a vast, drilled choir up there, deep voices blending in thrilling harmonies that hung and lingered on the soft air.

I sat entranced for a long time, till the light faded and the chill of nightfall made me close my window and drive away.

Years later I read that these Russians went home to death or captivity, and whenever I thought of their fate, I remembered that summer evening and the beautiful music they made in the peace of the Yorkshire hills.

Chapter
7

October 29, 1961

"Breakfast, Mr. Herriot."

I heard the mess boy's call and his knock on my cabin door. It was the first of many during this day. "Lunch, Mr. Herriot." "Dinner, Mr. Herriot." "Coffee time, Mr. Herriot." He is a fresh-faced lad of seventeen and takes care I don't miss anything.

I hurried to the mess room. To my surprise I found it was empty, but there was a large pot of coffee on the table, along with a stack of rye bread and a remarkable selection of cold meats and fish. I counted nine different platters on the table.

Well, it was an unusual breakfast but I was hungry, so I started operations immediately. The coffee was delicious, and I was happily washing down wonderful raw herring and onion, smoked ham and a particularly toothsome meat loaf when the mess boy appeared and smilingly deposited two fried eggs and bacon in front of me.

I was surprised but undeterred, and as I started my fresh attack with the ship heaving and pitching, I thanked providence that I had never known sea-sickness.

I was soon joined by two of the ship's officers, the mate, a tubby little man also called Rasmussen, and the engineer, Hansen, very dark with a humorous face.

Neither of them spoke much English, but we managed to

converse on various subjects including football pools which, when they had the chance, they both filled up assiduously without success.

After breakfast I went down to inspect my animals. The general picture was a happy one, but I noticed a sheep limping as it walked to its hay. I examined the feet and found a small area of footrot. I had been told that the Russian vets were meticulous in their examination, but they had missed that one. I directed a long jet of Terramycin aerosol at the affected spot; I was confident that a few more similar treatments would put that right before we reached Klaipeda.

Another animal blinked painfully at me as I passed its pen, and I found that its eyes were weeping and inflamed. It was the only one so affected, and I felt that it had probably picked up some irritant material on the journey to Hull. I squeezed some chloramphenicol eye ointment across the eyeballs and decided to do the same at midday and in the evening.

I finished my tour with the comforting thought that so far my stock of drugs was adequate.

Before lunch the captain asked me to drink a glass of lager with him in his cabin. He himself, despite being a man of natural refinement, drank straight from the bottle; later today I found that this was the approved method among the ship's officers, but he gave me a glass.

I sat down at the end of the table and poured the lager, and at that moment the ship gave a tremendous roll. My chair went over; I literally flew through the air, shot across the floor on my side and finished up underneath a desk in the corner. My glass was shattered, and a pool of the precious Carlsberg Special spread across the floor.

The captain leaped anxiously to my assistance. "Oh, Mr. Herriot, I hope you do not hurt yourself!" As I have said, his English is very good but occasionally little inaccuracies creep in.

"No, I'm fine," I replied, laughing. I got up and started on another bottle, but this time I kept my knees jammed against the legs of the table. I am beginning to learn.

After this little contretemps we went down to lunch, passing on the way the cook's galley. This was about the size of a large cupboard and was crammed with pans, stove, ovens and food. I wondered how anybody could possibly produce proper meals in that tiny place, and it occurred to me that perhaps that was the reason for the lavish breakfast. The other meals would probably be makeshift, and I mentally resigned myself to the fact that I would have to put up with a primitive diet during the voyage.

When we had gathered round the table in the little mess room, the first course arrived. It was an exquisite asparagus soup in which floated meat balls and large stalks of asparagus. This was followed by what the captain described as "boneless birds"— tender veal steaks wrapped around strips of bacon, parsley and spices, with anchovies draped across them. We finished off with a sago pudding thickly sprinkled with cinnamon and with peaches nestling on its bosom. As I sipped my coffee and nibbled delicious Danish cheese, I felt I might have been eating at the Ritz.

The cook, Nielsen by name, a large smiling man in a white apron, pushed his head round the door at the end of the meal, and I called out to him that his food was wonderful. He looked intensely gratified but also surprised because the other ship's officers seem to take it all for granted.

His smile grew wider, and he nodded his head rapidly. "Thank you, thank you, thank you." He stared at me as though he had been looking for me all his life. I have a feeling that I have made a friend there.

After lunch, back down to t'ween decks and lower hold, to give them their proper names, for another look at the sheep, but on the way I had to stop for a few minutes on the upper deck to take gulping breaths of the unbelievably fresh air that swept over the heaving miles of water. Walking around is difficult because I find it almost impossible to stand upright with the constant movement of the ship.

Down below I studied the animals carefully. There was something on my mind. Right at the beginning I had heard the odd cough, and I hadn't paid much attention because all sheep cough occasionally, but since we sailed, it had become more frequent and had a rasping quality that was only too familiar.

As I walked around I heard it again, and this time I traced it to the affected sheep. I climbed into the pen—all Lincolns—and began to stir them around, and after a few seconds there was a regular chorus of coughs. I knew now; they had husk.

I took a few temperatures, leaning back against the swaying wall to read the thermometer, but there was clearly no secondary infection; it was a straightforward parasitic bronchitis, and with my pitiful little stock of drugs in the suitcase upstairs there was nothing I could do about it.

Of course, as I sit here writing in my cabin, I realise it is only a mild attack and since they are off the pasture, in top condition, and with an abundant supply of good food, they will certainly throw it off in time. But for all that, I don't like it. The vets in Hull didn't spot it but those in Klaipeda probably will, and I want to present a batch of healthy animals to them.

Later, I had a most interesting hour with the captain on the bridge. He showed me how the radar and other gadgets worked and pointed out our position on the chart. We are off the coast of Holland but out of sight of land.

I was intrigued by the mariner's view of a map. The sea is a complicated mass of lines, words and figures, while the land is a white blank.

At 6:30 P.M. I began again on what I had thought was to be my frugal living. Mountains of roast chicken with a piquant stuffing I had never tasted before, surrounded by thin layers of cucumber done up with sugar and vinegar. Fruit followed, and, of course, there was the ever-present array of herring in tomato, salami, salt beef, pork, smoked ham, bacon and endless kinds of

Danish sliced sausages and cheeses. I haven't mentioned the two most popular things among the Danes themselves—the liver paste and trays of dripping.

The ship's officers seem to love these two items, especially the dripping which they spread on rye bread and eat at the end of the meal.

After dinner we settled down to a two-hour session of smoking and swopping yarns over the schnapps and beer. I gather that this is a regular custom in the evenings. The seamen are very interesting with their tales of many countries and peoples and the often startling adventures they have had on their travels.

Chapter
8

"It was Hemingway who said that, wasn't it?"

Norman Beaumont shook his head. "No, Scott Fitzgerald."

I didn't argue because Norman usually knew. In fact, it was one of the attractive things about him.

I enjoyed having veterinary students seeing practice with us. They helped with fetching and carrying, they opened gates and they were company on our lonely rounds. In return, they absorbed a lot of knowledge from us in our discussions in the car, and it was priceless experience for them to be involved in the practical side of their education.

Since the war, however, my relationships with these young men had undergone a distinct change. I found I was learning from them just about as much as they were learning from me.

The reason, of course, was that veterinary teaching had taken a leap forward. The authorities seemed to have suddenly discovered that we weren't just horse doctors and that the vast new field of small-animal work was opening up dramatically. Advanced surgical procedures were being carried out on farm animals, too, and the students had the great advantage of being able to see such things done in the new veterinary schools with their modern clinics and operating theatres.

New specialist textbooks were being written that made my own thumbed volumes with everything related to the horse seem like museum pieces. I was still a young man, but all the bursting knowledge I had nurtured so proudly was becoming irrelevant. Quittor, fistulous withers, poll evil, bog spavin, stringhalt—they didn't seem to matter much anymore.

Norman Beaumont was in his final year and was a deep well of information at which I drank greedily. But apart from the veterinary side we had a common love of books and reading.

When we weren't talking shop the conversation was usually on literary lines, and Norman's companionship lightened my days and made the journeys between farms seem short.

He was immensely likable, with a personality that was formal and dignified beyond his twenty-two years and which was only just saved from pomposity by a gentle humour. He was a solid citizen in the making if ever I saw one, and this impression was strengthened by his slightly pear-shaped physique and the fact that he was determinedly trying to cultivate a pipe.

He was having a little trouble with the pipe, but I felt sure he would win through. I could see him plainly twenty years from now, definitely tubby, sitting around the fireside with his wife and children, puffing at that pipe which he had finally subjugated; an upright, dependable family man with a prosperous practice.

As the dry stone walls rolled past the car windows, I got back onto the topic of the new operations.

"And you say they are actually doing Caesarians on cows in the college clinics?"

"Good Lord, yes." Norman made an expansive gesture and applied a match to his pipe. "Doing them like hot cakes, it's a regular thing." His words would have carried more weight if he had been able to blow a puff of smoke out after them, but he had filled the bowl too tightly and, despite a fierce sucking which hollowed his cheeks and ballooned his eyeballs, he couldn't manage a draw.

"Gosh, you don't know how lucky you are," I said. "The number of hours I've slaved on byre floors calving cows. Sawing up calves with embryotomy wire, knocking my guts out trying to

[63]

bring heads round or reach feet. I think I must have shortened my life. And if only I'd known how, I could have saved myself the trouble with a nice straightforward operation. What sort of a job is it, anyway?"

The student gave me a superior smile. "Nothing much to it, really." He relit his pipe, tamped the tobacco down and winced as he burned his finger. He shook his hand vigorously for a moment, then turned towards me. "They never seem to have any trouble. Takes about an hour, and no hard labour."

"Sounds marvellous." I shook my head wistfully. "I'm beginning to think I was born too soon. I suppose it's the same with ewes?"

"Oh yes, yes, indeed," Norman murmured airily. "Ewes, cows, sows—they're in and out of the place every day. No problem at all. Nearly as easy as bitch spays."

"Ah, well, you young lads are lucky. It's so much easier to tackle these jobs when you've seen a lot of them done."

"True, true." The student spread his hands. "But, of course, most bovine parturitions don't need a Caesarian, and I'm always glad to have a calving for my case book."

I nodded in agreement. Norman's case book was something to see; a heavily bound volume with every scrap of interesting material meticulously entered under headings in red ink. The examiners always wanted to see these books, and this one would be worth a few extra marks to Norman in his finals.

It was August Bank Holiday Sunday, and Darrowby market place had been bustling all day with holiday makers and coach parties. Each time we passed through I looked at the laughing throngs with a tiny twinge of envy. Not many people seemed to work on Sundays.

I dropped the student at his digs in late afternoon and went back to Skeldale House for tea. I had just finished when Helen got up to answer the phone.

"It's Mr. Bushell of Sycamore House," she said. "He has a cow calving."

[64]

"Oh damn. I thought we'd have Sunday evening to ourselves."
I put down my cup. "Tell him I'll be right out, Helen, will you?"
I smiled as she put down the receiver. "One thing, Norman will
be pleased. He was just saying he wanted something for his case
book."

I was right. The young man rubbed his hands in glee when I
called for him, and he was in excellent humour as we drove to the
farm.

"I was reading some poetry when you rang the bell," he said.
"I like poetry. You can always find something to apply to your life.
How about now, when I'm expecting something interesting.
'Hope springs eternal in the human breast.' "

"Alexander Pope, *Essay on Man*," I grunted. I wasn't feeling
so enthusiastic as Norman. You never knew what was ahead on
these occasions.

"Jolly good." The young man laughed. "You aren't easy to
catch out."

We drove through the farm gateway into the yard.

"You've made me think with your poetry," I said. "It keeps
buzzing in my head. 'Abandon hope all ye who enter here.' "

"Dante, of course, *The Inferno*. But don't be so pessimistic."
He patted me on the shoulder as I put on my Wellingtons.

The farmer led us into the byre, and in a stall opposite the
window a small cow looked up at us anxiously from her straw bed.
Above her head, her name, Bella, was chalked on a board.

"She isn't very big, Mr. Bushell," I said.

"Eh?" he looked at me enquiringly, and I remembered that he
was hard of hearing.

"She's a bit small," I shouted.

The farmer shrugged. "Aye, she allus was a poor doer. Had a
rough time with her first calvin', but she milked well enough after
it."

I looked thoughtfully at the cow as I stripped off my shirt and
soaped my arms. I didn't like the look of that narrow pelvis, and

I breathed the silent prayer of all vets that there might be a tiny calf inside.

The farmer poked at the light roan hairs of the rump with his foot and shouted at the animal to make her rise.

"She won't budge, Mr. Herriot," he said. "She's been painin' all day. Ah doubt she's about buggered."

I didn't like the sound of that either. There was always something far wrong when a cow strained for a long time without result. And the little animal did look utterly spent. Her head hung down and her eyelids drooped wearily.

Ah well, if she wouldn't get up, I had to get down. With my bare chest in contact with the ground, the thought occurred that cobbles didn't get any softer with the passage of the years. But when I slid my hand into the vagina, I forgot about my discomfort. The pelvic opening was villainously narrow, and beyond was something that froze my blood: two enormous hooves and, resting on their cloven surfaces, a huge expanse of muzzle with twitching nostrils. I didn't have to feel anymore, but with an extra effort I strained forward a few inches, and my fingers explored a bulging brow squeezing into the small space like a cork in a bottle. As I withdrew my hand, the rough surface of the calf's tongue flicked briefly against my palm.

I sat back on my heels and looked up at the farmer. "There's an elephant in there, Mr. Bushell."

"Eh?"

I raised my voice. "A tremendous calf, and no room for it to come out."

"Can't ye cut it away?"

"Afraid not. The calf's alive and, anyway, there's nothing to get at. No room to work."

"Well, that's a beggar," Mr. Bushell said. "She's a good little milker. Ah don't want to send 'er to the butcher."

Neither did I. I hated the very thought of it, but a great light was breaking beyond a new horizon. It was a moment of decision, of history. I turned to the student.

"This is it, Norman! The ideal indication for a Caesar. What a good job I've got you with me. You can keep me right."

I was slightly breathless with excitement, and I hardly noticed the flicker of anxiety in the young man's eyes.

I got to my feet and seized the farmer's arm. "Mr. Bushell, I'd like to do a Caesarian operation on your cow."

"A what?"

"A Caesarian. Open her up and remove the calf surgically."

"Tek it out o' the side, d'ye mean? Like they do wi' women?"

"That's right."

"Well that's a rum' un." The farmer's eyebrows went up. "I never knew you could do that wi' cows."

"Oh, we can now," I said airily. "Things have moved on a bit in the last few years."

He rubbed a hand slowly across his mouth. "Well, ah don't know. I reckon she'd die if you made a bloody great 'ole in her like that. Maybe she'd be better goin' for slaughter. I'd get a few quid for her and I allus think fust loss is best."

I could see my big moment slipping away from me. "But she's only a thin little thing. She wouldn't be worth much for meat, and with a bit of luck we might get a live calf out of her."

I was going against one of my steadfast rules—never to talk a farmer into doing something—but I was seized by a kind of madness. Mr. Bushell looked at me for a long time, then, without changing expression, he nodded.

"Awright, what do you want?"

"Two buckets of warm water, soap, towels," I replied. "And I'll bring some instruments into the house to boil, if I may."

When the farmer had departed, I thumped Norman on the shoulder. "This is just right. Plenty of light, a live calf to aim for and it's just as well poor Mr. Bushell doesn't hear too well. If we keep our voices down, I'll be able to ask you things as we go along."

Norman didn't say anything. I told him to set up some straw bales for our equipment and had him scatter loose straw around the cow while I boiled the instruments in a pan in the farm kitchen.

Soon all was ready—syringes, suture materials, scalpels, scissors, local anaesthetic and cotton wool laid in a row on a clean towel draped over one of the bales. I added some antiseptic to the water and addressed the farmer.

"We'll roll her over and you can hold the head down, Mr. Bushell. I think she's too tired to move much."

Norman and I pushed at the shoulder, and Bella flopped on her side without resistance. The farmer put his knee against her neck, and the long area of the left flank was exposed for our attention.

I nudged the student. "Where do I make the incision?" I whispered.

Norman cleared his throat. "Well, er, it's about . . ." he pointed vaguely.

I nodded. "Around the rumenotomy site, eh? But a bit lower, I suppose." I began to clip away the hair from a foot-long strip. It would need a big opening for that calf to come through. Then I quickly infiltrated the area with local.

We do these jobs under a local anaesthetic and in most cases the cow lies quietly on her side or even stands during the operation. The animal can't feel anything, of course, but I have a few extra grey hairs round my ears that owe their presence to the occasional wild cow suddenly rearing up halfway through and taking off with me in desperate pursuit, trying to keep her internal organs from flopping on the ground.

But that was all in the future. On this first occasion I had no such fears. I cut through skin, muscle layers and peritoneum, and was confronted by a protruding pink and white mass of tissue.

I poked at it with my finger. There was something hard inside. Could it be the calf?

"What's that?" I hissed.

"Eh?" Norman, kneeling by my side, jumped convulsively. "What do you mean?"

[68]

"That thing. Is it the rumen or the uterus? It's pretty low down, it could be the uterus."

The student swallowed a couple of times. "Yes . . . yes . . . that's the uterus all right."

"Good." I smiled in relief and made a bold incision. A great gout of impacted grass welled out, followed by a burst of gas and an outflow of dirty brown fluid.

"Oh, Christ!" I gasped. "It's the rumen. Look at all that bloody mess!" I groaned aloud as the filthy tide surged away down and out of sight into the abdominal cavity. "What the hell are you playing at, Norman?"

I could feel the young man's body trembling against mine.

"Don't just sit there!" I shouted. "Thread me one of those needles. Quick! Quick!"

Norman bounded to his feet, rushed over to the bale and returned with a trailing length of catgut extended in shaking fingers. Wordlessly, dry-mouthed, I stitched the gash I had made in the wrong organ. Then the two of us made frantic attempts to swab away the escaped rumenal contents with cotton wool and antiseptic, but much of it had run away beyond our reach. The contamination must be massive.

When we had done what we could, I sat back and looked at the student. My voice was a hoarse growl. "I thought you knew all about these operations."

He looked at me with frightened eyes. "They do quite a few of them at the clinic."

I glared back at him. "How many Caesarians have you seen?"

"Well . . . er . . . one, actually."

"One! To hear you speak I thought you were an expert! And, anyway, even if you'd seen only one, you should know a little bit about it."

"The thing is . . ." Norman shuffled his knees around on the cobbles. "You see . . . I was right at the back of the class."

I worked up a sarcastic snarl. "Oh, I understand. So you couldn't see very well?"

"That's about it." The young man hung his head.

"Well, you're a stupid young fool!" I said in a vicious whisper. "Dishing out your confident instructions when you know damn all. You realise you've killed this good cow. With all that contamination, she'll certainly develop peritonitis and die. All we can hope for now is to get the calf out alive." With an effort I turned my gaze from his stricken face. "Anyway, let's get on with it."

Apart from my first shouts of panic, the entire interchange had been carried out *pianissimo,* and Mr. Bushell kept shooting enquiring glances at us.

I gave him what I hoped was a reassuring smile and returned to the attack. Getting the calf out alive was easy to say, but it soon dawned on me that getting the calf out in any way whatsoever was going to be a mammoth task. Plunging my arm deep below what I now knew was the rumen, I encountered a smooth and mighty organ lying on the abdominal floor. It contained an enormous bulk with the hardness and immobility of a sack of coal.

I felt my way along the surface and came upon the unmistakable contours of a hock pushing against the slippery wall. That was the calf, all right, but it was far, far away.

I withdrew my arm and started on Norman again. "From your position at the back of the class," I enquired bitingly, "did you happen to notice what they did next?"

"Next? Ah, yes." He licked his lips, and I could see beads of sweat on his brow. "You are supposed to exteriorise the uterus."

"Exteriorise it? Bring it up to the wound, you mean?"

"That's right."

"Good God!" I said. "King Kong couldn't lift up that bloody uterus. In fact I can't move it an inch. Have a feel."

The student, who was stripped and soaped like myself, introduced his arm and for a few moments I watched his eyes pop and his face redden. Then he withdrew and nodded sheepishly. "You're right. It won't move."

[70]

"Only one thing to do." I picked up a scalpel. "I'll have to cut into the uterus and grab that hock. There's nothing else to get hold of."

It was very nasty, fiddling about away out of sight down in the dark unknown, my arm buried to the shoulder in the cow, my tongue hanging out with anxiety. I was terrified I might slash into something vital but, in fact, it was my own fingers that I cut, several times, before I was able to draw the scalpel edge across the bulge made by the hock. A second later I had my hand round the hairy leg. Now I was getting somewhere.

Gingerly, I enlarged the incision, inch by inch. I hoped fervently I had made it big enough, but working blind is a terrible thing, and it was difficult to be sure.

At any rate, I couldn't wait to deliver that calf. I laid aside my knife, seized the leg and tried to lift it, and immediately I knew that another little nightmare lay ahead. The thing was a tremendous weight and it was going to take great strength to bring it up into the light of day. Nowadays when I do a Caesar, I take care to have a big strong farm lad stripped off, ready to help me with this lifting job, but today I had only Norman.

"Come on," I panted. "Give me a hand."

We reached down together and began to pull. I managed to repel the hock and bring the foot round, and that gave us greater purchase, but it was still agonisingly laborious to raise the mass to the level of the skin incision.

Teeth clenched, grunting with effort, we hauled upwards till at last I was able to grasp the other hind leg. Even then, with a foot apiece in our hands, nothing wanted to move. It was just like doing a tough calving except it was through the side. And as we lay back, panting and sweating, pulling with every vestige of our strength, I had the sudden wave of illumination which comes to all members of our profession at times. I wished with all my heart and soul that I had never started this ghastly job. If only I had followed Mr. Bushell's suggestion to send the cow for slaughter I would now be driving peacefully on my rounds. Instead, here

I was, killing myself. And even worse than my physical torment was the piercing knowledge that I hadn't the slightest idea what was going to happen next.

But the calf was gradually coming through. The tail appeared, then an unbelievably massive rib cage and finally with a rush, the shoulders and head.

Norman and I sat down with a bump, the calf rolling over our knees. And like a gleam of light in the darkness, I saw that he was snorting and shaking his head.

"By gaw, he's a big 'un!" exclaimed the farmer. "And wick, too."

I nodded. "Yes, he's huge. One of the biggest I've ever seen." I felt between the hind legs. "A bull, as I thought. He'd never have come out the proper way."

My attention was whisked back to the cow. Where was the uterus? It had vanished. Again I started my frantic groping inside. My hand became entangled with yards of placenta. Oh hell, that wouldn't do any good floating around among the guts. I pulled it out and dropped it on the floor, but I still couldn't find the uterus. For a palpitating moment I wondered what would happen if I never did locate it, then my fingers came upon the ragged edge of my incision.

I pulled as much as possible of the organ up to the light, and I noticed with sinking disquiet that my original opening had been enlarged by the passage of that enormous calf and there was a long tear disappearing out of sight towards the cervix.

"Sutures." I held my hand out, and Norman gave me a fresh needle. "Hold the lips of the wound," I said and began to stitch.

I worked as quickly as I could and was doing fine until the tear ran out of sight. The rest was a kind of martyrdom. Norman hung on grimly while I stabbed around at the invisible tissue far below. At times I pricked the young man's fingers, at others my own. And to my dismay, a further complication had arisen.

The calf was now on its feet, blundering unsteadily around. The speed with which newly born animals get onto their legs has always fascinated me, but at this moment it was an unmitigated nuisance.

The calf, looking for the udder with that instinct which nobody can explain, kept pushing his nose at the cow's flank and at times toppling headfirst into the gaping hole in her side.

"Reckon 'e wants back in again," Mr. Bushell said with a grin. "By 'eck, he is a wick 'un."

"Wick" is Yorkshire for lively, and the word was never more aptly applied. As I worked, eyes half-closed, jaws rigid, I had to keep nudging the wet muzzle away with my elbow, but as fast as I pushed him back the calf charged in again, and with sick resignation I saw that every time he nosed his way into the cavity, he brought particles of straw and dirt from the floor and spread them over the abdominal contents.

"Look at that," I moaned. "As if there wasn't enough muck in there."

Norman didn't reply. His mouth was hanging open and the sweat ran down his blood-streaked face as he grappled with that unseen wound. And in his fixed stare I seemed to read a growing doubt as to his wisdom in deciding to be a veterinary surgeon.

I would rather not go into any more details. The memory is too painful. Sufficient to say that, after an eternity, I got as far down the uterine tear as I could, then we cleared away a lot of rubbish from the cow's abdomen and covered everything with antiseptic dusting powder. I stitched up the muscle and skin layers, with the calf trying all the time to get in on the act, and at last the thing was finished.

Norman and I got to our feet very slowly, like two old, old men. It took me a long time to straighten my back, and I saw the young man rubbing tenderly at his lumbar region. Then, since we were both plastered with caked blood and filth, we began the slow process of scrubbing and scraping ourselves clean.

Mr. Bushell left his position by the head and looked at the row of skin stitches. "Nice neat job," he said. "And a grand calf, too."

Yes, that was something. The little creature had dried off now, and he was a beauty, his body swaying on unsteady legs, his wide-set eyes filled with gentle curiosity. But that "neat job" hid things I didn't dare think about.

Antibiotics were still not in general use, but, in any case, I knew there was no hope for the cow. More as a gesture than anything else, I left the farmer some sulpha powders to give her three times a day. Then I got off the farm as quickly as I could.

We drove away in silence. I rounded a couple of corners, then stopped the car under a tree and sank my head against the steering wheel.

"Oh hell," I groaned. "What a bloody balls-up."

Norman replied only with a long sigh and I continued, "Did you ever see such a performance? All that straw and dirt and rumenal muck in among that poor cow's bowels. Do you know what I was thinking about towards the end? I was remembering the story of that human surgeon of olden times who left his hat inside his patient. It was as bad as that."

"I know." The student spoke in a strangled undertone. "And it was all my fault."

"Oh no, it wasn't," I replied. "I made a right bollocks of the whole thing all by myself, and I tried to blame you because I got in a panic. I shouted and nagged at you and I owe you an apology."

"Oh no, no . . ."

"Yes, I do. I am supposed to be a qualified veterinary surgeon, and I did nearly everything wrong." I groaned again. "And on top of it all, I behaved like an absolute swine towards you, and I'm sorry."

"You didn't really, you didn't . . . I . . ."

"Anyway, Norman," I broke in. "I'm going to thank you now. You were a tremendous help to me. You worked like a Trojan and I'd have got nowhere at all without you. Let's go and have a pint."

With the early-evening sunshine filtering into the bar parlour of the village inn, we dropped into a quiet corner and pulled deeply at our beer glasses. We were both hot and weary and there didn't seem to be anything more to say.

It was Norman who broke the silence. "Do you think that cow has any chance?"

I examined the cuts and punctures on my fingers for a moment. "No, Norman. Peritonitis is inevitable, and I'm pretty sure I've left a good-sized hole in her uterus." I shuddered and slapped my brow at the memory.

I was sure I would never see Bella alive again, but first thing next morning a morbid curiosity made me lift the phone to find out if she had survived so far.

The "buzz-buzz" at the other end seemed to last a long time before Mr. Bushell answered.

"Oh, it's Mr. Herriot. Cow's up and eatin'." He didn't sound surprised.

It was several seconds before I was able to absorb his words.

"Doesn't she look a bit dull or uncomfortable?" I asked huskily.

"Nay, nay, she's bright as a cricket. Finished off a rackful of hay, and I got a couple o' gallons of milk from 'er."

As in a dream I heard his next question. "When'll you take them stitches out?"

"Stitches . . . Oh yes." I gave myself a shake. "In a fortnight, Mr. Bushell, in a fortnight."

After the horrors of the first visit, I was glad Norman was with me when I removed the sutures. There was no swelling round the wound, and Bella chewed her cud happily as I snipped away. In a pen nearby the calf gambolled and kicked his feet in the air.

I couldn't help asking, "Has she shown any symptoms at all, Mr. Bushell?"

"Nay." The farmer shook his head slowly. "She's been neither up nor down. You wouldn't know owt had happened to 'er."

That was the way it was at my first Caesarian. Over the years Bella went on to have eight more calves normally and unaided, a miracle which I can still hardly believe.

But Norman and I were not to know that. All we felt then was an elation all the sweeter for being unexpected.

As we drove away I looked at the young man's smiling face. "Well, Norman," I said. "That's veterinary practice for you. You get a lot of nasty shocks, but some lovely surprises, too. I've often heard of the wonderful resistance of the bovine peritoneum, and thank heavens it's true."

"The whole thing's marvellous, isn't it?" he murmured dreamily. "I can't describe the way I feel. My head seems to be full of quotations like 'Where there is life there's hope.'"

"Yes, indeed," I said. "John Gay, isn't it—*The Sick Man and the Angel.*"

Norman clapped his hands. "Oh, well done."

"Let's see." I thought for a moment. "How about 'But t'was a famous victory.'"

"Excellent," replied the young man. "Southey, *The Battle of Blenheim.*"

I nodded. "Quite correct."

"Here's a good one," the student said. "'Out of this nettle, danger, we pluck this flower, safety.'"

"Splendid, splendid," I replied. "Shakespeare, *Henry Fifth.*"

"No, *Henry Fourth.*"

I opened my mouth to argue, but Norman held up a confident hand. "It's no good, I'm right. And this time I *do* know what I'm talking about."

Chapter
9

October 30, 1961

At 6:30 A.M. this morning we reached the Kiel Canal. There is a little town at the western end and a big lock gate. We had to wait for about half an hour to get through the lock, and during this time we took aboard a German policeman and a Dutch pilot. The policeman's job was to see that we did not pollute the canal by throwing out the manure and soiled bedding from the ship. He was very smart in a black leather coat with gold buttons and a neat blue uniform with two pips on the shoulder, and we spent a pleasant time chatting. He shamed me, as so many foreigners do, by speaking quite good English.

After passing through the lock gate it was a delight to be gliding along in still water for a change, and I stood out on the strip of deck, watching the many types of vessels that use the canal. There were several German warships, and the young sailors with their little caps on the side of their heads waved cheerily to me as they passed.

The countryside was flat with much farmland and woods, looking very pretty with their autumn tints. We passed many villages with attractive houses, most of which had long, steeply sloping roofs and dormer windows.

After about six hours we arrived at the eastern end of the canal. Here a German immigration official came aboard and stamped my passport. He also put a stamp on my name in the ship's articles, since this morning I was officially signed on as a member of the ship's company. It was odd to see the list of Danish names and then "James Herriot, Supercargo." I felt strangely uplifted. Me, a supercargo!

The sheep looked quite happy this morning, though there is still that nagging cough among the Lincolns. The one with the eye irritation is almost normal now, but the lame sheep has not improved; in fact, it has deteriorated slightly and is running a high temperature, so I have got it in a pen on its own and have given it a shot of penicillin as well as the antibiotic spray. Obviously the infection was deeper than I thought.

The sailor who is my constant helper is the same one who spoke to me on the first evening. His name is Raun and he is a flaxen-haired young husky with great shoulders and a flattened-nosed boxer's face, but when he smiles he radiates charm. He is warm-natured and an animal lover. When we had installed the lame sheep in its pen he knelt down, put his arms round the woolly neck and gave it a long hug. I have noticed him doing this with the other sheep, particularly the massive Romney Marsh rams. As I have said, they are like huge teddy bears, and Raun seems to find them irresistible. Anyway, I am delighted they have chosen such a man to be my assistant.

At the east end the canal widened out into the Baltic. I could see the town of Kiel just round the corner, and there was a tremendous amount of shipping. We passed an imposing memorial to the Germans killed in the First World War, and there were a few deserted sandy beaches with summer houses around them.

As we headed out into the sea I found a hidden corner of the deck and did a bit of hopping about and running on the spot. I must try to make a habit of this because the only exercise I get is clambering up and down the ladders to the hold, and I will have to work off Nielsen's abundant fare somehow.

I have decided that I will make a final inspection of the animals each night at ten o'clock and go round them with Raun to hold any I want to examine more closely. Tonight I was told that Raun was steering but that if I went up on the bridge he would soon be relieved.

The ship was pitching wildly as I staggered out onto the upper deck. This, I thought, was the real thing as I felt my way along in the inky blackness, drenched with sea spray, the boards heaving and slippery under my feet, my hands grabbing at anything to hold me upright.

I stumbled onto the bridge and found myself in a decidedly eerie atmosphere. The bridge is an entirely different place at night —absolutely dark—and I had to stand there for a long time before I could pick out the lonely figure at the wheel. That is a quiet job if ever there was one.

When Raun came down with me, I gave the ewe with the eye trouble what ought to be its final application of ointment and injected the lame sheep again. The animals that tried to stand were swaying and tumbling around, but they didn't seem any the worse. However, I wondered what they would be like in the morning because Raun told me he had heard the captain say there was a real storm blowing up.

"No matter," the big sailor said cheerfully. "You come and have a beer with me."

"Okay, thanks," I replied, and we went together to the crew's mess room. We sat down, he gave me a "Camels" cigarette and as we talked I looked around at the other members of the crew. Strangely, though the officers were dark, these were all of a type; thick yellow hair, fine physiques, tremendous men. All of them were cheerful and polite.

Raun told me about himself in his limited English. He is twenty-eight, has been at sea for fourteen years and is married, with two young children. He never stopped smiling, except at the end when he leaned across the table and tapped me on the chest.

"Doctor, on my last voyage we take two hundred cattles from Dublin to Lübeck. When we get to Lübeck, five cattles dead."

I whistled. "That's nasty. Didn't they have a vet with them?"

"No, no." His battered face was very serious. "No doctor for the cattles. Is good that you are here for the sheeps."

It made me think. Maybe I really was going to earn my keep.

I thanked him, said goodnight to everybody and made my way back to my quarters. Just outside my cabin is a door that opens onto a small platform on the stern of the ship. I like to go out there for a lungful of the good air before going to bed. Tonight, in the roaring wind, I could see only the creamy wash from the ship's propellors disappearing into the surrounding blackness. Above, there were a million stars, and I could pick out the plough and the pole star plainly. I didn't have to be an expert navigator to find our course. We are heading dead east.

I am finding it difficult to write my log tonight because the cabin keeps tilting steeply. I feel the captain is going to be right about the storm.

Chapter
10

To any conscientious veterinary surgeon, killing a patient is a terrible thought. I am not talking about euthanasia which is so often merciful, but of inadvertently killing when attempting to cure.

This has probably happened to many of us, and I think it happened to me. I can never be sure, but the memory still haunts me.

It all started when a young representative from a pharmaceutical company called at the surgery and started to talk about a wonderful new treatment for foul of the foot in cattle.

This condition was a headache in those early days. Judging by its name, it had been going on for centuries, and it happened when the interdigital space between the cleats of the cloven-footed bovine was invaded by the organism *Fusiformis necrophorus,* usually through some small wound or abrasion.

This resulted in the actual death of an area of tissue in the region along with swelling of the foot and extreme lameness. A good cow could lose condition at an alarming rate due simply to the pain. The medieval-sounding name came from the fact that the dead tissue gave off a particularly offensive smell.

The treatment we used to employ ranged from the tedious to the heroic. Cow's hind feet were never meant to be lifted up, and I was always relieved when it was a forefoot that was affected.

With hind feet, even applying antiseptics was a chore. If that didn't work, we bandaged on pads of cotton wool impregnated with caustics like copper sulphate, and a very popular treatment among the farmers was dressing the area with Stockholm tar and salt—a messy and unpleasant business with the feet whistling round the head of the operator.

So I couldn't believe it when the representative told me that an injection of M & B 693 into the vein would rapidly clear up the condition.

I actually laughed at the young man. "I know you chaps have to make a living, but this sounds like one of your tallest stories."

"It works, I tell you," he said. "It has been well tested, and I promise you it really does the trick."

"And you don't have to touch the foot at all?"

"No, only for diagnosis. Then you can forget about it."

"How long does it take to have an effect?"

"Just a few days. And I give you my word, the cow is sometimes much better within twenty-four hours."

It sounded like a beautiful dream. "Okay," I said. "Send some on. We'll give it a try."

He made a note on his pad, then looked up. "There's just one thing. This drug is very irritant. You must be sure you don't get it subcutaneous, or it could cause an abscess."

As he walked out of the door, I wondered if this really meant the end of one of our most disagreeable tasks. I had already had occasion to be thankful for the beneficent M & B tablets. They had wrought some minor miracles in our practice. But I found it hard to believe that an intravenous injection could cure a necrotic condition of the foot.

When the stuff arrived, I had the same trouble convincing the farmers. "What are you doin', injectin' the neck? You should be puttin' it into t'bloody foot." Or, "Is that all you're goin' to do? Aren't you goin' to give me summat to put on t'foot?" These were typical remarks, and my answers were halting because I had the same reservations as the stock owners.

[82]

But oh, how magically everybody's attitude changed because it was just as the young man said. Very often within a single day the beast was walking sound, the swelling had gone down, the pain had vanished. It was like witchcraft.

It was a giant step forward and I was at the height of my euphoria when I saw Robert Maxwell's cow. The reddened swollen foot, the agonised hopping, the stinking discharge—it was all there.

The fact is that it was so bad that I was delighted; I had found that the worst cases, with the acute lameness and the interdigital tissues pouting from toe or heel, were the ones that recovered quickest.

"We'll have some work on with this 'un," the farmer grunted. He was in his late forties, a dynamic little man and one of the bright farmers of the district. He was always to the fore in farmers' discussion groups, always eager to learn and teach.

"Not a bit of it, Mr. Maxwell," I said airily. "There's a new injection for this now. No foot dressing—that's gone for good."

"Well, that would be a blessin', anyway. It's savage amusement, hangin' onto cows' feet." He bent over the leg and looked down. "Where exactly do ye inject this new stuff, then?"

"In the neck."

"In the neck!"

I grinned. I never seemed to get tired of the reaction. "That's right. Into the jugular vein."

"Well, there's summat new every day now." Robert Maxwell shrugged and smiled, but he accepted it. The intelligent farmers like him were the ones who didn't argue. It was always the thickheads who knew everything.

"Just hold the nose," I said. "That's right, pull the head a little way round. Fine." I raised the jugular with my finger, and it stood out like a hosepipe as I slipped the needle into it. The M & B solution ran into the blood stream in about two minutes, and I pulled the needle out.

"Well, that's it," I said with a trace of smugness.

"Nothing else?"

"Not a thing. Forget about it. That cow will be sound in a few days."

"Well, I don't know." Robert Maxwell looked at me with a half-smile. "You young fellers keep surprising me. I've been in farmin' all me life, but you do things I've never dreamed of."

I saw him at a farmers' meeting about a week later.

"How's that cow?" I asked.

"Just like you said. Sound as a bell o' brass. That stuff shifts foul, all right, there's no doubt about it; it's like magic."

I was just expanding when his expression changed. "But there's a heck of a swelling on 'er neck."

"You mean, where I injected her?"

"Yes."

My happy feeling evaporated. I didn't like the sound of that. My first thought was that I must have got some of the solution under the skin, but I seemed to remember the blood still gushing from the needle when I pulled it out.

"That's funny," I said. "I can't see any reason for that."

Robert Maxwell shook his head. "I can't, either. I did that cow over with fly spray right after you left. Could some of that have got in your needle wound?"

"No . . . surely not. I've never heard of such a thing. I'd better have a look at her tomorrow."

I made it one of my first calls the next morning. The farmer had not been exaggerating. There was a marked swelling on the neck, but it was not confined to the injection site. It ran right along the course of the jugular. The vein itself had a solid, corded feel, and there was oedema around the swollen area.

"She's got phlebitis," I said. "The vein has somehow got infected through my injection."

"How would that happen?"

"I just don't know. I'm pretty sure none of the solution escaped, and my needle was clean."

The farmer peered closely at the cow's neck. "It's not like an abscess, is it?"

"No," I replied. "There's no abscess."

"And what's that long, hard lump goin' up to the jaw?"

"That's a thrombus."

"A what?"

"A thrombus. A big clot in the vein." I wasn't enjoying this little pathological lecture, considering that I had been responsible for the whole thing myself.

Robert Maxwell gave me a searching look. "Well, what's going to happen? What do we do?"

"Usually, collateral circulation develops within a few weeks. That is, other veins take over the job. And, in the meantime, I'll put her onto a course of mixed sulphonamide powders."

"Aye, well, she doesn't seem bothered," the farmer said.

That was one gleam of light. The cow had been looking round at us contentedly as we spoke, and now I saw her pulling a little hay from her rack.

"No . . . no . . . She doesn't look concerned at all. I'm sorry this has happened, but it should just be a question of time before she's right."

He scratched the root of the animal's tail for a moment. "Would bathin' with hot water do any good?"

I shook my head vigorously. "Please don't touch that place at all. It would be dangerous if that clot broke down."

I left the powders and drove away, but I had that nasty feeling I always have when I know I have boobed. I gripped the wheel and swore under my breath. What had I done wrong? The sterilised disposable needles and syringes which we take for granted now were unknown then, but Siegfried and I always boiled our hypodermics and carried them in cases where they were always immersed in surgical spirit. We could hardly do more. Had the farmer's fly spray done something? Hard to believe.

In any case, I comforted myself with the thought that the cow didn't look ill. These cases recovered in time. But the unpalatable fact remained. That animal had had a simple case of foul until James Herriot MRCVS took a hand, and now she had jugular phlebitis.

Helen had just put my breakfast in front of me on the following morning when the phone rang. It was Robert Maxwell.

"That cow's dead," he said.

I stared stupidly at the wall in front of me for several seconds before I could speak. "Dead . . . ?"

"Aye, found 'er laid in her stall this mornin'. Just as though she'd dropped down."

"Mr. Maxwell . . . I . . . er." I had to clear my throat more than once. "I'm terribly sorry. I never expected this."

"What's happened, then?" The farmer's voice was strangely matter-of-fact.

"There's only one explanation," I said. "Embolism."

"What's that?"

"It's when a piece of the clot breaks off and gets into the circulation. When an embolus reaches the heart, it usually means death."

"I see. That would do it, then."

I swallowed. "Let me say again, Mr. Maxwell, I'm very sorry."

"Ah, well . . ." There was a pause. "These things happen in farmin'. I just thought I'd let you know. Good mornin'."

I felt sick as I put the phone down, and the feeling persisted as I sat at the breakfast table, staring at my plate.

"Aren't you going to eat, Jim?" Helen asked.

I looked down sadly at the nice slice of home-fed ham. "Sorry, Helen, it's no good. I can't tackle it."

"Oh, come on." My wife smiled and pushed the plate nearer to me. "I know you worry about your work, but I've never known it to put you off your food."

I shrugged miserably. "But this is different. I've never killed a cow before."

Of course, I didn't know this for sure—I never will know—but the thing stayed with me for a long time. I am a great believer in Napoleon's dictum, "Throw off your worries when you throw off your clothes," and I had never known the meaning of insomnia, but for many nights, turgid jugular veins and floating emboli brought me gasping to wakefulness.

As time passed I continued to wonder at the farmer's attitude on the phone. Most people would have been furious at a disaster like this, and it would have been natural enough if Robert Maxwell had blasted me at great length. But he hadn't been rude, hadn't even tried to blame me.

Of course, there was always the possibility that he might be going to sue me. He was a nice man, but, after all, he had suffered a financial loss, and it would not take a legal genius to make out a good case that I was the villain.

But the solicitor's letter never arrived. In fact, I did not hear a word from the farmer for nearly a month, and since I had been a regular visitor on his place, I concluded that he had changed his veterinary surgeon. Well, I had lost the practice of a good client, and that was not a pleasant thought, either.

Then one afternoon the phone rang, and it was Robert Maxwell again, speaking in the same quiet voice. "I want you to come and look at one of me cows, Mr. Herriot. There's somethin' amiss with her."

A wave of relief went through me. Not a mention of the other thing, just a call for assistance as if nothing had happened. There were a lot of charitable farmers in the Dales, and this man was one of them. I just hoped I could make it up to him in some way.

What I wanted was a case I could cure quickly and, if possible, in a spectacular manner. I had a lot of ground to make up on this farm.

Robert Maxwell received me with his usual quiet courtesy.

"That was a good rain last night, Mr. Herriot. The grass was gettin' right parched." It was as though my last unhappy visit had never occurred.

The cow was a big Friesian, and when I saw her my hopes of

[87]   .

a cheap triumph vanished in an instant. She was standing, arch-backed and gaunt, staring at the wall in front of her. One thing I hate to see is a cow staring at the wall. As we approached she showed no interest, and I made a spot diagnosis. This was traumatic reticulitis. She had swallowed a wire. I would have to operate on her, and after my last experience in this byre the idea did not appeal.

Yet, when I began to examine her, I realised that things were not adding up. The rumen was working well, seething and bubbling under my stethoscope, and when I pinched her withers she did not grunt—just swivelled an anxiety-ridden eye in my direction before turning her attention to the wall again.

"She's a bit thin," I said.

"Aye, she is." Robert Maxwell dug his hands into his pockets and surveyed the animal gloomily. "And I don't know why. She's had nobbut the best of stuff to eat, but she's lost condition fast over the last few days."

Pulse, respiration and temperature were normal. This was a funny one.

"At first I thought she had colic," the farmer went on. "She kept tryin' to kick at her belly."

"Kicking at her belly?" Something was stirring at the back of my mind. Yes, that was often a symptom of nephritis. And as if to clinch my decision, the animal cocked her tail and sent a jet of bloody urine into the channel. I looked at the pool behind her. There were flecks of pus among the blood, and though I knew her trouble now, it did not make me happy.

I turned to the farmer. "It's her kidneys, Mr. Maxwell."

"Her kidneys? What's the matter wi' them?"

"Well, they're inflamed. They've become infected in some way. It's called pyelonephritis. Probably the bladder is affected, too."

The farmer blew out his cheeks. "Is it serious?"

How I wished I could give him, of all people, a light answer,

[88]

but there was no doubt that this was a usually fatal condition. I had a feeling of doom.

"I'm afraid so," I replied. "It is very serious."

"I had a feelin' there was somethin' far wrong. Can you do owt for her?"

"Yes," I said. "I would like to try her with some mixed sulphonamides."

He glanced at me quickly. That was what I had used for the phlebitis.

"It really is the best thing," I went on hurriedly. "Cows like this used to be hopeless to treat, but since the sulpha drugs came on the scene, we do have a chance."

He gave me one of his long, calm looks. "All right, then, we'd better get started."

"I'll keep an eye on her," I said as I handed over the powders.

And I did keep an eye on her. I was in the Maxwell byre every day. I desperately wanted that cow to live. But after four days there was no improvement; in fact, she was slowly sinking.

I was steeped in gloom as I stood by the farmer's side and looked at the animal's jutting ribs and pelvic bones. She was thinner than ever, and still she passed that blood-stained urine.

I could not bear the thought that another tragedy was going to follow so soon after the first one, but the certainty was growing in my mind that death was imminent.

"The sulphonamides are keeping her alive," I said, "but we need something stronger."

"Is there anythin' stronger?"

"Yes, penicillin."

Penicillin. The marvellous new drug, the first of the antibiotics, but as yet the veterinary profession had no injectable form. All we had were the tiny tubes, each containing 300 mg in an oily base, for the treatment of mastitis. The nozzle of the tube was inserted into the teat canal and the contents squeezed up into the udder. It was a magical improvement on any previous mastitis treatment, but at that stage of my career I had never injected an antibiotic into an animal hypodermically.

I am not usually inventive but I had a sudden idea. I went out to my car, found a box of twelve mastitis tubes and tried the nozzle in the base of a record hypodermic needle. It fitted perfectly.

I am no scientific theorist so I didn't know whether I was doing the right thing or not, but I plunged the needle into the cow's rump and squeezed tube after tube into the depths of the muscle until the box was empty. Would the penicillin be absorbed in that form? I didn't know. But there was comfort in the knowledge that at least it was in there. It was a spark of hope.

I kept this up for three days and on the third I knew I was doing some good.

"Look!" I said to Robert Maxwell. "Her back isn't arched now. She seems to have relaxed."

The farmer nodded. "You're right. She isn't as tucked up as she was."

The sight of the cow standing there peacefully, looking around her and occasionally pulling a mouthful of hay from her rack, was like a blast of trumpets to me. The pain in the kidneys was plainly subsiding, and the farmer had said that the urine was not as dark as it had been.

I seemed to go mad after that. With the scent of victory in my nostrils, I pumped my little tubes into the animal day after day. I didn't know the correct dose for a bovine—nobody did at that time—so I just whacked them in, willy-nilly, sometimes more, sometimes less, and all the time the improvement continued steadily.

There came the happy day when I was quite certain that the battle was won. As I worked on the cow, she straddled her legs and sent out a cascade of crystal-clear urine. I stepped back, and as if for the first time I contemplated the change in my patient. The gaunt frame of that first day was padded with flesh, and the cow's coat shone with the gloss of health. She had returned to normal just as quickly as she had fallen away. It was remarkable.

I threw down the empty box. "Well, Mr. Maxwell, I think we can say she's about right. I'll give her another treatment tomorrow, and that will be the end."

"You're comin' back tomorrow, then?"

"Yes, for the last time."

The farmer's face grew grave, and he stepped closer to me. "All right, then, I 'ave a complaint to make about you."

Oh God, at last he was going to tackle me about that phlebitis. And what a terrible moment to pick, just when I was flushed with success. Human nature could be very strange, and if he had decided to give me hell after all this time, there was nothing I could do about it. I would just have to take it.

"Oh, yes?" I replied shakily. "And what is that?"

He leaned forward and tapped my chest with his forefinger. His face was transfigured, heavy with menace. "D'ye think I've got nothin' better to do than sweep up after you every day?"

"Sweep up . . . what . . ." I stared at him stupidly.

He waved an arm over the byre floor. "Just look at all this dang mess! I've got to clear it away!"

I looked down at the scattering of empty penicillin tubes, the paper pamphlets which always went with them and the discarded box. Totally unheeding, I had hurled them far and wide as I worked.

"Gosh, I'm sorry," I muttered. "I didn't realise . . ."

I was interrupted by a great burst of laughter from the farmer.

"Nay, I'm just havin' ye on, lad. Of course you didn't realise. You were ower busy curin' me cow." He thumped me on the shoulder, and I knew it was his way of saying thanks.

That was my first experience of injecting an antibiotic, and even though the method was bizarre, I learned something from it. But I learned more on that farm about the way to live than I did about veterinary science. Over the following thirty years I knew him, the farmer never alluded to that disaster which he could so easily have laid at my door.

[91]

During that period there have been occasions when I have suffered misfortunes due to the shortcomings of others, when I have found people at fault and at my mercy if I wished to make trouble for them. At these times I had a standard of conduct to follow. I tried to behave like Robert Maxwell.

Chapter
11

"You know, Jim," said Tristan, pulling thoughtfully at his Woodbine, "I often wonder if there is any other household where the mark of a lady's favour is expressed in goat shit."

In quiet moments I often thought about the old bachelor days in Skeldale House, and it was at one of these times that I recalled Tristan's observation. I could remember looking up at him from the day book in surprise. "Well, isn't that funny? I've just been thinking the same thing. It certainly is rather an odd business."

We had just come through from the dining room, and my memory of the breakfast table was very clear. Mrs. Hall always placed our letters next to our plates, and there, at Siegfried's place, dominating the scene like an emblem of triumph, stood the tin of goat droppings from Miss Grantley.

We all knew what it was, despite its wrapping of brown paper, because Miss Grantley always used the same container, an empty cocoa tin about six inches high. Either she collected them from friends or she was very fond of cocoa.

One indisputable thing was that she was very fond of goats. In fact, they seemed almost to rule her existence, which was strange because the care of goats was an unlikely hobby for a blond beauty who could have stepped effortlessly into the film world.

Another odd thing about Miss Grantley was that she had never married. Each time I had been at her house I had marvelled that anybody like her was able to keep the men away. She would be about thirty, with a nicely rounded figure and elegant legs and sometimes when I looked at the fine contours of her face, I wondered whether that rather firm jaw might have frightened prospective suitors. But no, she was cheerful and charming; I decided that she just didn't want to get married. She had a lovely home and obviously plenty of money. She appeared to be perfectly happy.

There was no doubt at all that the goat droppings were a mark of favour. Miss Grantley took her stock keeping very seriously and insisted on regular laboratory examination of faeces samples for internal parasites or any other abnormality that might be found.

These samples were always addressed personally to Mr. Siegfried Farnon and I had attached no importance to this until one morning, a few days after I had pleased her immensely by removing an embedded piece of chaff from one of her Billies' eyes, the familiar tin appeared by my breakfast plate and I read, "James Herriot Esq., MRCVS," on the label.

That was when I realised it was an accolade, a gesture of approval. In ancient days the feudal knights would carry a glove at their saddle bow or a scarf on their lance point as a symbol of their lady's esteem, but with Miss Grantley it was goat droppings.

On the occasion when I got mine, Siegfried's face showed the slightest flicker of surprise and I suppose I might have shown a trace of smugness, but he needn't have worried. Within a week or two the tin reappeared at his end of the table.

And after all, it was the natural thing, because if sheer male attractiveness entered into this situation, there was no doubt that Siegfried was out in front by a street. Tristan pursued the local girls enthusiastically and with considerable success; I had no reason to complain about my share of female company, but Siegfried was in a different class. He seemed to drive women mad.

He didn't have to chase them; they chased him. I hadn't known him long before I realised that the tales I had heard about the irresistible appeal of tall, lean-faced men were true. And when you added his natural charm and commanding personality, it was inevitable that the goat droppings would land regularly by his plate.

In fact, that is how it was for a long time even though Tristan and I paid almost as many visits to Miss Grantley's goats as Siegfried. As I said, she seemed to be quite rich because she called us out to the slightest ailment and was as good a client as some of our big farmers.

However, when I heard her voice on the telephone one morning, I knew that this time it wasn't for something trivial. She sounded agitated.

"Mr. Herriot, Tina has caught her shoulder on a nail and torn herself rather badly. I do hope you can come out immediately."

"Yes, as it happens, I can. There is nothing urgent at the moment. I'll leave right away."

A mild glow of satisfaction rippled through me. This would be just another stitching job and I liked stitching. It was easy and always impressed the client. I would be on happier ground there than when Miss Grantley was quizzing me about goat diseases. They had taught me practically nothing about goats at college, and though I had tried to catch up by snatches of reading here and there, I realised uncomfortably that I was no expert.

I was leaving the room when Tristan levered himself slowly from the depths of the armchair where he spent a lot of his time. Since breakfast I had been aware of his presence only by the rustle of the *Daily Mirror* under a cloud of Woodbine smoke.

He yawned and stretched. "Miss Grantley's, eh? Think I'll come with you. Just feel like a ride out."

I smiled. "Okay, come on, then." He was always good company.

Miss Grantley met us in a tight-fitting pale-blue boiler suit of some silky material which did nothing to diminish her attractions.

"Oh, thank you so much for coming," she said. "Please follow me."

Following her was rewarding. In fact, on entering the goat

[95]

house Tristan failed to see the step and fell onto his knees. Miss Grantley glanced at him briefly before hurrying to a pen at the far end.

"There she is," she said and put a hand over her eyes. "I can't bear to look."

Tina was a fine white Saanen, but her beauty was ravaged by a huge laceration that had pulled the skin down from her shoulder in a long V, exposing the naked smoothness of the supraspinatus and infraspinatus muscles. The bony spine of the scapula gleamed white through the blood.

It was a mess, but I had to stop myself rubbing my hands. It was all superficial, and I could put it right and look very good in the process. Already I could see myself inserting the last stitch and pointing to the now almost-invisible wound. "There, now, that looks a lot better, doesn't it?" Miss Grantley would be in raptures.

"Yes . . . yes . . ." I murmured in my most professional manner as I probed the damaged area. "It's nasty, really nasty."

Miss Grantley clasped her hands together. "But do you think you can save her?"

"Oh, yes." I nodded weightily. "It will be a big stitching job and take rather a long time, but I feel sure she will pull through."

"Oh, thank heaven." She gave a long sigh of relief. "I'll fetch some hot water."

Soon I was ready for action. My needles, cotton wool, scissors, suture materials and forceps laid out on a clean towel, Tristan holding Tina's head, Miss Grantley hovering anxiously, ready to help.

I cleaned the whole area thoroughly, sprinkled dusting powder with a liberal hand, then began to stitch. Miss Grantley was soon in action, passing me the scissors to clip each suture. It was a nice smooth start, but it was a very large wound and this was going to take some time. I searched my mind for light conversation.

Tristan chipped in, apparently thinking the same thing. "Wonderful animal, the goat," he said lightly.

"Ah, yes." Miss Grantley looked across at him with a bright smile. "I do agree."

"When you think about it, they are probably the earliest of the domestic animals," he went on. "It always thrills me to realise that there is ample evidence of domestication of goats in prehistoric times. There are cave paintings of goats and later, ancient books from all over the world mention their existence. They have been part of the world of man since recorded time. It is a fascinating thought."

From my squatting position I looked up at him in surprise. In my relationship with Tristan I had discovered several things which fascinated him, but goats were not one of them.

"And another thing," he went on. "They have such a marvellous metabolism. They will consume food other animals won't look at, and they will produce abundant milk from that food."

"Yes, indeed," breathed Miss Grantley.

Tristan laughed. "They're such characters, too. Tough and hardy under all climatic conditions, absolutely fearless and ready to tackle any other animal, no matter how large. And, of course, it is a known fact that they can eat with impunity many poisonous plants which would kill most creatures in a very short time."

"Oh, they *are* amazing." Miss Grantley gazed at my friend and passed the scissors to me without turning her head.

I felt I ought to make some contribution. "Goats certainly are extremely . . ." I began.

"But really, you know," Tristan was in full flow again, "I think that the thing which appeals to me most about them is their affectionate nature. They are friendly and sociable, and I feel that that is why people become so deeply attached to them."

Miss Grantley nodded gravely. "How true, how true."

My colleague stretched out a hand and fingered the hay in the animal's rack. "I see you feed them properly. There's all sorts of rough stuff in here—thistles and bits of shrubs and coarse plants.

[97]

Obviously you know that goats prefer such things to grass. No wonder your animals are so healthy."

"Oh thank you." She blushed faintly. "Of course I give them concentrates, too."

"Whole grain, I hope?"

"Oh yes, always."

"Good, good. Keeps up the pH of the rumen. You know, you can get hypertrophy of the rumenal walls and inhibition of cellulose-digesting bacteria with a low pH?"

"Well, no . . . I didn't really understand it in those terms." She was staring at him as if he were a prophet.

"Ah, no matter," Tristan said airily. "You are doing all the right things, and that is the important point."

"Can I have the scissors, please?" I grunted. I was beginning to feel cramped in my bent-over position and also a little piqued at the growing impression that Miss Grantley had forgotten all about me.

But I stitched on doggedly, one-half of my mind watching thankfully as the skin gradually covered the denuded area, the other listening in amazement as Tristan pontificated on the construction of goat houses, their dimensions, ventilation and relative humidity.

A long time later Miss Grantley hardly noticed as I inserted the last suture and straightened up wearily. "Well, now, that looks better, doesn't it?" I said, but there wasn't the expected impact because Tristan and my client were deeply involved in a discussion of the relative merits of the different breeds of goats.

"Are you really in favour of the Toggenburg and Anglo-Nubian?" she asked.

"Oh yes." Tristan inclined his head judicially. "Excellent animals, both of them."

Miss Grantley suddenly became aware that I had finished. "Oh, thank you so much," she said absently. "You have taken such pains. I am most grateful. Now you must both come in for a cup of coffee."

As we balanced our cups on our knees in the elegant sitting room, Tristan carried on, unabated. He dealt in depth with reproductive problems, obstetrics and the feeding of weaned kids, and he was well into a little treatise on anaesthesia for dehorning when Miss Grantley turned towards me. She was clearly still under his spell but no doubt felt that it would be only polite to bring me into the conversation.

"Mr. Herriot, one thing worries me. I share a pasture with the farmer next door, and very often my goats are grazing with his ewes and lambs. Now, I have heard that his sheep are troubled with coccidiosis. Is there any chance that my goats could contract it from them?"

I took a long pull at my coffee cup to give myself time to think. "Well . . . er . . . I would say . . ."

My friend broke in again effortlessly. "Most unlikely. It seems that most types of coccidiosis are specific to their individual hosts. I don't think you need worry on that account."

"Thank you." Miss Grantley addressed me again, as though deciding to give me a last chance. "And how about worms, Mr. Herriot? Can my goats become infected with worms from the sheep?"

"Ah now, let's see . . ." My cup rattled in the saucer, and I could feel a light perspiration breaking out on my brow. "The thing is . . ."

"Quite so," murmured Tristan, gliding once more to my aid. "As Mr. Herriot was about to say, helminthiasis is a different proposition. There is a very real danger of infection, since the common nematodes are the same in both species. You must always worm regularly, and if I can give you a brief programme . . ."

I sank deeper in my chair and let him get on with it, only half hearing erudite remarks about the latest anthelmintics and their actions on trichostrongyles, haemonchus and ostertagia.

It came to an end at last, and we went out to the car. "I'll come back in ten days to remove the stitches," I said as Miss Grantley showed us off the premises. It struck me that it was just about the only sensible thing I had said.

I drove a few hundred yards along the road, then I stopped the car.

"Since when have you been a goat lover?" I demanded bitterly. "And where the hell did you get all that high-powered stuff you were preaching back there?"

Tristan giggled, then threw back his head and laughed immoderately. "Sorry, Jim," he said when he had recovered. "I have exams coming up in a few weeks, as you know, and I heard that one of the examiners is really goat-orientated. Last night I boned up on every bit of goat literature I could find. Uncanny how I had the opportunity to trot it all out so soon after."

Ah, well, that made sense. Tristan had the kind of brain that absorbed information like a sponge. I could believe that he would have to read those chapters only once, and they would be his for good. In my student days I often had to go over a thing about six times before it sank in.

"I see," I said. "You'd better let me see those things you read last night. I didn't realise I was so ignorant."

There was an interesting little sequel about a week later. Siegfried and I were going in to breakfast when my partner stopped in mid-stride and stared at the table. The familiar brown-wrapped cocoa tin was there, but it was at his brother's place. Slowly he walked over and examined the label. I had a look, too, and there was no mistake. It read, "Mr. Tristan Farnon."

Siegfried said nothing but sat down at the head of the table. Very soon the young man himself joined us, examined the tin with interest and started on his meal.

Not a word was spoken and the three of us sat in silence, but over everything the undeniable fact hung heavy in the room. Tristan, for the moment, at least, was top man.

Chapter
12

October 31, 1961

Getting into bed last night wasn't easy. With every passing minute the ship's movements became more violent, and I fell down several times while undressing.

Once in the bunk I was thrown from side to side, not in the gentle roll of the other nights but with an unpleasant jarring bump. I turned onto my stomach, braced arms and legs against the wood and after about half an hour I managed to fall asleep.

Around two o'clock in the morning I was jerked from a troubled slumber into a world gone mad. I was being tossed about like a rubber ball, the wind howled, driving rain spattered against the cabin window and a frightful din rose from all over the ship. The banging and clattering were deafening. I could hear the pans in the galley flying around against the walls, a loose iron door clanged repeatedly on its hinges and from everywhere came a medley of undefined rattles and groans.

I switched on the light and looked out on a scene of chaos. My money, keys, pipe and tobacco were rolling about on the floor; the desk drawers were shooting out to their full extent, then slamming back again; the chair and my suitcase were sliding from one side to another.

Reeling about in the pandemonium, falling down repeatedly, I did my best to clear up the mess. Then I got back into bed. But

I couldn't stand the thumping of the drawers against the chair so I got out again, jammed the chair against the drawers and my suitcase between chair and bunk, and clambered wearily up again. But though this cured most of the local noise, the uproar outside was unabated, and I got very little sleep after that.

At dawn a cheerless sight greeted me as I looked out of my window. All around was an empty waste of grey water tossed up into mighty green- and white-topped waves that broke up into clouds of spray as the wind caught them. It gave me an uncomfortable thrill to see our little ship climb up one monstrous wave after another and then drop into a series of deep watery valleys beyond. The Baltic was really playing up.

My first thought was for the sheep, but I heard the knock on my door and the familiar voice of the mess boy. "Breakfast, Mr. Herriot."

I hurried to the mess room. I would have a quick bite and then collect Raun. The captain was seated alone at the table when I entered.

"Good morning, Mr. Herriot," he said and gave me a long appraising stare, which I couldn't quite understand.

I sat down and waited. I was impatient to get down to the hold, and I wished the breakfast would arrive. On top of that I was distinctly peckish, and I jabbed busily at the smoked ham, herring and salt beef. The captain watched me with narrowed eyes all the time.

After a few minutes the mess boy appeared. His face was as green as grass, and he averted his eyes from the piled plateful of sausages, scrambled eggs and fried potatoes.

I grabbed a piece of rye bread and fell upon the savoury mound without delay. I was hacking at a sausage when the captain spoke again.

"Are you feeling all right, Mr. Herriot?"

I looked up in surprise and replied with my mouth full, "Mm, yes, fine, thanks, a bit tired, maybe. I didn't get much sleep last night."

"But you are hungry, yes?"

"I am, yes, I certainly am. All that bouncing around seems to have stimulated my appetite."

"This is most unusual," the captain said in his precise way. "We have just come through a force-nine gale, and I was sure you would be seasick this morning. You are a very good sailor."

I laughed. "Well, thank you. I don't suppose there's anything very clever about that. I'm just made that way. Motion of any kind has never troubled me."

"Yes, yes . . ." The captain nodded gravely. "Still, it is remarkable. Didn't you notice Peter's face?"

"Peter?"

"Yes, the mess boy. All mess boys are called Peter, by the way, no matter what their real name is. He is feeling very ill; in fact, he is always ill in bad weather."

"Oh, poor lad. It *was* pretty rough last night, wasn't it?"

"Yes, Mr. Herriot, and I might say that we were sailing with the wind behind us. If we have to come back in weather like that with the wind against us, then heaven help us. It will be much worse."

"Really? I didn't know that. I . . ."

Raun's face, poking round the door, cut me off in mid-sentence.

"Doctor, come queek. The sheeps . . . the sheeps are bad!"

I bolted the last of the sausage and followed him to the hold as quickly as the heaving of the ship would allow me.

"Look, Doctor!" The big Dane pointed excitedly at one of the Romney Marsh rams.

The sheep was standing with some difficulty, legs straddled wide. It was panting violently, its mouth gaped and a bubbling saliva poured from its lips. The normally docile eyes were wide and charged with terror as the animal fought for breath.

All the euphoria I had felt since boarding the *Iris Clausen* evaporated as I rushed feverishly around the pens. A lot of the other sheep were behaving in exactly the same way, and I realised with a sense of shock that I wasn't on a pleasure cruise after all.

I suppressed a rising panic as I examined the animals. They all looked as though they were going to die, and I had a strong conviction that those unknown Russians waiting at the other end were not going to be amused when the expert veterinary attendant presented them with a heap of carcasses. A fine start it would be to my first venture at sea.

But as I went round the pens again, I began to calm down. None of the sheep looked happy, but it was only the biggest that were affected in this way—all the rams and one or two of the larger ewes, about a dozen in all. So, though it might be a tragedy, it wasn't going to be total disaster. With Raun hanging onto the necks, I took the temperatures. They were all around 107.

I leaned back against the wooden rail and tried to rationalise my thoughts. This was stress—a classical example. It must be; up in my case I had a few bottles of the new wonder drug, cortisone, and one of its indications was just this.

I was up to my cabin and down again quicker than I thought was possible and in the pockets of my working coat the precious bottles bumped against each other. The brand name was Predso-lan; it was one of the first of the steroid products and though I had used it for arthritic and inflammatory conditions, I had never tried it in a case like this.

It wasn't only the ship's pitching that made my hand shake and wobble as I drew the liquid into my syringe. The supply was very limited, and heaven only knew how many more sheep would go down. I rationed the injections to 3 c.c. per sheep, and as I went round the stricken animals, my spirits sank lower. Only three of them could stand; the others were slumped on their chests, necks craning forward, eyes starting from their heads, their flanks heaving uncontrollably.

As I worked, Raun stroked the woolly heads and muttered endearments in Danish. It was the first time I had seen him look unhappy, and I knew how he felt. I hadn't been seasick, but I was sick now with apprehension.

[104]

These beautiful pedigree animals. And it was the rams, the most valuable of all, which were struck down. I could only wait now, but I was convinced that the whole business was hopeless. I realised that I couldn't bear to stand there watching them any longer, and I hurried up the iron ladders to the top deck, which was running with water and slanting at crazy angles. It was clearly no place for me, and I went up to the bridge.

The captain, as always, greeted me courteously, and when I told him about the sheep he looked thoughtful. Then he smiled.

"I know they are in good hands, Mr. Herriot. Do not be upset. I am sure you will cure them."

I couldn't share his optimism, and, in any case, I was pretty certain he was only trying to cheer me up. To take my mind off my troubles he again showed me our position on the chart and began to talk of maritime things.

"We are out of the sea lanes now," he said. He waved a hand round the desolation on all sides. "You see no ships now, and I think you see no ships all day."

As we talked we looked out through the glass at the bows of the ship, dipping into each gulf, then climbing up the green mountain on the other side. This was the best position to appreciate the size of those mighty waves, and a part of me never stopped being surprised as our tiny vessel fought her way up again and again.

The captain fell silent for a few minutes and gazed impassively at the endless stretch of sea beyond the glass.

"I tell you again, Mr. Herriot, we are running before the wind now, and if it is like this on our return journey, we are in big trouble." He turned and smiled. "You see, once we are unloaded, we must come back straightaway. A ship is doing no good lying in harbour."

All the time I was hanging on grimly to a rail, and it fascinated me to see the mate stroll casually onto the bridge, pipe in mouth, hands in pockets, and begin to move around effortlessly. At times his body seemed to be at an angle of forty-five degrees to the ground. I have noticed that all the crew are wonderfully adept at this, but for me it is frankly very dangerous to walk anywhere at all without support.

After two hours I had to give in to my gnawing anxiety. It would be too soon to expect any improvement in my patients, but at least I could check to see that they were no worse.

I struggled, a foot at a time, back to my cabin to get my gear, and on the way I passed the galley. The cell-like room was a chaos of tumbled pans and plates, and the walls were almost entirely covered with soup which Nielsen, the cook, was wiping away with a cloth. When he saw me, he nodded and smiled as he worked. He didn't seem in the least put out; this was probably a common occurrence for him.

Down those iron ladders again; they really are uncomfortable when the world is whirling and wet. I rushed straight to the pen that held the first ram, and for a moment I was sure I had gone to the wrong place, because a large woolly head was regarding me placidly over the rails. A few strands of hay hung from the mouth, then the jaws began to move in a contented chew.

I was standing there, bewildered, when from the deep straw in the pen the massive figure of Raun rose like a golden-maned genie and began to wave his arms about.

"Look, Doctor, look!" His boxer's face vibrated in every feature as he gestured at the ram, then at the other patients in the hold.

I moved among them like a man in a dream. They were all normal. Not just improved, but right back to where they were before the trouble started, and all within two hours.

Over my veterinary career, I have learned about new things in various odd places, and I learned about cortisone in the bowels of a little cattle ship on the way to Russia.

And it was sweet, made sweeter by the ecstatic response of Raun to the little miracle. He vaulted over the rails from pen to pen, hugging the sheep as though they were dogs, and laughing nonstop.

"Is wonderful, Doctor, is wonderful! So queek—they dying,

now they live. So queek, how you do it?" He stared at me with undisguised admiration.

Just then, I felt a pang of envy for Danish vets. I have had my black moments in practice, but I have also pulled off the occasional spectacular cure without seeing anything like this reaction from the Yorkshiremen. But then, maybe Danish farmers don't leap about with joy, either. After all, Raun is a sailor.

Anyway, I was filled with the exhilaration every veterinary surgeon knows when the curtain of despair is unexpectedly lifted. The pre-lunch beer with the captain tasted like nectar, and lunch itself in the swaying mess room was a celebration.

Somehow, the wonder man in the galley had conjured up a glorious vegetable soup with pieces of sausage and dumpling floating around in it. This was followed by "Fregadillas," which were delicious and, I was told, are made from chopped pork and veal rolled into balls bound together with egg and highly spiced.

As I write, I am conscious that my journal is in danger of degenerating into a kind of Cattle Boat Cook Book, but how Nielsen manages to produce this kind of food in a cubbyhole and in stormy weather is a constant source of wonder to me. I am going to find it difficult to resist making references to his artistry.

He has a habit of poking his head round the door halfway through every meal. He looks only at me, the one who recognises him as a culinary genius, and when I put my fingers to my lips and close my eyes, his sweating face beams with delight. He thinks I am wonderful.

My cabin is almost opposite the galley, and between meals he experiments on me constantly with his own special tidbits. I admit I am a willing subject.

The bad weather continued throughout the day, and, as the captain had prophesied, we did not see another ship at any time. I kept a close eye on the sheep and a few more showed the beginnings of the stress symptoms, but I was on them immediately with my Predsolan and crushed the trouble before it became alarming.

Tonight, the ritual after-dinner session with the schnapps and lager was particularly pleasant. The ship's officers are such likable men. They showed me pictures of their families and of the places they have visited, and the conversation never flagged. At the end, the captain raised a finger and looked at me smilingly. "Would you like to telephone your wife?"

I laughed. "You're joking, aren't you?"

"No, no, it is quite simple."

He took me up to the bridge, and within a few minutes I was talking to Helen and daughter Rosie in the darkness. With a sense of unreality, I heard their voices giving me the news of home, of Jimmy at the university, of the latest football scores. It put the final touch on a rewarding day.

I have made a close inspection of the sheep before I came to my cabin, because tomorrow we will be in Klaipeda and I will have to hand them over, then. They look fine. No more stress; the lame animal has recovered, as has the one with the discharging eyes. There is just that cough among the Lincolns, and it is a worry. What will those Russians make of it? I know that it is just a touch of parasitic bronchitis, that it is getting better all the time and that it will soon be gone completely. But will I be able to explain that to the Russian vets? I will soon know.

Chapter
13

The farm man moved between the cows and took hold of my patient's tail, and when I saw his haircut, I knew immediately that Josh Anderson had been on the job again. It was a Sunday morning and everything fitted into place. I really didn't have to ask.

"Were you in the Hare and Pheasant last night?" I enquired carelessly as I inserted my thermometer.

He ran a hand ruefully over his head. "Aye, bugger it, ah was. Ye can see straight off, can't ye? T'missus has been playin' 'ell with me ever since."

"I suppose Josh had had one too many, eh?"

"Aye, he had. I should've known better, pickin' a Saturday night. It's me own fault."

Josh Anderson was one of the local barbers. He liked his job, but he also liked his beer. In fact he was devoted to it, even to the extent of taking his scissors and clippers to the pub with him every night. For the price of a pint, he would give anybody a quick trim in the gents' lavatory.

Habitués of the Hare and Pheasant were never surprised to find one of the customers sitting impassively on the toilet seat with Josh snip-snipping round his head. With beer at sixpence a pint it was good value, but Josh's clients knew they were taking a chance. If the barber's intake had been moderate, they would escape relatively unscathed because the standard of hair styling in the Darrowby district was not very fastidious, but if he had imbibed beyond a certain point, terrible things could happen.

Josh had not as yet been known to cut off anybody's ear, but if you strolled around the town on Sundays and Mondays, you were liable to come across some very strange coiffures.

I looked again at the farm man's head. From my experience, I judged that Josh had been around the ten-pint mark when he did that one. The right sideburn had been trimmed off meticulously just below eye level, while the left was nonexistent. The upper hair seemed to have been delved into at random, leaving bare patches in some parts and long dangling wisps in others. I couldn't see the back, but I had no doubt it would be interesting, too. There could be a pigtail or anything lurking behind there.

Yes, I decided, definitely a ten-pinter. After twelve to fourteen pints, Josh was inclined to cast away all caution and simply run over his victim's head with the clippers, leaving a tuft in front. The classical convict's crop necessitated wearing a cap, well pulled down at all times, for several weeks thereafter.

I always played safe, and when my hair needed cutting, I went to Josh's shop where he operated in a state of strict sobriety.

I was sitting there a few days later, waiting my turn with my dog, Sam, under my seat, and as I watched the barber at work, the wonder of human nature seemed to glow with a particular radiance. There was a burly man in the chair, and his red face, reflected in the mirror above the enveloping white sheet, was contorted every few seconds with spasms of pain. Because the simple fact was that Josh didn't cut hair, he pulled it out.

He did this not only because his equipment was antiquated and needed sharpening, but because he had perfected a certain flick of the wrist with his hand clippers which wrenched the hairs from their follicles at the end of each stroke. He had never got round to buying electric clippers, but with his distinctive technique I doubt whether it would have made any difference.

One wonder was that anybody went to Josh for a haircut

because there was another barber in the town. My own opinion was that it was because everybody liked him.

Sitting there in his shop I looked at him as he worked. He was a tiny man in his fifties with a bald head that made a mockery of the rows of hair restorer on his shelves, and on his face rested the gentle smile which never seemed to leave him. That smile and the big, curiously unworldly eyes gave him an unusual attraction.

And then there was his obvious love of his fellow men. As his client rose from the chair, patently relieved that his ordeal was over, Josh fussed around him, brushing him down, patting his back and chattering gaily. You could see that he hadn't been just cutting this man's hair, he had been enjoying a happy social occasion.

Next to the big farmer, Josh looked smaller than ever, a minute husk of humanity, and I marvelled as I had often done at how he managed to accommodate all that beer.

Of course, foreigners are often astonished at the Englishman's ability to consume vast quantities of ale. Even now, after forty years in Yorkshire, I cannot compete. Maybe it is my Glasgow upbringing, but after two or three pints, discomfort sets in. The remarkable thing is that, throughout the years, I can hardly recall seeing a Yorkshireman drunk. Their natural reserve relaxes and they become progressively jovial as the long cascade goes down their throats, but they seldom fall about or do anything silly.

Josh, for instance. He would swallow around eight pints every night of the week, except Saturday when he stepped up his intake to between ten and fourteen, yet he never looked much different. His professional skill suffered, but that was all.

He was turning to me now. "Well, Mr. Herriot, it's good to see you again." He warmed me with his smile and those wide eyes with their almost mystic depths caressed me as he ushered me to the chair. "Are you very well?"

"I'm fine, thank you, Mr. Anderson," I replied. "And how are you?"

"Nicely, sir, nicely." He began to tuck the sheet under my chin, then laughed delightedly as my little beagle trotted in under the folds.

"Hullo, Sam, you're there as usual, I see." He bent and stroked the sleek ears. "By gum, Mr. Herriot, he's a faithful friend. Never lets you out of 'is sight if he can help it."

"That's right," I said. "And I don't like to go anywhere without him." I screwed round in my chair. "By the way, didn't I see you with a dog the other day?"

Josh paused, scissors in hand. "You did an' all. A little bitch. A stray—got 'er from the Cat and Dog Home at York. Now that our kids have all left home, t'missus and I fancied gettin' a dog, and we think the world of her. I tell ye, she's a grand 'un."

"What breed is she?"

"Eee, now you're askin'. Nobbut a mongrel, I reckon. I can't see any pedigree about her, but money wouldn't buy 'er."

I was about to agree with him when he held up a hand. "Hang on a minute and I'll bring 'er down."

He lived above the shop, and his feet clumped on the stairs as he returned with a little bitch in his arms. "There you are, Mr. Herriot. What d'you think of that?" He stood her on the floor for my inspection.

I looked at the little animal. She was a light grey in colour, with very long crinkled hair. In fact, at a quick glance she looked like a miniature Wensleydale sheep. Definitely a hound of baffling lineage, but the panting mouth and swishing tail bore witness to her good nature.

"I like her," I said. "I think you've picked a winner there."

"That's what we think." He stooped and fondled his new pet, and I noticed that he kept picking up the long hairs and rubbing them gently between finger and thumb again and again. It looked a little odd, then it occurred to me that that was what he was used to doing with his human customers. "We've called her Venus," he said.

"Venus?"

"Aye, because she's so beautiful." His tone was very serious.

"Ah yes," I said. "I see."

He washed his hands, took up his scissors again and grasped a few strands of my hair. Again, I saw that he went through the same procedure of rubbing the hairs between his fingers before cutting them.

I couldn't understand why he did this, but my mind was too preoccupied to give the matter much thought. I was steeling myself. Still, it wasn't too bad with the scissors—just an uncomfortable tug as the blunt edges came together.

It was when he reached for the clippers that I gripped the arms of the chair as though I were at the dentist. It was all right as long as he was running the things up the back of my neck; it was that jerk at the end, plucking the last tuft from its roots, that set my face grimacing at me in the mirror. Once or twice an involuntary "Ooh!" or "Aah!" escaped me, but Josh gave no sign of having heard.

I remembered that for years I had sat in that shop listening to the half-stifled cries of pain from the customers, but at no time had the barber shown any reaction.

The thing was that, though he was the least arrogant or conceited of men, he did consider himself a gifted hairdresser. Even now, as he gave me a final combing, I could see the pride shining from his face. Head on one side, he patted my hair repeatedly, circling the chair and viewing me from all angles, making a finicky snip here and there before holding up the hand mirror for my inspection.

"All right, Mr. Herriot?" he enquired with the quiet satisfaction that comes from a job well done.

"Lovely, Mr. Anderson, just fine." Relief added warmth to my voice.

He bowed slightly, well pleased. "Aye, you know, it's easy enough to cut hair off. The secret is knowin' what to leave on."

I had heard him say it a hundred times before, but I laughed dutifully as he whisked his brush over the back of my coat.

My hair used to grow pretty fast in those days, but I didn't have time to pay another visit to the barber before he arrived on my front doorstep. I was having tea at the time and I trotted to the door in answer to the insistent ringing of the bell.

He was carrying Venus in his arms but she was a vastly different creature from the placid little animal I had seen in his shop. She was bubbling saliva from her mouth, retching and pawing frantically at her face.

Josh looked distraught. "She's chokin', Mr. Herriot. Look at 'er! She'll die if you don't do summat quick!"

"Wait a minute, Mr. Anderson. Tell me what's happened. Has she swallowed something?"

"Aye, she's 'ad a chicken bone."

"A chicken bone! Don't you know you should never give a dog chicken bones?"

"Aye, ah know, ah know, everybody knows that, but we'd had a bird for our dinner and she pinched the frame out of the dustbin, the little beggar. She had a good crunch at it afore I spotted 'er, and now she's goin' to choke!" He glared at me, lips quivering. He was on the verge of tears.

"Now just calm down," I said. "I don't think Venus is choking. By the way she's pawing, I should say there's something stuck in her mouth."

I grabbed the little animal's jaws with finger and thumb and forced them apart. And I saw with a surge of relief the sight familiar to all vets—a long spicule of bone jammed tightly between the back molars and forming a bar across the roof of the mouth.

As I say, it is a common occurrence in practice and a happy one because it is harmless and easily relieved by a flick of the forceps. Recovery is instantaneous, skill minimal and the kudos most warming. I loved it.

I put my hand on the barber's shoulder. "You can stop worrying, Mr. Anderson, it's just a bone stuck in her teeth. Come through to the consulting room and I'll have it out in a jiffy."

[114]

I could see the man relaxing as we walked along the passage to the back of the house. "Oh, thank God for that, Mr. Herriot. I thought she'd had it, honest, I did. And we've grown right fond of the little thing. I couldn't bear to lose 'er."

I gave a light laugh, put the dog on the table and reached for a strong pair of forceps. "No question of that, I assure you. This won't take a minute."

Jimmy, aged five, had left his tea and trailed after us. He watched with mild interest as I poised the instrument. Even at his age, he had seen this sort of thing many a time and it wasn't very exciting. But you never knew in veterinary practice; it was worth hanging around because funny things could happen. He put his hands in his pockets and rocked back and forth on his heels, whistling softly as he watched me.

Usually it is simply a matter of opening the mouth, clamping the forceps on the bone and removing it. But Venus recoiled from the gleaming metal and so did the barber. The terror in the dog's eyes was reproduced fourfold in those of its owner.

I tried to be soothing. "This is nothing, Mr. Anderson. I'm not going to hurt her in the least, but you'll just have to hold her head firmly for a moment."

The little man took a deep breath, grasped the dog's neck, screwed his eyes tight shut and turned his head as far away as he could.

"Now, little Venus," I cooed, "I'm going to make you better."

Venus clearly didn't believe me. She struggled violently, pawing at my hand, to the accompaniment of strange moaning sounds from her owner. When I did get the forceps into her mouth, she locked her front teeth on the instrument and hung on fiercely. And as I began to grapple with her, Mr. Anderson could stand it no longer and let go.

The little dog leaped to the floor and resumed her inner battle there while Jimmy watched appreciatively.

I looked at the barber more in sorrow than in anger. This was just not his thing. He was manually ham-fisted, as his hairdressing

[115]

proved, and he seemed quite incapable of holding a wriggling dog.

"Let's have another go," I said cheerfully. "We'll try it on the floor this time. Maybe she's frightened of the table. It's a trifling little job, really."

The little man, lips tight, eyes like slits, bent and extended trembling hands towards his dog, but each time he touched her she slithered away from him until, with a great shuddering sigh, he flopped facedown on the tiles. Jimmy giggled. Things were looking up.

I helped the barber to his feet. "I tell you what, Mr. Anderson, I'll give her a short-acting anaesthetic. That will cut out all this fighting and struggling."

Josh's face paled. "An anaesthetic? Put her to sleep, you mean?" Anxiety flickered in his eyes. "Will she be all right?"

"Of course, of course. Just leave her to me and come back for her in about an hour. She'll be able to walk, then." I began to steer him through the door into the passage.

"Are you sure?" He glanced back pitifully at his pet. "We're doing the right thing?"

"Without a doubt. We'll only upset her if we go on this way."

"Very well, then, I'll go along to me brother's for an hour."

"Splendid." I waited till I heard the front door close behind him, then quickly made up a dose of pentothal.

Dogs do not put on such a tough front when their owners are not present and I scooped Venus easily from the floor onto the table. But her jaws were still clamped tight and her front feet at the ready. She wasn't going to stand for any more messing with her mouth.

"Okay, old girl, have it your own way," I said. I gripped her leg above the elbow and clipped an area from the raised radial vein. In those days, Siegfried or myself were often left to anaesthetise dogs without assistance. It is wonderful what you can do when you have to.

Venus didn't seem to care what I was about as long as I kept away from her face. I slid the needle into the vein, depressed the plunger and within seconds her fighting pose relaxed, her head dropped and her whole body sagged onto the table. I rolled her over. She was fast asleep.

"No trouble now, Jimmy, lad," I said. I pushed the teeth apart effortlessly with finger and thumb, gripped the bone with the forceps and lifted it from the mouth. "Nothing left in there—lovely. All done."

I dropped the piece of chicken bone into the waste bin. "Yes, that's how to do it, my boy. No undignified scrambling. That's the professional way."

My son nodded briefly. Events had gone dull again. He had been hoping for great things when Mr. Anderson draped himself along the surgery floor, but this was tame stuff. He had stopped smiling.

My own satisfied smile, too, had become a little fixed. I was watching Venus carefully, and she wasn't breathing. I tried to ignore the lurch in my stomach, because I have always been a nervous anaesthetist and am not very proud of it. Even now, when I come upon one of my younger colleagues operating, I have a nasty habit of placing my hand on the patient's chest wall over the heart and standing wide-eyed and rigid for a few seconds. I know the young surgeons hate to have me spreading alarm and despondency, and one day I am going to be told to get out in sharp terms, but I can't help it.

As I watched Venus, I told myself as always that there was no danger. She had received the correct dose and anyway, you often did get this period of apnoea with pentothal. Everything was normal, but just the same I wished to God she would start breathing.

The heart was still going all right. I depressed the ribs a few times—nothing. I touched the unseeing eyeball—no corneal reflex. I began to rap my fingers on the table and stare closely at the little animal, and I could see that Jimmy was watching me just as keenly. His deep interest in veterinary practice was built upon a fascination for animals, farmers and the open air, but it was

[117]

given extra colour by something else; he never knew when his father might do something funny or something funny might happen to him.

The unpredictable mishaps of the daily round were all good for a laugh and my son, with his unerring instinct, had a feeling that something of the sort was going to happen now.

His hunch was proved right when I suddenly lifted Venus from the table, shook her vainly a few times above my head, then set off at full gallop along the passage. I could hear the eager shuffle of the little slippers just behind me.

I threw open the side door and shot into the back garden. I halted at the narrow part—no, there wasn't enough room there —and continued my headlong rush till I reached the big lawn.

Here I dropped the little dog onto the grass and fell down on my knees by her side in an attitude of prayer. I waited and watched as my heart hammered, but those ribs were not moving and the eyes stared sightlessly ahead.

Oh, this just couldn't happen! I seized Venus by a hind leg in either hand and began to whirl her round and round my head. Sometimes higher, sometimes lower, but attaining a remarkable speed as I put all my strength into the swing. This method of resuscitation seems to have gone out of fashion now, but it was very much in vogue then. It certainly met with the full approval of my son. He laughed so much that he fell down and sprawled on the grass.

When I stopped and glared at the still immobile ribs, he cried, "Again, Daddy, again." And he didn't have to wait more than a few seconds before Daddy was in full action once more, with Venus swooping through the air like a bird on the wing.

It exceeded all Jimmy's expectations. He probably had wondered about leaving his jam sandwiches to see the old man perform, but how gloriously he had been rewarded. To this day the whole thing is so vivid: my tension and misery lest my patient should die for no reason at all; and, in the background, the helpless, high-pitched laughter of my son.

I don't know how many times I stopped, dropped the inert form on the grass, then recommenced my whirling, but at last, at one of the intervals, the chest wall gave a heave and the eyes blinked.

With a gasp of relief I collapsed facedown on the cool turf, peering through the green blades as the breathing became regular and Venus began to lick her lips and look around her.

I dared not get up immediately because the old brick walls of the garden were still dancing around me and I am sure I would have fallen.

Jimmy was disappointed. "Aren't you going to do any more, Daddy?"

"No, son, no." I sat up and dragged Venus onto my lap. "It's all over now."

"Well, that was funny. Why did you do it?"

"To make the dog breathe."

"Do you always do that to make them breathe?"

"No, thank heaven, not often." I got slowly to my feet and carried the little animal back to the consulting room.

By the time Josh Anderson arrived, his pet was looking almost normal.

"She's still a little unsteady from the anaesthetic," I said. "But that won't last long."

"Eee, isn't that grand! And that nasty bone, is it . . . ?"

"All gone, Mr. Anderson."

He shrank back as I opened the mouth. "You see?" I said. "Not a thing."

He smiled happily. "Did ye have any bother with her?"

Well, my parents brought me up to be honest rather than clever, and the whole story almost bubbled out of me. But why should I worry this sensitive little man? To tell him that his dog had been almost dead for a considerable time would not cheer him, nor would it bolster his faith in me.

I swallowed. "Not a bit, Mr. Anderson. A quite uneventful

[119]

operation." The whitest of lies, but it nearly choked me, and the aftertaste of guilt was strong.

"Wonderful, wonderful. I am grateful, Mr. Herriot." He bent over the dog, and again I noticed the strange rolling of the strands of hair between his fingers.

"Have ye been floatin' through the air, Venus?" he murmured absently.

The back of my neck prickled. "What . . . what makes you say that?"

He turned his eyes up to me, those eyes with their unworldly depths. "Well . . . I reckon she'd think she was floatin' while she was asleep. Just a funny feeling I had."

"Ah, yes, well, er . . . right." I had a very funny feeling myself. "You'd better take her home now and keep her quiet for the rest of the day."

I was very thoughtful as I finished my tea. Floating . . . floating.

A fortnight later I was again seated in Josh's barber's chair, bracing myself for the ordeal. To my alarm he started straight in with the dread clippers. Usually he began with the scissors and worked up gradually, but he was throwing me in at the deep end this time.

In an attempt to alleviate the pain, I began to chatter with an edge of hysteria in my voice.

"How is—ouch—Venus going on?"

"Oh fine, fine." Josh smiled at me tenderly in the mirror. "She was neither up nor down after that job."

"Well—ooh, aah—I really didn't expect any trouble. As I said, it was—ow—just a trifling thing."

The barber whipped out another tuft with that inimitable flick of his. "The thing is, Mr. Herriot, it's grand to 'ave faith in your vet. I knew our little pet was in good 'ands."

"Well, thank you very much, Mr. Anderson, it's—aaah—very nice to hear that." I was gratified, but that guilt feeling was still there.

[120]

I got tired of trying to speak while watching my twitching features in the mirror, so I tried to concentrate on something else. It is a trick I adopt at the dentist's and it doesn't work very well, but as the little man tugged away, I thought as hard as I could about my garden at Skeldale House.

The lawns really did want mowing, and there were all those weeds to get at when I had a minute to spare. I had got round to considering whether it was time to put some fertiliser on my outdoor tomatoes when Josh laid down the clippers and lifted his scissors.

I sighed and relaxed. The next part was only mildly uncomfortable, and, who knew, he might have had the scissors sharpened since last time. My mind was wandering over the fascinating subject of tomatoes when the barber's voice pulled me back to reality.

"Mr. Herriot." He was twiddling away at a wisp of my hair with his fingers. "I like gardening, too."

I almost jumped from the chair. "That's remarkable. I was just thinking about my garden."

"Aye, ah know." There was a faraway look in his eyes as he rolled and rolled with finger and thumb. "It comes through the hair, ye know."

"Eh?"

"Your thoughts. They come through to me."

"What!"

"Yes, just think about it. Them hairs go right down into your head, and they catch summat from your brain and send it up to me."

"Oh, really, you're kidding me." I gave a loud laugh that nevertheless had a hollow ring.

Josh shook his head. "I'm not jokin' nor jestin', Mr. Herriot. I've been at this game for nearly forty years, and it keeps happenin' to me. You'd be flabbergasted if I told ye some of the thoughts that's come up. Couldn't repeat 'em, I tell ye."

[121]

I slumped lower in my white sheet. Absolute rubbish and nonsense, of course, but I made a firm resolve never to think of Venus's anaesthetic during a haircut.

Chapter
14

November 1, 1961

When I awoke this morning everything was wonderfully still. It was a blessed relief because last night was as the others, and I was thrown about in my bunk like a rag doll.

I went up on deck and found we were anchored in the mouth of a river or inlet. A few hundred yards away I could see the Russian port of Klaipeda.

I couldn't believe the calm — only a gentle swell rocked the ship—but half a mile back, the great sea waves still dashed themselves against the entrance to the harbour.

Up on the bridge I found the captain, pale and unshaven. He told me he had had a terrible job bringing the ship between the concrete walls at the entrance to the harbour. He had signalled repeatedly for a pilot but none had come, and finally he was forced to bring the ship in himself. Doing this, in the dark, in unfamiliar waters and during a storm, must have been a great strain.

He said we were waiting now for a pilot to take us through the great concrete breakwaters to a berth at the quayside. At length one arrived, a little stubbly-chinned man of about thirty-five, in a very Russian-looking overcoat a couple of sizes too big for him and a large peaked cap.

He was very nervous as he guided us in. He kept hopping about the bridge, peering here and there, and then dashing to have a look over the ship's side. I was astonished to hear that he gave his commands in English and it was strange to hear him cry, "Starrboard," and the big Dane at the wheel reply, "Starrboard," then, "Meedsheeps," followed by the answering call, "Meedsheeps."

Up in the bows, the mate and a sailor were gazing down into the water and signalling back to the bridge—apparently testing the depth and looking for obstructions.

To my untutored eyes it seemed that the captain brought the ship in himself. He was as always, calm and self-contained, and as we approached another ship or part of the breakwater, he would say, "Perhaps a little astern, Mr. Pilot," or, "Port side, perhaps, Mr. Pilot," in a quiet voice while the little man rushed about the bridge in a panic.

On either side of the estuary, the banks were thickly clothed in pine trees, and further ahead I could see tenement buildings, and then the cranes and quays of the port.

Once we had been moored by the quayside, I looked eagerly ashore, almost into the eyes of a young Russian soldier. There were two of them standing by the gangway of the *Iris Clausen,* and at least two guarding each of the other ships in the port.

They all had automatic guns slung on their backs and were wearing long, greenish coats, crinkly, Wellington-type boots and furry hats turned up at the front and sides.

Leaning over the rail of our little ship, I was only a few yards away from my soldier. I raised my hand and gave him a wave.

"Good morning," I cried cheerfully.

His expression never changed. He looked back at me with a completely impassive, dead countenance.

I moved along the rail and tried his colleague. "Hello," I called, waving again.

The response was exactly the same. A blank, unsmiling stare.

Just then it started to rain, and they both reached back and pulled hoods over their heads.

I felt it was not a happy start, and I looked past them at a sight that was not much more cheering: a network of railway lines with wagons; a forest of huge cranes; and, around the perimeter, tall watch towers, each with its armed soldier looking down at us. Beyond the port itself rose an assortment of dilapidated houses.

Klaipeda is, of course, the old Lithuanian port of Memel, and I have previously read that when the Russians took over, a proportion of the native population was deported and replaced by Russians. I am unable to ascertain the extent of this, and since Klaipeda is now part of the Soviet Union, I shall refer to all the people I meet as Russians.

Very soon a large number of officials came aboard, and I was relieved to find that they were cheerful and smiling. There was much shaking of hands and loud laughter and everybody addressed me as Doktor in a guttural tone with the accent on the second syllable. Most of them were from the customs and immigration authorities, and among them were several young women, one of whom spoke very good English. In fact, nearly all of them seemed to be able to get along in English; the other language in which they conversed with the captain was German.

The exception in this merry company was a tall, lugubrious sanitary inspector, wearing breeches and a cowboy hat. I had to go down into the hold with him, where he looked around him sadly but said nothing.

Immediately afterwards, a little fat woman beckoned to me to accompany her to where the animals' food was kept. There were several tons of this surplus, and it was all to be left for the Russians, free of charge. But it seemed that they suspected some catch in this because, to my astonishment, the little woman began to slash open the bags of super-quality sheep nuts and the bales of sweet hay. She pushed her hand into the centre of each bag and bale and dropped some of the contents into a series of polythene bags. Apparently these samples had to go to a laboratory to be examined before they would accept the food.

I went back up to the captain's room, where the officials were still signing forms and smoking and drinking. They had been joined by the chief of "Saufratt," which deals with all the incom-

[125]

ing and outgoing cargoes, and like the others, he was polite, friendly and ready to roar with laughter at the slightest excuse.

I was interested in the dress of these men who are obviously important people. They all wore smartly cut dark suits, and some had greenish gabardine macintoshes, but the materials of their clothes looked cheap and shoddy. Still, they were trim and neatly turned out, but the whole effect was spoiled by the fact that every man sported an abominable off-white tweedy cloth cap pulled right down to his ears. This was clearly the fashion in these parts, but to me the result was truly ghastly.

However they were very pleasant, and I found their conversation fascinating. I was struck forcefully by their tremendous willingness to work and their desire to learn. They told me that most of them had begun as factory workers but had studied at night and in every available moment to rise to their present positions.

Of course all the time I was anxiously awaiting the veterinary examination of the sheep. The veterinary surgeon turned out to be a little fat woman very like the one who had inspected the food. Unlike the officials she could not speak a word of English, but she marched up to me, tapped her chest and said, "Doktor." As we shook hands as colleagues she burst into an infectious, bubbling laugh.

She had a helper with her, a big, tough-looking chap in blue dungarees and we all went down to the hold together. I was intrigued by her method of examining the sheep. The man penned five animals in a corner while she opened a little bag and took out a whole bunch of thermometers. These were strange-looking flat things with centigrade markings and attached to each was a piece of string with a clip on the end.

She methodically dipped each nozzle in a jar of vaseline before inserting it in the rectum and clipping the string to the wool. Then she stood looking at her watch for what seemed an age. Finally, she removed the thermometers and took the readings.

After that she had another five caught up, and again we had the lengthy wait and the reading before moving to another pen.

[126]

The realisation burst on me with a sense of shock that these were two-minute thermometers, unlike our half-minute ones, and also that she was going to examine ten sheep in every pen. This was going to take an awfully long time.

Gallantly holding her jar of vaseline, I tried to alleviate the boredom by making conversation. It was difficult since neither of us spoke a word of the other's language, but I managed to get over to her that most of the sheep were of the Romney Marsh breed. This appeared to delight her because thereafter, when she pushed the thermometer up a sheep's rectum, she would cry, "Rromnee Marrsh!" and laugh happily, then on to the next one and again the thrust of the thermometer and the joyous, "Rromnee Marrsh!"

It lightened the proceedings to a certain extent, but after an hour and a half we had covered only one side of the 'tween decks hold—about a quarter of the sheep—and I quailed at the thought of another four and a half hours of this.

But there was no doubt she was a pleasant little woman. She was dressed in a cheap-looking, navy-blue raincoat and the kind of velour hat you see in jumble sales in England, and her chubby face never stopped smiling.

The only time she looked serious was when she heard a cough from one of the Lincolns. It was the moment I had been dreading, and she turned to me questioningly.

"Ah-ah, ah-ha, ah-ha," she said in a fair imitation of the parasitic bark and raised her eyebrows.

I shrugged my shoulders. What could I do? How could I explain?

The animal's temperature was normal and she appeared reassured, but some time later another sheep coughed.

"Ah-ah, ah-ha, ah-ha?" she asked, and again I shrugged and gave a noncommittal smile.

About halfway through, we were joined by another vet, obviously the little woman's superior. He was very well dressed in dark overcoat and black trilby hat, and his handsome, high-cheek-boned, Asiatic face radiated charm as he shook my hand and thumped me on the back.

"Salaam aleikum," he said, somewhat to my surprise.

He, too, spoke no English, and when he heard the cough he swung round on me.

"Ah-ah, ah-ha, ah-ha?" he enquired.

I spread my hands and shook my head, and he laughed suddenly. He seemed a happy-go-lucky fellow and was clearly in a hurry to be off. He waved goodbye to his colleague, shook my hand warmly and smiled, then he strode from the hold.

I was still baffled by the oriental greeting and turned to the little woman. *"Salaam aleikum?"*

"Irkutsk, Tartar," she replied.

I realised that he came from the other end of this vast country, and, to let her know I understood, I pulled the corners of my eyes outwards.

She burst into a high-pitched giggle. She did love to laugh.

But the strain of hanging around with the pot of vaseline was beginning to tell. I tried to get rid of the tension by saying things like, "Look, this is driving me right up the bloody wall," at which she would give me a nod and a sweet, uncomprehending smile, but at last I could stand it no longer. I gave her back the vaseline and fled to the sanctuary of my cabin. I heard later that it took her five hours to get round the sheep.

The unloading berth is occupied by another ship, the *Ubbergen*, which is discharging a cargo of cattle and taking on a lot of little cob-like horses, so we cannot start our unloading until she moves. My immediate ambition was to get ashore, but the customs and immigration people had taken our passports, and until they came back nobody could leave the ship.

When the passports were returned I looked around for a companion, because John Crooks had warned me not to go ashore alone. The mate and engineer would not budge as they were worried about relations between Denmark and Russia, following a verbal attack on the Scandinavian countries by Khrushchev which they had heard on the radio in the Danish news. In fact, as I went around, it soon became obvious that none of the ship's company had any intention of going ashore.

It was the captain, gentlemanly as always, who stepped in. He could see that I was disappointed and said that, if I gave him a few minutes to wash and change, he would come with me.

As I waited on the deck the daylight faded rapidly to dusk, and lights began to appear in the tenements beyond the port. They all seemed like forty-watt bulbs, and the general effect was dreary in the extreme.

By the time the captain was ready, it was quite dark. I had been strongly advised by the man from Saufratt to visit the seamans' club called Interklub and I decided to do this and leave the exploration of the town until tomorrow.

We went down the gangway, showed our passports to the soldiers and I took my first step onto Russian soil. I said, "Interklub?" and the soldiers pointed vaguely along the railway lines into the distance. They still preserved the deadpan look I had seen in the morning, and it struck me that they were just about the only unsmiling Russians I had met all day. I wondered why they acted so very differently.

There were floodlights shining down from the cranes, and we began to pick our way along by their light. But it was slow going. We were in a maze of sheds, cranes and wagons, and the quayside seemed to stretch indefinitely ahead.

I soon became impatient. "Look," I said to the captain. "The town's just over there." I pointed to the high fence that surrounded the harbour. "Surely there's a gate of some kind here."

The captain shook his head. "I think not. There will be a gate house somewhere along at the end. We must go through there."

Now, I believe I am fundamentally a fairly solid citizen, but every now and then I do something daft. This was one of those times. I decided to look for a shortcut.

I groped my way into the darkness behind a row of wagons, and I was studying the dim silhouette of the fence when suddenly an enormous dog shot out at me from the gloom. It was of an Alsatian type, and it came at me with a terrifying baying sound. I caught a glimpse of a snarling mouth and white teeth, but I didn't wait to make a closer examination. I took off at great speed, but after a few yards I tripped over a railway line and fell flat on my face.

At that moment I was sure it was all over with me. I am not going to suggest that my past life flashed before my eyes, but in that second or two I did have a vivid impression of the incongruity of my situation. I, James Herriot, Yorkshire Dales veterinary surgeon and dog lover, meeting my end by being torn to pieces by a dog behind a railway wagon on a dark night in Russia.

I was waiting for the first crunch when I heard the animal twang to a stop at the end of its chain, and as I looked back, I could see it fighting to get at me, the great teeth, gleaming in the floodlights, about six inches from my leg.

I scrabbled along on my stomach to where the captain was waiting. That usually calm man was visibly shaken, and he helped me up, gripped my arm and hurried me along the road we had first taken.

As I struggled to regain my breath, I felt I had learned my first lesson. Do not go nosing about in dark places in Russia. Keep to the proper path.

When we came to the gate house, I had to smile to myself. My nerves were still vibrating after my encounter with that creature back there, but when I saw the groups of soldiers around the brightly lit room and more soldiers behind a sliding window carrying out an interminable, hard-eyed scrutiny of our passports and ourselves, the absurdity of my idea of a shortcut was forced on me. Before passing through, I took a last glance at the long stretch of quayside behind us, and I wondered how many more four-legged killers were lurking in the shadows under the fence.

Once in the street, we asked a young fellow in the inevitable light cloth cap about Interklub, and he politely marched us to the door before shaking hands and leaving us.

Inside we found a very comfortable, even mildly luxurious club. Russian time is two hours ahead of ours so most of the activities had ceased for the night, but nevertheless the little man in charge was effusive in his welcome.

The captain spoke to him in German and told him who we were, and he kept bowing and smiling as though we were his long-lost brothers.

He insisted on taking us on a tour of the establishment and ushered us into each room with a deferential, "Please, please"— a common and much-used word among the people I have met here.

There were a little cinema, dance hall, bar, and a billiard room where some young German sailors were knocking balls about. We saw several cosy lounges, in one of which a large radio was giving a commentary of Tottenham Hotspur in the European Cup.

Our guide led us into a library and reading room where there were newspapers in all languages, and I hastened to the English section, hoping to catch up with some of the latest news. However, I found only a pile of the *Daily Worker,* and the most recent was a fortnight old. I was moodily reading about the long-past England v. Wales football match when the little man bustled up, all smiles, and began to load me with a huge quantity of books and pamphlets, all in English.

These books were all beautifully produced, and one of them, *Khrushchev in the U.S.A.,* would be very expensive to buy in England. I was also presented with a roll of cine film of the same visit and a little badge which I must keep for Rosie.

We left on a wave of cordiality, and as I came out into the night and looked at the gaunt tenements nearby, it struck me how sharply they contrasted with that club.

Tonight, as I complete my journal, two thoughts are uppermost in my mind. First, my bed will keep still for a change, and second, it has been an eventful day.

Chapter
15

"This is Amber," Sister Rose said. "The one I wanted you to examine."

I looked at the pale, almost honey-coloured shading of the hair on the dog's ears and flanks. "I can see why you've given her that name. I bet she'd really glow in the sunshine."

The nurse laughed. "Yes, funnily enough it was sunny when I first saw her, and the name just jumped into my mind." She gave me a sideways glance. "I'm good at names, as you know."

"Oh yes, without a doubt," I said, smiling. It was a little joke between us. Sister Rose had to be good at christening the endless stream of unwanted animals passing through the little dog sanctuary that lay behind her house and which she ran and maintained by organising small shows and jumble sales, and by spending her own money.

And she didn't only give her money, she gave her precious time, because as a nursing sister she led a full life of service to the human race. I often asked myself how she found the time to fight for the animals, too. It was a mystery to me, but I admired her.

"Where did this one come from?" I asked.

Sister Rose shrugged. "Oh, found wandering in the streets of Hebbleton. Nobody knows her, and there have been no enquiries to the police. Obviously abandoned."

I felt the old tightening of anger in my throat. "How could they do this to such a beautiful dog? Just turn it away to fend for itself."

"Oh, people like that have some astonishing reasons. In this case I think it's because Amber has a little skin disease. Perhaps it frightened them."

"They could at least have taken her to a vet," I grunted as I opened the door of the pen.

I noticed some bare patches around the toes, and as I knelt and examined the feet, Amber nuzzled my cheek and wagged her tail. I looked up at her, at the flopping ears, the pronounced jowls and the trusting eyes that had been betrayed.

"It's a hound's face," I said. "But how about the rest of her? What breed would you call her?"

Sister Rose laughed. "Oh, she's a puzzle. I get a lot of practice at guessing, but this one beats me. I wondered if a fox hound had got astray and mated with something like a Labrador or Dalmatian, but I don't know."

I didn't know, either. The body, dappled with patches of brown, black and white, was the wrong shape for a hound. She had very large feet, a long thin tail in constant motion and everywhere on her coat the delicate sheen of gold.

"Well," I said. "Whatever she is, she's a bonny one, and good-natured, too."

"Oh, yes, she's a darling. We'll have no difficulty in finding a home for her. She's the perfect pet. How old do you think she is?"

I smiled. "You can never tell for sure, but she's got a juvenile look about her." I opened the mouth and looked at the rows of untainted teeth. "I'd say nine or ten months. She's just a big pup."

"That's what I thought. She'll be really large when she reaches full size."

As if to prove the sister's words, the young bitch reared up and planted her forefeet on my chest. I looked again at the laughing mouth and those eyes. "Amber," I said. "I really like you."

"Oh, I'm so glad," Sister Rose said. "We must get this skin

trouble cleared up as quickly as possible, and then I can start finding her a home. It's just a bit of eczema, isn't it?"

"Probably . . . probably . . . I see there's some bareness around the eyes and cheeks, too." Skin diseases in dogs, as in humans, are tricky things, often baffling in origin and difficult to cure. I fingered the hairless areas. I didn't like the combination of feet and face, but the skin was dry and sound. Maybe it was nothing much. I banished to the back of my mind a spectre that appeared for a brief instant. I didn't want to think of that, and I had no intention of worrying Sister Rose. She had enough on her mind.

"Yes, probably eczema," I said briskly. "Rub this ointment well into the parts, night and morning." I handed over the box of zinc oxide and lanolin. A bit old-fashioned, maybe, but it had served me well for a few years and ought to do the trick, in combination with the nurse's good feeding.

When two weeks passed without news of Amber, I was relieved. I was happy, too, at the thought that she would now be in a good home among people who appreciated her.

I was brought back to reality with a bump when Sister Rose phoned one morning.

"Mr. Herriot, those bare patches aren't any better. In fact, they're spreading."

"Spreading? Where?"

"Up her legs and on the face."

The spectre leaped up, mouthing and gesticulating. Oh, not that, please. "I'll come right out, Sister," I said, and on my way to the car I picked up the microscope.

Amber greeted me as she had before, with dancing eyes and lashing tail, but I felt sick when I saw the ragged denudation of the face and the naked skin staring at me on the legs.

I got hold of the young animal and held her close, sniffing at the hairless areas.

Sister Rose looked at me in surprise. "What are you doing?"

"Trying to detect a mousy smell."

"Mousy smell? And is it there?"

"Yes."

"And what does that mean?"

"Mange."

"Oh, dear." The nurse put a hand to her mouth. "That's rather nasty, isn't it." Then she put her shoulders back in a characteristic gesture. "Well, I've had experience of mange before, and I can tackle it. I've always been able to clear it up with sulphur baths, but there's such a danger of infection to the other dogs. It really is a worry."

I put Amber down and stood up, feeling suddenly weary. "Yes, but you're thinking of sarcoptic mange, Sister. I'm afraid this is something rather worse."

"Worse? In what way?"

"Well, the whole look of the thing suggests demodectic mange."

She nodded. "I've heard of that—and it's more serious?"

"Yes. . . ." I might as well bite the bullet. "Very often incurable."

"Goodness me, I had no idea. She wasn't scratching much, so I didn't worry."

"Yes, that's just it," I said wryly. "Dogs scratch almost nonstop with sarcoptic mange and we can cure it, but they often show only mild discomfort with demodectic, which usually defeats us."

The spectre was very large in my mind now, and I use the word literally because this skin disease had haunted me ever since I had qualified. I had seen many fine dogs put to sleep after the most prolonged attempts to treat them.

I lifted the microscope from the back of the car. "Anyway, I may be jumping the gun. I hope I am. This is the only way to find out."

There was a patch on Amber's left foreleg which I squeezed and scraped with a scalpel blade. I deposited the debris and serum on a glass slide, added a few drops of potassium hydroxide and put a cover-slip on top.

Sister Rose gave me a cup of coffee while I waited, then I rigged

[135]

up the microscope in the light from the kitchen window and looked down the eyepiece. And there it was. My stomach tightened as I saw what I didn't want to see—the dread mite, demodex canis; the head, the thorax with its eight stumpy legs and the long, cigar-shaped body. And there wasn't just one. The whole microscopic field was teeming with them.

"Ah, well, that's it, Sister," I said. "There's no doubt about it. I'm very sorry."

The corners of her mouth drooped. "But . . . isn't there anything we can do?"

"Oh, yes, we can try. And we're going to try like anything because I've taken a fancy to Amber. Don't worry too much. I've cured a few demodex cases in my time, always by using the same stuff." I went to the car and fished around in the boot. "Here it is—Odylen." I held up the can in front of her. "I'll show you how to apply it."

It was difficult to rub the lotion into the affected patches as Amber wagged and licked, but I finished at last.

"Now do that every day," I said, "and let me know in about a week. Sometimes that Odylen really does work."

Sister Rose stuck out her jaw with the determination that had saved so many animals. "I assure you I'll do it most carefully. I'm sure we can succeed. It doesn't look so bad."

I didn't say anything, and she went on. "But how about my other dogs? Won't they become infected?"

I shook my head. "Another odd thing about demodex. It very rarely spreads to another animal. It is nothing like as contagious as the sarcops, so you have very little cause for worry in that way."

"That's something, anyway. But how on earth does a dog get the disease in the first place?"

"Mysterious again," I said. "The veterinary profession is pretty well convinced that all dogs have a certain number of demodex mites in their skins, but why they should cause mange in some and not in others has never been explained. Heredity has got something to do with it because it sometimes occurs in several dogs in the same litter. But it's a baffling business."

I left Sister Rose with her can of Odylen. Maybe this would be one of the exceptions to my experiences with this condition. I had to hope so.

I heard from the nurse within a week. She had been applying the Odylen religiously but the disease was spreading further up the legs.

I hurried out there, and my fears were confirmed when I saw Amber's face. It was disfigured by the increasing hairlessness, and when I thought of the beauty that had captivated me on my first visit, the sight was like a blow. Her tail-wagging cheerfulness was undiminished, and that seemed to make the whole thing worse.

I had to try something else, and in view of the fact that a secondary subcutaneous invasion of staphylococci was an impediment to recovery, I gave the dog an injection of staph toxoid. I also started her on a course of Fowler's solution of arsenic, which at that time was popular in the treatment of skin conditions.

When ten days passed I had begun to hope, and it was a bitter disappointment when Sister Rose telephoned just after breakfast.

Her voice trembled as she spoke. "Mr. Herriot, she really is deteriorating all the time. Nothing seems to do any good. I'm beginning to think that . . ."

I cut her off in mid-sentence. "All right, I'll be out there within an hour. Don't give up hope yet. These cases sometimes take months to recover."

I knew as I drove to the sanctuary that my words were only meant to comfort. They had no real substance. But I had tried to say something helpful because there was nothing Sister Rose hated more than putting a dog to sleep. Of all the hundreds of animals that had passed through her hands, I could remember only a handful that had defeated her. Very old dogs, in a hopeless plight with chronic kidney or heart conditions, or young ones with distemper. With all the others she had battled until they were fit

[137]

to go to their new homes. And it wasn't only Sister Rose—I myself recoiled from the idea of doing such a thing to Amber. Something about that dog had taken hold of me.

When I arrived I still had no idea what I was going to do, and when I spoke I was half-surprised at the things I said.

"Sister, I've come to take Amber home with me. I'll be able to treat her myself every day, then. You've got enough to do, looking after your other dogs. I know you have done everything possible, but I'm going to take on this job myself."

"But . . . you are a busy man. How will you find the time?"

"I can treat her in the evenings and any other spare moments. This way I'll be able to check on her progress all the time. I'm determined to get her right."

And, driving back to the surgery, I was surprised at the depth of my feeling. Throughout my career I have often had this compulsive desire to cure an animal, but never stronger than with Amber. The young bitch was delighted to be in the car with me. Like everything else, she seemed to regard this as just another game, and she capered around, licking my ear, resting her paws on the dash and peering through the windscreen. I looked at her happy face, scarred by the disease and smeared with Odylen, and thumped my hand on the wheel. Demodectic mange was hell, but this was one case that was going to get better.

It was the beginning of a strangely vivid episode in my life, as fresh now as it was then, more than thirty years ago. We had no facilities for boarding dogs—very few vets had at that time—but I made up a comfortable billet for her in the old stable in the yard. I penned off one of the stalls with a sheet of plywood and put down a bed of straw. Despite its age, the stable was a substantial building and free from draughts. She would be snug in there.

I made sure of one thing. I kept Helen out of the whole business. I remembered how stricken she had been when we adopted Oscar the cat and then lost him to his rightful owner, and I knew she would soon grow too fond of this dog. But I had forgotten about myself.

[138]

Veterinary surgeons would never last in their profession if they became too involved with their patients because I knew from experience that most of my colleagues were just as sentimental over animals as the owners, but before I knew what was happening, I became involved with Amber.

I fed her myself, changed her bedding and carried out the treatment. I saw her as often as possible during the day, but when I think of her now, it is always night. It was late November, when darkness came in soon after four o'clock, and the last few visits were a dim-sighted fumbling in cow byres; when I came home, I always drove round to the yard at the back of Skeldale House and trained my headlights on the stable.

When I threw open the door, Amber was always there, waiting to welcome me, her forefeet resting on the plywood sheet, her long yellow ears gleaming in the bright beam. That is my picture of her to this day. Her temperament never altered, and her tail swished the straw unceasingly as I did all the uncomfortable things to her: rubbing the tender skin with the lotion, injecting her with the staph toxoid, taking further skin scrapings to check progress.

As the days and the weeks went by and I saw no improvement, I became a little desperate. I gave her sulphur baths, derris baths, although I had done no good with such things in the past, and I also began to go through all the proprietary things on the market. In veterinary practice every resistant disease spawns a multitude of quack "cures," and I lost count of the shampoos and washes I swilled over the young animal in the hope that there might be some magic element in them, despite my misgivings.

Those nightly sessions under the headlights became part of my life, and I think I might have gone on blindly for an indefinite period, until one very dark evening with the rain beating on the cobbles of the yard I seemed to see the young dog for the first time.

The condition had spread over the entire body, leaving only tufts and straggling wisps of hair. The long ears were golden no longer. They were almost bald, as was the rest of her face and head. Everywhere, her skin was thickened and wrinkled and had assumed a bluish tinge. And when I squeezed it, a slow ooze of pus and serum came up around my fingers.

I flopped back and sat down in the straw while Amber leaped around me, licking and wagging. Despite her terrible state, her nature was unchanged.

But this couldn't go on. I knew now that she and I had come to the end of the road. As I tried to think, I stroked her head, and her cheerful eyes were pathetic in the scarecrow face. My misery was compounded of various things. I had grown too fond of her, I had failed and she had nobody. Only Sister Rose and myself. And that was another thing. What was I going to tell that good lady after all my brave words?

It took me until the following lunchtime to summon the will to telephone her. In my effort to be matter-of-fact about the thing, I fear I was almost brusque.

"Sister," I said, "I'm afraid it's all over with Amber. I've tried everything, and she has got worse all the time. I do think it would be the kindest thing to put her to sleep."

Shock was evident in her voice. "But . . . it seems so awful. Just for a skin disease."

"I know, that's what everybody thinks. But this is a dreadful thing. In its worst form it can ruin an animal's life. Amber must be very uncomfortable now, and soon she is going to be in pain. We can't let her go on."

"Oh . . . well, I trust in your judgment, Mr. Herriot. I know you wouldn't do anything that wasn't necessary." There was a long pause, and I knew she was trying to control her voice. Then she spoke calmly. "I think I would like to come out and see her when I can get away from the hospital."

"Please, Sister," I said gently. "I'd much rather you didn't."

Again the pause, then, "Very well, Mr. Herriot. I leave everything to you."

I had an urgent visit immediately afterwards, and a rush of work kept me going all afternoon. I never really stopped thinking about what I had to do later, but at least the other pressures stopped it from obsessing me. It was, as always, pitch-dark when I drove into the yard and opened the garage doors.

And it was like all the other times. Amber was there in the beam, paws on the plywood, body swinging with her wagging, mouth open and panting with delight, welcoming me.

I put the barbiturate and syringe into my pocket before climbing into the pen. For a long time I made a fuss of her, patting her and talking to her as she leaped up at me. Then I filled the syringe.

"Sit, girl," I said, and she flopped obediently onto her hindquarters. I gripped her right leg above the elbow to raise the radial vein. There was no need for clipping—all the hair had gone. Amber looked at me interestedly, wondering what new game this might be as I slipped the needle into the vein. I realised that there was no need to say the things I always said. "She won't know a thing." "This is just an overdose of anaesthetic." "It's an easy way out for her." There was no sorrowing owner to hear me. There were just the two of us.

And as I murmured, "Good girl, Amber, good lass," while she sank down on the straw, I had the conviction that if I *had* said those things, they would have been true. She didn't know a thing between her playfulness and oblivion, and it was indeed an easy way out from that prison which would soon become a torture chamber.

I stepped from the pen and switched off the car lights, and in the cold darkness the yard had never seemed so empty. After the weeks of struggle, the sense of loss and failure was overpowering, but at the end I was at least able to spare Amber the ultimate miseries: the internal abscesses and septicaemia that await a dog suffering from a progressive and incurable demodectic mange.

For a long time I carried a weight around with me, and I feel some of it now after all these years. Because the tragedy of Amber was that she was born too soon. At the present time we can cure

[141]

most cases of demodectic mange by a long course of organo-phosphates and antibiotics, but neither of these things was available then when I needed them.

It is still a dread condition, but we have fought patiently with our modern weapons and won most of the battles over the past few years. I know several fine dogs in Darrowby who have survived, and when I see them in the streets, healthy and glossy-coated, the picture of Amber comes back into my mind. It is always dark, and she is always in the headlight's beam.

Chapter
16

"Just look at that," the farmer said.

"At what?" I was "cleansing" a cow (removing the afterbirth), and my arm was buried deep in the cow's uterus. I turned my head to see him pointing at the byre floor beneath my patient. I saw four white jets of milk spurting onto the concrete from the animal's udder.

He grinned. "That's a funny thing, isn't it?"

"It isn't, really," I said. "It's a reflex action caused by my hand twiddling the uterus about. This acts on a gland in the brain which causes the milk to flow. I often see cows letting their milk down like that when I'm cleansing them."

"Well, that's a rum 'un." The farmer laughed. "Any road, you'd better get finished quick or you'll have a few pints of milk to knock off your bill."

That was in 1947, the year of the great snow. I have never known snow like that before or since, and the odd thing was that it took such a long time to get started. Nothing happened in November and we had a green Christmas, but then it began to get colder and colder. All through January a north-east wind blew, apparently straight from the Arctic; usually after a few days of this sort of unbearable blast, snow would come and make things a bit warmer. But not in 1947.

Each day we thought it couldn't get any colder, but it did, and then, borne on the wind, very fine flakes began to appear over the last few days of the month. They were so small you could hardly see them, but they were the forerunners of the real thing. At the beginning of February, big, fat flakes started a steady, relentless descent on our countryside, and we knew, after all that buildup, that we were in for it.

For weeks and weeks the snow fell, sometimes in a gentle, almost lazy curtain that remorselessly obliterated the familiar landmarks, at others in fierce blizzards. In between, the frost took over and transformed the roads into glassy tracks of flattened snow over which we drove at fifteen miles an hour.

The long garden at Skeldale House disappeared under a white blanket. There was a single deep channel by the wall-side where I fought my way daily to my car in the yard at the top.

The yard itself had to be dug out every day and the opening of the big double doors into the yard was a back-breaking job. One day I found the doors were jammed immovably in high mounds of frozen snow. There was nothing I could do about it so they were left standing open for the rest of the winter.

To get to our cases we did a lot of walking since so many of the farm tracks were blocked wall to wall. On the very high country there were some farms we couldn't reach at all, and that was very sad because there was no doubt that many animals died for lack of veterinary help. It was around the middle of March when helicopters were dropping food on these isolated spots that Bert Kealey telephoned me.

He was one of those out of reach on a high moor that was bleak even in summertime, and I was surprised to hear his voice.

"I thought your phone wires would be down, Bert," I said.

"Naw, they've survived, God knows how." The young farmer's voice was cheerful, as always. He ran a small suckling herd on the high tops and was one of the many who scratched a living from the unfriendly soil.

"But ah'm in trouble," he went on. "Polly's just had a litter, and she hasn't a drop of milk."

[144]

"Oh dear, that's unfortunate," I said. Polly was the only pig on the Kealey farm.

"Aye, it's a beggar. Bad enough losin' the litter—there's twelve smashin' little pigs—but it's Tess I'm bothered about."

"Yes . . . yes . . ." I was thinking of Tess, too. She was Bert's eight-year-old daughter, and she had a thing about little pigs. She had persuaded her father to buy her an in-pig sow for her birthday so that she could have a litter of her own. I could remember Tess's excitement when she showed me her birthday gift a few days after its arrival.

"That's Polly Pig," she said, pointing to the sow nuzzling the straw in its pen. "She's mine. My dad gave her to me."

I leaned over the pen. "Yes, I know. You're a lucky girl. She looks a fine pig to me."

"Oh, she is, she is." The little girl's eyes shone with pleasure. "I feed her every day, and she lets me stroke her. She's nice."

"I bet she is. She looks nice."

"Yes, and do you know something else?" Tess's face grew serious, and her voice took on a conspiratorial tone. "She's going to have babies in March."

"Well, I never!" I said. "Is that so? You'll have a whole lot of little pink pigs to look after." I held my hands a few inches apart. "Just about this size."

She was so thrilled at the thought that she was lost for words. She just smiled happily, got hold of the wall of the pen and began to jump up and down.

All this came back to me as I listened to Bert Kealey's voice on the phone.

"Do you think she's got mastitis, Bert? Is the udder red and swollen? Is she off her food?"

"No, nowt like that. She's eatin' her head off, and her udder's not a bit inflamed."

"Well, then, it's a straight case of agalactia. She needs a shot of pituitrin, but how the heck is she going to get it? Your district's been cut off for weeks now."

It takes a lot to make a Yorkshire farmer admit that his farm is inaccessible because of the weather, but these were exceptional circumstances and Bert had to agree.

"I know," he said. "Ah've tried diggin' me road out, but it fills up as fast as I clear it. Anyway, top road's blocked for two miles, so I'm wastin' me time."

I thought for a moment. "Have you tried getting some cow's milk into the piglets? An egg mixed with a quart of milk and a teaspoonful of glucose isn't a bad milk substitute. I know you got some glucose for those scouring calves."

"I've tried 'em with that," Bert replied. "Put it in a Yorkshire puddin' tin and dipped their noses in it, but they wouldn't look at it. If only they could have a good suck at their mother and get summat into their bellies it would start them off, and then they'd maybe have a go at t'substitute."

He was right. There was nothing to compare with that first suck. And if they didn't get it, those tiny creatures with their empty stomachs could start dying at an alarming rate.

"Looks like they're all goin' to go down t'nick," Bert said. "Ah don't know what little Tess is goin' to say. She'll be heartbroken."

I tapped my fingers against the receiver. An idea was forming in my mind. "There's just one possibility," I said. "I know I can get to the top of Dennor Bank because the road is open to there. After that it's all flat going to your place. I could maybe get there on skis."

"Skis?"

"Yes, I've been doing a bit of that lately. But I've not tackled anywhere as far off as your farm. I can't be sure that I'll make it, but I'll try."

"By 'eck, I'd be very grateful if you would, Mr. Herriot. It's t'little lass ah'm thinkin' of."

"Same here, Bert. Anyway, I'll have a go. I'll leave now."

On the summit of Dennor Bank I manoeuvered my car as close as possible to the tall white walls the snow ploughs had thrown up, got out and buckled on my skis. I have to admit I was

[146]

beginning to fancy myself a bit on skis, because one bonus of the long spell of snow and frost was that some nice little slopes had become available. With a few other enthusiasts I had been rushing out to the hillsides at every opportunity and I had found that gliding down again and again in the frosty air was one of the most exhilarating things I had ever known. I had bought a book on the subject and thought I was becoming quite skilful.

All I needed was the bottle of pituitrin and a syringe, and I put them in my pocket.

To get to the Kealey farm in normal conditions you drove a couple of miles along a very straight road, turned right and made for the high-lying village of Branderley. Bert's farm lay in an isolated position about halfway along this second road.

But today, although I had travelled this region a hundred times, I might have been in a strange country, somewhere I had never seen before. The stone walls had been deeply engulfed, so there were no fields, no roads, nothing but a yawning white expanse with the tops of telegraph poles sticking up here and there. It was uncanny.

Without skis there was no saying how far I might have sunk into the billowing drifts. I felt a twinge of misgiving, but I had promised to try. Anyway, I would be able to travel cross-country. It would be like cutting off two sides of a triangle, and I was pretty sure the farm lay in one of the hollows just below the dark skyline.

I am afraid this is not a glorious episode in my history. I had slithered amateurishly for about half a mile when the snow started again. It seemed to come from nowhere and was by no means a blizzard, just a white veil that cut me off completely from my surroundings. There was no point in going on because I had lost all sense of direction; the swirling screen of flakes was impenetrable. There is no disguising the fact that I was scared. As I stood stock-still in the cold with my eyes half-closed, I wondered what would happen to me if the snow didn't stop. In fact, I still wonder about that, because I could have blundered for miles in that empty wilderness without coming upon a house.

[147]

It is a question that will never be answered because the flurry stopped as suddenly as it had begun. My heart thumped as I stared around me, and the dark smudge of my car roof in the white distance was a sweet sight. I headed back to it with a speed worthy of an Olympic skier, and I am sure my eyes were popping as I kept them fixed on my link with home.

Relief flowed through me as I threw my skis into the back and started the engine, and I had left Dennor Bank behind and was well on the way to Darrowby before my pulse rate returned to normal.

"Bert," I said on the phone. "I'm terribly sorry but I just couldn't make it. I got caught by a snow shower and had to turn back."

"Well, ah'm glad ye did turn. I've been a bit worried since ye left. Fellers have got lost and died in the snow up here. I shouldn't have let you try."

He paused for a moment, then said wistfully, "If only there was some other way to make Polly let 'er milk down."

As he spoke, the picture flashed into my mind of that cow I was cleansing and the white jets striking the byre floor. And there were other memories—when I was doing uterine examinations on sows, the same thing had happened.

"Maybe there is a way," I blurted out.

"What d'ye mean?"

"Bert, have you ever had your hand inside a sow?"

"Eh?"

"Have you ever examined a sow internally?"

"You mean . . . in 'er pig bed?"

"Yes."

"Nay, nay, ah leave that to you chaps."

"Well, I want you to start now. Get some warm water and soap and . . ."

"Hey, hang on, Mr. Herriot. I'm sure there's no more pigs left in 'er."

"I don't suppose there are, Bert, but do as I say. Soap your arm

[148]

well and use any household antiseptic you have. Then feel your way into the vagina till you come to the cervix. She's only just farrowed, so the cervix should still be open. Put a finger inside and waggle the pig bed around a bit."

"Oh, 'eck, I don't fancy this. What's it all about?"

"It often brings the milk down, that's what it's about, so get going."

I put down the phone and went through to have lunch. Helen kept glancing at me during the meal as I answered little Jimmy's questions in a preoccupied way. She knew something was on my mind, and I don't suppose she was surprised when I leaped to my feet at the sound of the phone ringing.

It was Bert. He sounded breathless but triumphant. "It worked, Mr. Herriot! I 'ad a good waggle round like you said, then I tried the udder. I could draw milk out of every tit and there wasn't a drop there before. It was like magic."

"Are the piglets feeding?"

"Not half! They were fightin' to get a drink before, but they're all laid quiet in a row, suckin' hard. It's lovely to see them."

"Well, that's great," I said. "But we haven't won yet. The piglets have had that vital first feed, but Polly will probably dry up again by tomorrow or even tonight. You'll have to get your hand in again."

"Oh, crumbs." A lot of the enthusiasm went out of Bert's voice. "I thought I'd finished wi' that."

The poor man did indeed have to perform his unusual task several times and, in fact, Polly never did come fully to her milk, but the piglets were kept going until they were able to drink the milk substitute from the tin. The litter was saved.

The great snow of 1947 was followed by the most glorious summer I can remember, but in late April in the high country, the white streaks still lay behind the walls, standing out against the green moorland like the ribs of a great beast. But the roads were clear, and my journey to see one of Bert Kealey's heifers had none of the drama of last time.

When I had finished my job, young Tess took me through to see her beloved Polly and family.

"They're pretty, aren't they?" she said as we looked into the pen at the twelve chunky little pigs playing around their mother.

"They certainly are, Tess," I replied. "Your first attempt at pig breeding has been a big success, but I really think you have to thank your father for it. He did a wonderful job."

Bert gave a wry smile, then screwed up his face at the memory. "Aye, maybe so, and I reckon it was worth it. Aye, well, it's wonderful what ye can do when you have to."

Chapter
17

"Are you all right, Helen?"

I looked round anxiously as my wife fidgeted in her seat. We were in the one- and-ninepennies in the La Scala cinema in Brawton, and I had a strong conviction that we had no right to be there.

I had voiced my doubts that morning. "I know it's our half-day, Helen, but with the baby due anytime, don't you think it would be safer to stay around Darrowby?"

"No, of course not." Helen laughed incredulously at the very idea of missing our outing. And I could see her point because it was an oasis of relaxation in our busy lives. For me it was an escape from the telephone and the mud and the Wellington boots, and for my wife it meant a rest from her own hard slog, plus the luxury of having meals cooked and served by somebody else.

"But, honestly," I said. "What if the thing comes on quickly? It's all right you laughing. We don't want our second child to be born in Smith's book shop or the back of a car."

The whole business had me worried. I wasn't as bad as when Jimmy was on his way. I was in the R.A.F. then, and I went into a sort of decline during which I lost two stones in weight, which wasn't all due to the hard training. People make jokes about this syndrome, but I didn't find it funny. There was something about having babies that really got through to me, and lately I had spent a lot of time flapping around watching Helen's every move, much to her amusement. I just couldn't be calm about the thing. There isn't much of the yogi in my make-up at any time, and over the last two days the tension had built up.

But Helen had been adamant this morning. She wasn't going to be done out of her half-day by such a trifle, and now here we were in the La Scala, with Humphrey Bogart competing vainly for my attention and my blood pressure rising steadily as my wife squirmed around and occasionally ran a thoughtful hand over her swollen abdomen.

As I scrutinised her keenly from the corner of my eye, she gave a convulsive jerk and her lips parted in a soft moan. An instant dew of perspiration had already sprung out all over me before she turned and whispered, "I think we'd better go now, Jim."

Stumbling over the outstretched legs in the darkness, I guided her up the sloping aisle, and such was my panic that I felt sure the crisis would be upon us before we reached the usherette standing at the back with her torch.

I was thankful to reach the street and see our little car standing only a few yards away. As we set off, I seemed to notice the rattles and bumping of the old springs for the first time. It was the only time in my life that I wished I had a Rolls Royce.

The twenty-five miles to Darrowby seemed to take an eternity. Helen sat very quiet by my side, occasionally closing her eyes and catching her breath, while my heart beat a tattoo against my ribs. When we reached our little town I turned the car to the right towards the market place.

Helen looked at me in surprise. "Where are you going?"

"Well, to Nurse Brown's, of course."

"Oh, don't be so silly. It's not time for that yet."

"But . . . how do you know?"

"I just know." Helen laughed. "I've had a baby before, don't you remember? Come on, let's go home."

Heavy with misgiving, I drove to Skeldale House, and as we mounted the stairs I marvelled at Helen's composure.

It was the same when we got into bed. She lay there, obviously not very comfortable but quite patient, and there was about her a calm acceptance of the inevitable which I could not share.

I suppose I kept dropping into what is termed a fitful slumber because it was 6 A.M. when she nudged my arm.

"Time to go, Jim." Her tone was very matter-of-fact.

I shot from the bed like a jack-in-the-box, threw on my clothes and shouted across the landing to Auntie Lucy who was staying with us for the occasion, "We're off!"

A faint reply came through the door. "All right, I'll see to Jimmy."

When I returned to our bedroom, Helen was dressing methodically.

"Get that suitcase out of the cupboard, Jim," she said.

I opened the cupboard door. "Suitcase?"

"Yes, that one. It's got my nighties and toilet things and baby clothes and everything I'll need. Go on, bring it out."

Suppressing a groan, I carried the case out and stood waiting. .I had missed all this last time because of the war and had often regretted it, but at that moment I wasn't at all sure whether I wouldn't rather be elsewhere.

Outside, it was a glorious May morning, the air limpid with the new-day freshness that had soothed the irritation of many an early call, but it was all lost on me today as I drove across the empty market place.

We had only about half a mile to go, and I was pulling up outside Greenside Nursing Home within minutes. There was a touch of grandeur about the name, but, in fact, it was just the small dwelling house of Nurse Brown. Upstairs there were a couple of bedrooms which for many years had seen the arrival of the local children.

I knocked at the door and pushed it open. Nurse Brown gave me a quick smile, put her arm round Helen's shoulders and led her upstairs. I was left in the kitchen feeling strangely alone and helpless, but a voice cut in on my jumbled thoughts.

[153]

"Now then, Jim, it's a grand mornin'."

It was Cliff, Nurse Brown's husband. He was sitting in the corner of the kitchen eating his breakfast, and he spoke to me casually as though we had encountered each other in the street. He wore the broad grin that never seemed to leave his face, but I suppose I half expected that he would leap from the table, seize my hand and say, "There, there," or something of the sort.

However, he continued to work his way phlegmatically through the stack of bacon, eggs, sausages and tomatoes on his plate, and I realised that over the years he must have seen hundreds of quivering husbands standing in that kitchen. It was old stuff to Cliff.

"Yes, Cliff . . . yes. . . ." I replied. "I think it will turn out hot later."

He nodded absently and pushed his plate to one side to join an empty porridge bowl before turning his attention to bread and marmalade. Nurse Brown was a noted cook as well as a baby expert, and it was evident that she believed in ensuring that her husband, a very big man and a lorry driver for one of the local contractors, would not grow faint from hunger during the morning.

Watching him slapping on the marmalade, I cringed inwardly at the creaking sounds from the floorboards above. What was happening in that bedroom?

As he chewed, Cliff seemed to notice that I was perhaps one of the more distraught type of husbands because he turned his big, kind smile on me. He was and is one of the nicest men in our town, and he spoke gently.

"Don't worry, lad," he said. "It'll be right."

His words were mildly soothing, and I fled. In those days it was unheard of for the husband to be present at the birth, and though it is now the in thing to observe it all, I marvel at the fortitude of these young men. I know beyond all doubt that Herriot would be carried away unconscious at some time during the proceedings.

When Siegfried arrived at the surgery, he was very thoughtful.

"You'd better stick around, James. I'll get through the morning round on my own. Take it quietly, my boy. All will be well."

It was difficult to take it quietly. I found that expectant fathers really did pace the floor for long periods, and I varied this by trying to read the newspaper upside down.

It was around eleven o'clock when the long-awaited telephone call came. It was my doctor and good friend, Harry Allinson. Harry always spoke in a sort of cheerful shout, and his very presence in a sickroom was a tonic. This morning the booming voice was like the sweetest music.

"A sister for Jimmy!" His words were followed by a burst of laughter.

"Oh great, Harry. Thank you, thank you. That's marvellous news." I held the receiver against my chest for a few moments before putting it down. I walked with dragging steps to the sitting room and lay back in a chair until my nerves had stopped vibrating.

Then, on an impulse, I leaped to my feet. I believe I have said before that I am a fairly sensible man with a propensity for doing daft things, and I decided that I had to go round to the nursing home immediately.

At that time, a husband was not welcome straight after the birth. I knew it because I had gone to see Jimmy too soon and had not been well received. But still I went.

When I burst into her establishment, Nurse Brown's usual smile was absent. "You've done it again, haven't you?" she said with some asperity. "I told you with Jimmy that you should have given us time to get the baby washed, but it seems you took no notice."

I hung my head sheepishly, and she relented. "Oh, well, now you're here you might as well come upstairs."

Helen had the same tired, flushed look that I remembered before. I kissed her thankfully. We didn't say anything, just smiled at each other. Then I had a look in the cot by the bed.

Nurse Brown regarded me with tight lips and narrowed eyes as

[155]

I peered down. Last time I had been so aghast at Jimmy's appearance that I had mortally offended her by asking if there was anything wrong with him, and heaven help me, I felt the same now. I won't go into details but the new little girl's face was all squashed and red and bloated, and the sense of shock hit me as it had done before.

I looked up at the nurse, and it was only too clear that she was waiting for me to say something derogatory. Her normally laughing face was set in a threatening scowl. One wrong word from me and she would have kicked me on the shins—I was sure of that.

"Gorgeous," I said weakly. "Really gorgeous."

"All right." She had seen enough of me. "Out you go."

She ushered me downstairs, and as she opened the outside door, she fixed me with a piercing eye. That bright little woman could read me without effort. She spoke slowly and deliberately, as though addressing a person of limited intelligence.

"That . . . is . . . a . . . lovely . . . healthy . . . baby. . . ." she said and closed the door in my face.

And, bless her heart, her words helped me, because as I drove away, I knew she must be right. And now, all these years later, when I look at my handsome son and my beautiful daughter, I can hardly believe my own stupidity.

When I returned to the surgery, there was one visit waiting for me, high in the hills, and the journey up there was like a happy dream. My worry was over, and it seemed that all nature was rejoicing with me. It was the ninth of May, 1947, the beginning of the most perfect summer I can remember. The sun blazed; soft breezes swirled into the car, carrying their fragrance from the fells around; an elusive breath of the bluebells, primroses and violets scattered everywhere on the grass, flowing among the shadows of the trees.

After I had seen my patient, I took a walk on the high tops along a favourite path of beaten earth on the hill's edge, with Sam trotting at my heels.

I looked away over the rolling patchwork of the plain, sleeping in the sun's haze, and at the young bracken on the hillside, springing straight and green from last year's dead brown stalks. Everywhere new life was calling out its exultant message, and it was so apt with my new little daughter lying down there in Darrowby.

We had decided to call her Rosemary. It is such a pretty name and I still love it, but it didn't last long. It became Rosie at a very early stage and though I did make one or two ineffectual stands, it has remained so to this day. She is now Dr. Rosie in our community.

On that May day I caught myself just in time. It has always been my practice to recline in the sunshine on the springy bed of heather that clusters on these hillsides, and I was just settling down when I remembered I had other things to do today. I sped back to Skeldale House and began to telephone my glad news all over the country.

It was received rapturously by all, but it was Tristan who grasped the essentials of the situation.

"We've got to wet this baby's head, Jim," he said seriously.

I was ready for anything. "Of course, of course, when are you coming over?"

"I'll be there at seven," he replied crisply, and I knew he would be.

Tristan was concerned about the venue of the celebration. There were four of us in the sitting room at Skeldale House— Siegfried, Tristan, Alex Taylor and myself. Alex was my oldest friend—we started school together in Glasgow at the age of four —and when he came out of the army after five years in the western desert and Italy, he came to spend a few weeks with Helen and me in Darrowby. It wasn't long before he had fallen under the spell of country life, and now he was learning farming and estate agency with a view to starting a new career. It was good that he should be with me tonight.

Tristan's fingers drummed on the arm of his chair as he thought aloud. His expression was fixed and grave, his eyes vacant.

"We'd normally go to the Drovers but they've got that big party on tonight, so that's no good," he muttered. "We want a bit of peace and quiet. Let's see, now, there's the George and Dragon—Tetley's beer, splendid stuff, but I've known them a bit careless with their pipes and I've had the odd sour mouthful. And, of course, we have the Cross Keys. They pull a lovely pint of Cameron's, and the draught Guinness is excellent. And we mustn't forget the Hare and Pheasant—their bitter can rise to great heights, although the mild is ordinary." He paused for a moment. "We might do worse than the Lord Nelson—very reliable ale—and, of course, there's always . . ."

"Just a minute, Triss," I broke in. "I went round to Nurse Brown's this evening to see Helen, and Cliff asked if he could come with us. Don't you think it would be rather nice to go to his pub since the baby was born in his house?"

Tristan narrowed his eyes. "Which pub is that?"

"The Black Horse."

"Ah, yes, ye-es." Tristan looked at me thoughtfully and put his fingertips together. "Russell and Rangham's. A good little brewery, that. I've had some first-rate pints in the Black Horse, though I've noticed a slight loss of nuttiness under very warm conditions." He looked anxiously out of the window. "It's been a hot day today. Perhaps we'd . . ."

"Oh, for heaven's sake!" Siegfried leaped to his feet. "You sound like an analytical chemist. It's only beer you're talking about, after all."

Tristan looked at him in shocked silence, but Siegfried turned to me briskly. "I think that's a pleasant idea of yours, James. Let's go with Cliff to the Black Horse. It's a quiet little place."

And indeed, as we dropped to the chairs in the bar parlour, I felt we had chosen the ideal spot. The evening sunshine sent long golden shafts over the pitted oak tables and the high-backed settles where a few farm men sat with their glasses. There was nothing smart about this little inn, but the furniture which hadn't been changed for a hundred years gave it an air of tranquillity. It was just right.

Reg Wilkey, the diminutive landlord, welcomed us and charged our glasses from his tall white jug.

Siegfried raised his pint. "James, may I be the first to wish a long life, health and happiness to Rosemary."

"Thank you, Siegfried," I said, feeling suddenly very much among friends as the others said, "Here, here," and began to drink.

Cliff, his face wreathed in his eternal smile, lowered the level in his glass by half, then turned to the landlord. "It gets better, Reg," he said reverently. "It gets better."

As Reg bowed modestly, Cliff said, "Ye know, Jim, I've said for years that me two best friends are Mr. Russell and Mr. Rangham. I think the world of 'em."

Everybody laughed, and the stage was set for a happy celebration. With my anxieties over, I felt wonderful.

After a couple of pints, Siegfried patted me on the shoulder. "I'm off, James. Have a good time. Can't tell you how pleased I am."

I watched him go, and I didn't argue. He was right. There was a veterinary practice out there, and somebody had to watch the shop. And this was my night.

It was one of those cosy evenings when everything seemed perfect. Alex and I recalled our childhood in Glasgow, Tristan came up with some splendid memories of Skeldale House in the bachelor days and over everything, like a beneficent moon, hung the huge smile of Cliff Brown.

A great love of my fellow men mounted in me, and I kept buying drinks for the local people around us. Finally I grew tired of fumbling for money and handed my wallet to the landlord. It was stuffed with notes because I had made a special visit to the bank that afternoon.

"Here, Reg," I said. "Just keep taking the drinks out of that."

"Aye, right, Mr. Herriot," he replied without changing expression. "It'll mek it easier."

It did make it a lot easier. Men whom I hardly knew raised their glasses and toasted my new daughter repeatedly, and all I had to do was smile and raise mine in return.

When closing time was announced, it didn't seem possible that it was all coming to an end.

As the little pub emptied, I approached the landlord. "We can't go home yet, Reg."

He looked at me quizzically. "Well, ye know the law, Mr. Herriot."

"Yes, but this is a special night, isn't it?"

"Aye, it is, I suppose." He hesitated for a moment. "Tell ye what. I'll lock up, then we could go down and 'ave one or two in the cellar, just to finish off."

I put my arm round his shoulders. "Reg, what a delightful idea. Let's go down there."

We descended a few steps into the pub cellar, switched on the light and pulled the trapdoor closed after us. As we disposed ourselves among the barrels and crates, I looked around the company. Apart from the original four, we were now augmented by two young farmers, one of the local grocers and an official from the Darrowby Water Board. We were a warmly knit little group.

It was much easier down there. No need to bother the landlord with his jug. We just went to a barrel and turned the tap.

"Still plenty in the wallet, Reg?" I shouted.

"Aye, there's plenty 'ere, don't worry. Help yourselves."

We kept doing that, and the party never flagged. It must have been past midnight when we heard the thumping on the outside door. Reg listened for a few moments, then went upstairs. He returned soon but was preceded through the trapdoor by the long blue legs, tunic, cadaverous face and helmet of Police Constable Hubert Goole.

A silence fell on the merry gathering as the constable's melancholy gaze passed slowly over us.

[160]

"Drinkin' a bit late, aren't ye?" he enquired tonelessly.

"Ah, well." Tristan gave a gay little laugh. "It's a special occasion, you see, Mr. Goole. Mr. Herriot's wife gave birth to a daughter this morning."

"Oh, aye?" The Old Testament countenance looked down on my friend from its bony perch. "I don't remember Mr. Wilkey applyin' for an extended licence for tonight."

It was the nearest he could get to making a joke, because P. C. Goole never made jokes. He was known in the town as a stern and unbending man, one who went by the book. It was no good riding a bike at night without lights when P. C. Goole was around. He was particularly merciless on this offence. He sang in the church choir, his morals were impeccable, he was active in community work, he did everything right. It was strange that in his mid-fifties he was still an ordinary constable.

Tristan bounced back. "Ah, yes, ha-ha, very good. But, of course, this was a totally impromptu thing. Spur of the moment, you know."

"Ye can call it what ye like, but you're breakin' the law and you know it." The big man unbuttoned his breast pocket and flipped open his notebook. "I'll have to 'ave your names."

I was sitting on an upturned crate, and I gripped my knees tightly. What an end to the happy evening. Nothing much happened in the town, and this would make headlines in the *Darrowby and Houlton Times.* It would look great, with all my friends involved, too. And poor little Reg standing sheepishly in the background—he would really get it in the neck, and it was all my fault.

Tristan, however, was not beaten yet. "Mr. Goole," he said coldly, "I'm disappointed in you."

"Eh?"

"I said I'm disappointed. I'd have expected you to show a different attitude on an occasion like this."

The constable was unmoved. He poised his pencil. "I'm a policeman, Mr. Farnon, and I 'ave my duty to do. We might as well start with your name." He wrote carefully, then looked up. "What's your address, now?"

"It seems to me," said Tristan, ignoring the question, "that you have forgotten all about little Julie."

"What about Julie?" The long face showed a certain animation for the first time. Tristan's mention of P. C. Goole's beloved Yorkshire terrier had found a tender spot.

"Well, as I recall," Tristan went on, "Mr. Herriot sat up for several hours during the night with Julie when she was having pups. In fact, if it hadn't been for him, you might have lost the pups and Julie, too. I know it's a few years ago, but I remember it distinctly."

"Now, then, that has got nowt to do with tonight. I've told ye, I have my duty to do." He turned to the official of the Water Board.

Tristan returned to the attack. "Yes, but surely you could have a drink with us on a night like this when Mr. Herriot has become a father for the second time. It's the same thing, in a way."

P. C. Goole paused, and his face softened. "Julie's still goin' strong."

"Yes, I know," I said. "Wonderful little thing for her age."

"And I still have one of them pups."

"Of course. You've had him in to see me a few times."

"Aye . . . aye . . ." P. C. Goole hitched up his tunic, delved in his trouser pocket and brought out a large watch. He studied it thoughtfully. "Well, I'm off duty about now. Suppose I could have a drink with ye. I'll just phone in to the office first."

"Oh, good!" Tristan moved quickly to the barrel and drew another pint.

When the constable returned from the phone, he raised the glass solemnly. "Here's wishin' t'little lass all the best," he said and took a long swallow.

"Thank you, Mr. Goole," I replied. "You're very kind."

He sat down on one of the lower steps, placed his helmet on a crate and had another deep drink. "Both well, I 'ope?"

"Yes, just grand. Have another."

It was surprising how soon he seemed to forget all about his notebook, and the party picked up again rapidly. The relief of the escape added greatly to the festivities, and joy reigned unrestrained.

"It's bloody 'ot down 'ere," P. C. Goole remarked after some time and removed his tunic. With this symbolic gesture, the last barrier went down.

And yet, over the next two hours, nobody got really plastered. Nobody, that is, except P. C. Goole. With the rest of us it was a case of laughter, reminiscing and an undoubted heightening of the senses, but the policeman passed through various phases on the road to a fairly profound inebriation.

The first was when he insisted on a Christian-name relationship, then he became almost tearfully affectionate as he rhapsodised on the wonders of birth, human and canine. The latest phase was more sinister. He was turning aggressive.

"You're 'avin' another, Jim." It was a statement rather than an enquiry as the tall, shirt-sleeved figure bent, swaying slightly, over the tap of the barrel, glass at the ready.

"No thanks, Hubert," I replied. "I've had enough."

He blinked at me owlishly. "You're not 'avin' another?"

"No, honestly, Hubert, I've had it. I started long before you."

He sent another pint frothing into his glass before continuing. "Then you're a bloody piker, Jim," he said. "And if there's one thing I can't shtand, if there's one thing I can't bloody well shtand, it's a bloody piker."

I tried an ingratiating smile. "I'm terribly sorry, Hubert, but I'm up to here, and, anyway, it's half-past two. I really think we ought to be going."

It seemed to be a general sentiment because the assembly all began to get to their feet.

"Goin'?" Hubert glared at me belligerently. "Whassa matter with you? The night's young yet." He slurped down another mouthful of beer indignantly. "You ask a feller to 'ave a

[163]

drink with you, and next minute ye say we're goin'. Itsh not right."

"Now, now, Hubert," said little Reg Wilkey, sidling up to him, smiling and radiating the bonhomie that came from thirty years' practice at easing reluctant clients from his premises. "Be a good lad, now. We've all 'ad a grand time and it's been lovely seein' you, but everybody's settin' off 'ome. Now where's your jacket?"

The constable muttered and grumbled as we helped him into his tunic and balanced his helmet on his head but allowed us to lead him up the steps into the darkness of the pub. Outside, I installed him in the back of my car, with Tristan and Alex on either side. Cliff sat with me in front.

Before we left, the landlord passed my wallet through the window. It had slimmed down to the point of emaciation, and it occurred to me that my bank manager, who was always advising me in the kindest possible way to watch my overdraft, would be tossing uneasily in his bed if he knew.

I drove through the sleeping town and turned down the narrow street towards the market place. As we approached, I could see that the cobbled square was deserted except for two figures standing at the edge of the roadway under a street light. With a twinge of alarm I recognised Inspector Bowles and Sergeant Rostron, our two head policemen. They were standing, very erect and trim-looking, hands behind their back, glancing around them keenly. They looked as though they wouldn't miss any misdemeanours in their vicinity.

A sudden scream from the back seat almost sent me through a shop window. Hubert had seen them, too.

"It's that bugger Rostron!" he yelled. "I 'ate that bugger! He's 'ad it in for me for years, and I'm goin' to tell 'im what I think about 'im!"

There was a thrashing of arms in the back as he wound down the window and started his tirade at the top of his voice. "You bloody rotten . . . !"

For the second time that night an icy dread swept me that something awful was going to happen because of me.

"Quell him!" I shouted. "For God's sake, quell him!"

However, my friends in the rear had anticipated me. Hubert's cries were suddenly switched off as Tristan and Alex bundled him to the floor and fell on top of him. Tristan was actually sitting on his head when we came up to the two policemen, and only muffled sounds drifted from below.

As we passed, the inspector nodded and smiled, and the sergeant gave me a friendly salute. It was not difficult to read their minds as they docketed away another item of information. Mr. Herriot, returning from yet another night call. A dedicated vet, that young man.

With their colleague writhing on the floor behind me, I could not relax until we had turned off the square, out of sight and sound. Hubert, when allowed to get up, seemed to have lost a lot of his belligerence. In fact he was reaching the sleepy stage and when he arrived at his home, he walked quietly and fairly steadily up his garden path.

Back in Skeldale House, I went up to our bedroom. The big room with the double bed, wardrobe and dressing table was eerily empty without Helen.

I opened the door to the long, narrow apartment that had been the dressing room in the great days of the old house. It was where Tristan had slept when we were all bachelors together, but now it was Jimmy's room, and his bed stood in exactly the same place as my old friend's.

I looked down on my son as I had often looked down on Tristan in his slumbers. I used to marvel at Tristan's cherubic innocence, but even he could not compete with a sleeping child.

I gazed at little Jimmy, then glanced at the other end of the room where a cot stood to receive Rosie.

Soon, I thought, I would have two in here. I was becoming rich.

Chapter
18

November 2, 1961

We learned this morning that we would not start unloading the sheep until this evening as the *Ubbergen* was still occupying the berth, so this gave me plenty of opportunity to explore the town.

Shortly after breakfast an important person came aboard, the head director of "Inflot," which deals with the movement of all ships in the harbour.

He was a kindly-looking man of about fifty, with an attractive smile. He wore very thick glasses, and he told me that his weak eyesight had been caused by hours of studying at night. His English was very good.

Maybe it was because he was so pleasant that I was emboldened to broach the question of the school. Another reason, of course, was that I was somewhat puffed up by my own importance. When I was recently elected chairman of the Darrowby Parent-Teachers' Association, it gave my ego a definite boost, and when our headmaster expressed an interest in Russian education, he started an idea in my mind.

Anyway, whatever the cause, I was about to do another of my daft things.

"Do you think I could possibly see inside a Russian school?" I asked him.

The eyes behind the glasses stopped twinkling, and he gave me a long, thoughtful stare. After a few moments he nodded. "I think it will be all right if you ask permission when you get to the school. As it happens, my wife is a teacher, and if you go to Skola Number Two, you could ask for Madame Juowskaya."

I could hardly wait to get ashore, but again I couldn't find any volunteers to come with me. When I finally approached the captain, he probably felt like throwing me over the side. He was short of sleep after our stormy voyage and weary with his long negotiations with the officials but still he had the goodness to humour me.

He smiled and said, "Of course, Mr. Herriot." As he settled his peaked hat on his silvery head and pulled on a smart navy-blue coat, I thought how very distinguished he looked.

Down the gangway again, past the unsmiling soldiers and along the railway tracks towards the gate. But I just had to solve the mystery of the man-eating dog. As we passed the wagon of last night I caught the captain's arm.

"Just a minute," I said. "I want to have a peep behind here."

For a moment he lost his poise and his eyes widened. "Mr. Herriot, no! What are you doing?"

"It's all right." I smiled reassuringly. "I only want a quick look."

With the greatest care I edged my way behind the wagon, but the dog was gone. There was only an empty kennel. Then I noticed there was a kennel about every fifty yards and a chain attached by a ring to a wire that stretched along the entire length of the fence.

As I re-emerged, to the obvious relief of the captain, I saw in the distance groups of dogs being led towards us. We passed them on the way to the gate house; large, stringy creatures loping along on the end of their leads, looking neither to right nor left. They were of the Alsatian type but taller, and they certainly had a lean and hungry look.

[167]

I looked around at the soldiers by the water's edge and in the watch towers, and back again at the dogs. Best of luck, I thought, to anybody who tried to get in or out of here after dark.

As we walked along, loudspeakers blared at us from all directions. This has gone on all the time the ship has been in Klaipeda; it is not music, but talking. Talk, talk, talk, all day. I do not know if it is political indoctrination or news of Soviet achievements, but it goes on without stopping, and I am getting tired of it.

Once outside the harbour, we began to make our way through the streets. Klaipeda is a town of 100,000 inhabitants, and we headed for what we thought was the centre of the place.

The streets on the outskirts were simply packed-down earth, and this applied also to the footpaths. Great muddy puddles stood everywhere, and there were holes, sometimes three- or four-feet-deep, dug in the footpaths and apparently just left with the heap of soil beside them.

Apart from the tenements there were the old Lithuanian houses, and these were in a very poor state of repair, with the paint flaking and roof tiles loose or missing. Many of the houses had little balconies in front of the upper windows.

There were quite a few people about, picking their way over the reddish clay.

We walked until we reached the main street, Montes Street. This had a cobbled surface and proper pavements, and there were shops on either side.

The book shops seemed to sell only technical literature. There was a store full of bicycles, scooters and mopeds and a sports shop with roller skates— of a different type from ours—fencing foils and table-tennis sets in the window. One shop was apparently devoted entirely to chessmen and chessboards.

We saw what looked like one of our licenced grocers, with lots of tinned and bottled goods and bottles of wine on show, but the place that really intrigued me was the fish shop. Its window was filled with large imitation fish of all colours. These models were covered with dust and were enough to put one off fish for life.

[168]

Inside, I could see a high counter, with white enamel bowls filled with the real things.

A characteristic of all the shops was their general dinginess. The windows were all dirty and unwashed, and there was no attempt to display their wares attractively.

There was very little traffic—mainly commercial vehicles, with an occasional private car or taxi.

There were a lot of people in the town centre, most of the women in head scarves and undistinguished clothes. It occurred to me then that I had not seen a single smartly dressed woman since my arrival. In fact, women seemed to do a lot of the rough jobs. Back in the harbour, women, dressed in cloaks and hoods, operated some of the mighty cranes that served the ships. I noticed, too, on a building site a group of girls throwing bricks from one to another, as our bricklayers do. Their hands must have been hard and rough.

A column of youngsters marched by, led by a tall man, probably a teacher. They were laughing and singing and looked very like English children, except that many of the boys had peaked army-style caps and the little girls without exception wore long, brown woollen stockings of the sort girls used to wear in our country in my early schooldays. All the children looked healthy and happy.

I stopped a young man in the street and showed him the slip of paper with the name of the school written in Russian. Again there was the polite response. He went out of his way and led us to the door of the school.

It was a large, old-fashioned type of building set flush on the roadside, with no sign of a playground. It looked more like a big block of offices.

The man from Inflot had told me to ask permission, but there didn't seem to be anybody about, so I did my second daft thing of the trip: I just barged inside, followed dutifully by the captain.

Once through the door there was something I noticed immediately—the intense silence, unusual in a school. We were in a long passage, with walls hung with brightly coloured paintings of every

[169]

conceivable sporting activity and of Russian feats of arms. These latter were done in a very romantic style: soldiers with bandaged foreheads, bayonets outstretched, handsome faces gazing fearlessly ahead. There was a glass case containing diplomas and certificates.

Many doors led off the passage, and I began to work my way along, knocking first, then trying the handle. They all seemed to be locked, and when I reached one near the end I had given up hope. I turned the handle without knocking, and it flew open.

I almost fell into a big room with a lot of startled women looking at me. They were all seated around a long table, and at the top was a big, impressive man with craggy features. He was staring at me harder than any of them.

I was obviously in the staff room, and I realised that I must have presented a strange sight. I had brought only my working clothes with me on the voyage and was clad in the black plastic macintosh I wore round the farms. This coat was frayed at cuffs and collar, and tattered by many horn thrusts. When horns tore off buttons and ripped pockets, I didn't like to pass it on to Helen to repair, because despite my efforts to keep it clean it carried the powerful odour of the farmyard deep in its seams. So I always did the sewing myself, using the thick, bright-blue nylon with which I stitched cows' wounds. This, with the ends of the coloured threads hanging loose, gave the garment an even more bizarre appearance.

They all continued to stare, but the man at the head of the table had clearly seen enough. He rose from his chair and hurried through a door at the far end. It didn't need a lot of intuition to know that he had gone to the telephone.

A realisation of my imprudence was dawning on me, but I swallowed a lump in my throat, gave what I hoped was a winning smile and said, "Madame Juowskaya?"

One of the women nodded; the others looked at her questioningly, and she turned deathly pale. She must have thought I was somebody sinister because she was undoubtedly frightened.

[170]

The captain could see it was time he took over. He stepped in front of me and addressed the company rapidly in German. He told them that I was chairman of the P.T.A. in Darrowby, but this information, not surprisingly, evoked no gasps of awe.

I stood there, the centre of all those female eyes. They were a very attractive lot of young women, for all the world like teachers in Britain except for one dark-skinned Mongolian miss, but it was easy to see that they were not similarly impressed with me.

The captain, a man of infinite resource, came to the rescue again and asked which one was the English teacher. The prettiest of them all came forward, and I was just about to speak to her when the door behind me burst open and two Russian army officers marched in.

They were massive men, very smart in their high-shouldered uniforms, epaulettes with stars, breeches and shiny high boots. They began to speak rapidly with the man who had returned to the top of the table, glaring over at me every few seconds. The man was wide-eyed, throwing his arms around, shaking his head, and I required no knowledge of Russian to divine that he was telling them that I had rushed in here from nowhere, he had no idea who the devil I was and he didn't like the look of me one little bit.

I do not wish to be over-dramatic, but I am convinced that if Captain Rasmussen had not been with me, I would have been hustled off to the local jail, but he stepped in once more with a flurry of explanations in German.

Another thing that saved me was that the little English teacher began to talk to me about the school. I sat down by her side at the table, and the officers moved close to me as we spoke together. All the time I was very conscious of their towering presence; they hung over me, looking me up and down, no doubt mystified at my eccentric apparel.

On an inspiration, I asked the English teacher her name. It was a real jawbreaker and I couldn't make much of it, but she said she was known as what sounded like "Kitty." She told me she was married, with a child of six.

She clapped her hands together. "Oh, I am so excited," she said. "I have taught English for so long, but I have never spoken to a real Englishman before. You must tell me if my pronunciation is very bad."

"I give you my word, you speak better English than I do," I replied. And with my thick Glaswegian, it was the literal truth. Kitty was delighted.

She told me that the director of the school had taken all the 1200 children away for the day on what was a regular visit to some local institution, where they saw a film show and listened to talks. This accounted for the silence. The big man at the head of the table was the deputy director.

As we swapped information, the other teachers pulled their chairs closer to us and listened with the greatest interest as Kitty passed everything on to them. Even the forbidding deputy director could not contain his curiosity and leaned across the table, elbows on the wood, watching me intently.

As the atmosphere grew more cordial, I was relieved to see the two officers move away and lean against the wall. Their previous hostile expressions were now merely impassive.

A hectic question-and-answer ensued, with Kitty relaying my words round the table.

"At what age do your children start school?" she asked.

When I replied, "At four or five years old," it caused general amazement.

"Ours do not start till seven or eight years old," she said, and I was similarly surprised.

The deputy director got quite heated on this point. He banged his hand on the table and declared that, according to the principles of education, it was impossible to teach children of five. What could they possibly learn? he wanted to know.

When I told him they learned simple sums and words to start with, he shook his head vigorously in disbelief.

All the teachers were astonished, too, to hear about the normal school hours in Britain. Kitty told me that younger Russian children go from 8:30 A.M. till 2:30 P.M., and the fifth and sixth formers go from 2:30 P.M. till 7 P.M. or 8 P.M. at night.

Their classes average about thirty in number, and they teach all the mathematical subjects, physics, chemistry, biology, geography and Russian history. The principal foreign language at that school is English, then German and Lithuanian. French or Latin is not taught.

I had to get in a question about sport. "Do you have games in your curriculum?"

Kitty raised her hands and laughed. "Many, many games. Volley ball is the most popular, but there is also swimming, hockey, skating, football, P.E. and gymnastics.

"Also," she went on, "we have many school clubs and outside activities. Do you have pioneers in your country?"

I presumed that this meant camping and hiking. I said yes, we did this, too, in our schools, and I launched into an explanation of the Duke of Edinburgh's Award Scheme. I struck an unexpected snag here because none of them had even heard of the Duke of Edinburgh.

I laughed. "Oh, surely you must know him. Our Queen's husband?"

Blank faces and shrugs all round.

"Edinbor? Edinbor?" Kitty queried.

"Yes, of course," I replied. "The capital of Scotland."

"But Dublin is the capital of Scotland," she said, so I decided to drop that topic.

Just about then, the army officers, seeing the teachers grouped around me, laughing and talking animatedly, apparently decided I was harmless and left the room. The atmosphere, which had thawed remarkably, became still more cordial, and the questioning went on at top speed.

"Do you teach religion?" I asked. Of course, I knew very well that they didn't, but I was interested to see what they would say.

Their reaction was pretty uniform—a kind of pitying amusement. One big dark girl, smiling sarcastically, put a question through Kitty.

"Do you teach about Darwin, too?"

I nodded. "Yes, we teach religion, and also about evolution and the scientific explanations of the beginnings of the world and of man."

This caused general puzzlement.

We discussed their attitude to religion, and I gathered that it is regarded as a private thing and people can go to church if they wish. It is not banned, nor is there any propaganda against it in the schools. The teachers seemed to be of the opinion that it would just quietly die out. There are three churches in Klaipeda, but in some towns of a similar size there are many more.

The teachers commiserated with me on the tremendous unemployment and poverty in Britain, and I got the impression that they thought I came from a land of starvation and soup kitchens. When I told them that British workers enjoyed a steady improvement in their living standards and that many of them owned cars, they looked at me with frank incredulity. Obviously they thought I was purveying capitalist propaganda.

And in one way, I couldn't blame them. I could see their eyes flickering over my ragged coat with the torn-down pockets and the buttons with their blue garlands. If this was a British professional man, what were the ordinary workers like?

"But your teachers do not have our standard of living," one of them declared.

I wondered if she had a point. These women were all beautifully dressed and clearly prosperous. I had the feeling that the teacher is a very prestigious person in Russia.

"What is the eleven-plus examination?" was the next question.

I tried to explain it as well as I could, but they really grilled me on this. The deputy director burst in, his deep-chested voice booming like an organ note amid the female chatter.

"There is absolutely no point in classing children according to

[174]

ability as you describe!" He was clearly a man of immovable opinions.

I looked across at him. "Well, do you have all levels in one class?"

The answer came back through Kitty. "All Russian children are clever." This was said with complete conviction and quite seriously.

In the ensuing discussion, I gathered that a very high proportion of the pupils go on to universities and that further education in the form of night schools is very popular. In fact, many Russians obtain a complete education up to university standard by working in these night schools.

"How about school meals?" I asked.

"Oh, yes," Kitty replied. "All the children stay for meals." She mentioned the number of kopeks they paid each day, and it worked out to about one shilling per meal.

"For this," Kitty went on, "they get a glass of tea, bread and sausage."

This did not sound as substantial as the food in English schools.

A volley of Russian from the deputy director was translated as an attack on the private school system in Britain. In the course of my reply I mentioned that the private schools were called public schools, which made them all look blank. The big man kept hammering home his point that only the children of the rich got a proper education in Britain, but when I pointed out that through university grants everybody in our country could receive a full education no matter what their financial position, he narrowed his eyes suspiciously. I don't think he believed me.

However, the party was really going with a bang, with lots of laughter, banter and give-and-take. It was a pity in one way that the children were away, but on the other hand I should never have had this priceless opportunity of a long discussion with all the teachers.

I was enjoying it so much that I could have stayed all day, but I saw the captain glancing anxiously at his watch and knew he was worried about getting back to the ship. Poor chap, he must be praying that he never has to sail with another veterinary attendant like me.

We took our leave in the friendliest spirit, with laughter and handshakes all round. Little Kitty was particularly nice.

"Oh, I am so thrilled. I will always remember meeting a real live Englishman," she said as we parted.

The deputy director also revealed an unexpected vein of massive charm as he led us out formally to the main door. His powerful features relaxed into a pleasant smile as he shook hands, bowed and waved us off down the street.

As we left the school, I saw some of the children coming back. They were all boys about twelve years old, and many had a greenish, military-style uniform and peaked cap. I saw one with a stripe on his arm. Whether this was a school uniform or whether they were members of a cadet corps, I do not know.

Back at the ship, trouble awaited me. A woman—who, I was told, was a farm commissar—had been asking to see me.

She was huge, well over six feet and broad in proportion, and as she towered over me, two hard eyes in a rough-hewn countenance regarded me coldly from under a black beret. She obviously meant business.

She spoke no English but came to the point straightaway.

"Ah-ha, ah-ha, ah-ha!" The other Russians had simulated the sheep's cough very closely, but this, rumbling from deep in her mighty rib-cage, was the best effort yet.

I tried my shrug and vacant smile, but they didn't work with this one. She seized my arm in steel claws and propelled me effortlessly towards the hold.

Down there among the sheep, she pointed an accusing finger at the Lincolns and went through the coughing routine again and again, while I replied with a series of reassuring grins that became more and more exhausting.

She produced a thermometer, and I wondered if she were a vet. If so, I greatly preferred her chubby little colleague of the morning. She needed no assistance to hold the sheep but jammed a great knee against each animal, trapping them against the wall as though they were puppy dogs. All the readings were normal, and she grew more and more impatient.

As she charged around the pens, she made frequent contact with me. I am a fairly solidly built man of around five feet ten, but she never even noticed as I bounced off her, and the thought occurred to me that if we both donned boxing gloves and got into a ring together, I would be lucky to last a three-minute round.

Finally she produced a tiny Russian-English dictionary and tried me out with various incomprehensible words. The nearest she came to the root of the matter was "broncheetees," but by then she had lapsed into a discontented muttering. I had the feeling that she was no longer aware of my presence, so I took my opportunity and made a bolt for my cabin.

I was almost there when Nielsen's head poked out from his cooking cell.

"You miss your lunch, Mr. Herriot. You have tough time, you look tired. Wait there." He held up a hand. "I make you something."

I stood in the doorway as he laid out a slice of rye bread and began to chop onto it tiny pieces of raw steak. He slashed away like lightning, his huge knife glinting with expert movements. Then he began to whittle away at a raw onion till the meat was covered with the fragments, then followed this by cracking an egg onto the top of the pile. He finished by dusting the whole mound with salt and black pepper before holding the final result proudly in my direction.

"Beef tartare!" His voice had a triumphant ring. "You eat, Mr. Herriot. You feel better!"

I shrank back a pace. How could I possibly eat this concoction? Raw meat, uncooked egg—it was unthinkable. I was desperately scouring my mind for some excuse to decline when I looked up again at Nielsen's beaming face. He was my friend, this unsung genius of the galley, and he was trying to succour me in my time of need. I would undoubtedly be ill later, but I couldn't say no.

It took courage, but I thanked him, seized the heaped slice of bread and bit resolutely into it. I thought if I held my breath throughout I wouldn't taste anything, but there was too much of it, and as I exhaled I got the full flavour. It was delicious.

The cook's expression became more and more ecstatic as he saw the growing wonder in my face. Then, as I chewed steadily, he must have noticed a fleeting doubt, a moment of disbelief in my eyes because he rested a hand anxiously on my shoulder.

"A leetle more pepper, maybe?"

I swallowed and regarded him for a moment. "Well . . . yes, possibly . . . just a touch."

He plied the grater, and as I started again on the delicacy, he began to pour me a glass of lager, his face a picture of delight.

I was sorry when I came to the end of the beef tartare, but the strong Carlsberg was just right to wash it down. Nielsen's taste was impeccable, as always.

It was dark—about 8 P.M.—when the *Ubbergen* moved out. Our ship took its place, and the discharging of the cargo commenced. Wagons drew up on the railway lines alongside the ship, a great crane lowered a gangway and my poor little sheep were driven up the ramps.

I had literally lived with them for six days, and even though I knew that as pedigree breeding animals they would get the best of treatment, it tugged at my heart to see them go. Those beautiful Romney Marsh with their teddy bear heads trotting under the glaring lights and disappearing into the black interiors of the wagons—I didn't like it at all. They had come from the green fields of Kent, and as the doors closed behind them, I wondered where they were going.

A throng of black-capped Russian workers swarmed on the quayside, wheeling the wagons from the darkness into the light thrown by the cranes. They all looked frail, dark and washed-out in contrast with the strapping Danes on the ship. My faithful helper, Raun, was in the thick of the action, all six feet four of him, his mop of golden hair flapping as he ushered the animals along the ramp.

Another striking figure was Jumbo, the youngest seaman on the ship. Apparently the youngest member of the crew is always called Jumbo, pronounced "Yoombo," and this chap is just about the bonniest lad I have ever seen. Seventeen years old, immensely tall and with massive shoulders, yet he has an angelic face, with large blue eyes and thick yellow hair growing down over his ears.

His job was the unloading of the surplus fodder, and I marvelled at the effortless way he roped and hoisted the heavy bags and bales onto the hook which swung down again and again from the crane on the quay. I cannot help thinking of the Vikings when I see these men. If they are typical, the Danes are a wonderful people.

Finally, at about midnight, the last sheep had trotted from sight and the last bale of hay and bag of nuts had been lifted out. The man in charge of the Russian workers waved up at me as I looked down from the rail of the ship.

"Doktor, goodbye," he cried and went off into the night.

I walked around the empty holds, feeling a sense of loss; then I went up to the captain's cabin to await a representative from Saufratt to sign my acceptance forms.

He came at about 2 A.M., and that is 4 A.M. Russian time. He was a young chap of about twenty-five and had been hard at it all day, checking the sheep and supervising the unloading. He was exhausted, white-faced and grimy, and I noticed that his nails were bitten right back. But he was no fool. He could speak and write English very well, and he had the authority to sign for £20,000 worth of sheep.

On the first form he wrote, "About twenty percent of Lincoln sheeps have cough." Gently I pointed out that it should be "sheep," and though he was so tired that he could hardly keep his eyes open, he launched into an interrogation as to why the singular should be the same as the plural and wanted to know all the other English words which had this peculiarity. It was another

[179]

symptom of the passion for learning that I had found repeatedly in Klaipeda.

He was followed by the customs and immigration people who cleared our passports; then the Inflot representatives came aboard and presented their bills to the captain—so many rubles for pilot, berthing and so forth.

The captain gave them hell in his gentlemanly way and said they charged far too much, but they only shrugged their shoulders and laughed heartily.

The very last Russian to come aboard was the pilot, a different one this time.

His face was grave as he spoke to the captain. "There is big storm blowing out beyond the estuary—force six–eight and getting worse. I advise you to pull away from the berth and anchor in the harbour till morning." He wagged a finger as he made his final admonition. "It will not be so good out there for you tonight."

The captain paced up and down the cabin, trying to make up his mind. He badly wanted to be off, but dare he risk the storm?

At last he said, "I think you are right, Mr. Pilot. We had better stay here tonight."

Leaving the cabin, I bumped into the mate. He had overheard the conversation, and he looked at me ruefully.

"I tell you this, Mr. Herriot, I have heard this before. We will leave tonight. Captain Rasmussen, he is not afraid of storms. Prepare yourself."

Sitting here over my log, I am very sleepy and my bunk looks very inviting. Still and peaceful, it beckons to me. It has been a long, long day.

Chapter
19

"This is Biggins 'ere."

I gripped the telephone tightly and dug the nails of my other hand into my palm. Mr. Biggins's vacillations always tried me sorely. He regarded calling out the vet as a final desperate measure, and it was always sheer torture for him to make up his mind to take it. On top of that he was extremely pig-headed about taking my advice if I did manage to fight my way onto his farm, and I knew beyond doubt that I had never ever managed to please him.

He had made me suffer during my pre-R.A.F. days, and now, with the war well over, he was still there, a bit older and a bit more pig-headed.

"What's the trouble, Mr. Biggins?"

"Well . . . I 'ave a heifer badly."

"Right, I'll have a look at her this morning."

"Haud on, just a minute." Mr. Biggins was still not sure if he wanted me out there, even though he had got as far as lifting the phone. "Are you sure she needs seein'?"

"Well, I don't know. What is she doing?"

There was a long pause. "Just laid out, like."

"Laid out?" I said. "That sounds rather serious to me. I'll be along as soon as possible."

"Now then, now then, she 'asn't allus been laid out."

"Well, how long, then?"

"Just this last couple o' days."

"You mean she just dropped down?"

"Nay, nay, nay." His voice took on an edge of exasperation at my thick-headedness. "She's been off her grub for a week, and now she's gone down."

I took a long breath. "So she's been ill for a week, and now she's collapsed and you've decided to call me?"

"Aye, that's right. She were pretty bright about t'head till she went off 'er legs."

"Right, Mr. Biggins, I'll be with you very soon."

"Ah, but . . . but . . . are ye sure there's any need . . . ?"

I put down the receiver. I knew from hard experience that this conversation could go on for a long time. I also knew that I was probably visiting a hopeless case, but if I got there immediately I might be able to do something.

I was on the farm within ten minutes, and Mr. Biggins met me with his typical attitude—hands in pockets, shoulders hunched, eyes regarding me suspiciously from under a thick fringe of greying eyebrows.

"Ye're ower late," he grunted.

I stopped with one foot out of the car. "You mean she's dead?"

"Nay, but just about. Ye're too late to do owt about it now."

I gritted my teeth. This animal had been ill for a week, I had arrived ten minutes after being summoned, but the farmer's tone was unequivocal; if it died it would be my fault. I had come ower late.

"Ah, well," I said, trying to relax. "If she's dying there's nothing I can do." I began to get back into the car.

Mr. Biggins lowered his head and kicked at a cobblestone with a massive boot. "Are ye not going to look at 'er while you're 'ere?"

"I thought you said it was too late."

"Aye . . . aye . . . but you're the vitnery."

"Right, if that's what you want." I climbed out again. "Where is she?"

[182]

He hesitated. "Will ye charge me extra?"

"No, I won't. I've made the journey to your farm, and if I can't do anything more, that's all you'll pay for."

It was a sadly familiar sight. The skinny young beast lying in a dark corner of the fold yard. Eyes sunken and glazed and moving every few seconds with the slow nystagmus of approaching death. Temperature was 99°F.

"Yes, you're right, Mr. Biggins," I said. "She's dying." I put my thermometer away and began to leave.

The farmer was a picture of gloom, with his head sunk deep in his shoulders as he looked down at the beast. Then he glanced at me quickly. "Where are ye goin'?"

I looked back in surprise. "I'm going on my round. I'm truly sorry about your heifer, Mr. Biggins, but she's beyond human aid."

"So you're just goin' to walk away without doin' owt?" He gave me a truculent stare.

"But she's dying. You said so yourself."

"Aye, but you're t'vet, not me. And I've allus heard that where there's life there's hope."

"Not in this case, I assure you. She could go any minute."

He continued to stare down at the animal. "Look, she's breathin', isn't she? Aren't you goin' to give her a chance?"

"Well . . . if you like, I can try giving her a stimulant injection into her vein."

"It's not what ah like. You're t'one that's supposed to know."

"Very well, I'll have a go." I trailed out to the car for the injection.

The heifer, in a deep coma, knew nothing as I slipped the needle into the jugular vein. As I depressed the plunger, Mr. Biggins gave tongue again.

"Expensive things, them injections. How much is this goin' to cost me, then?"

"I honestly don't know." My brain was beginning to reel.

[183]

"You'll know awright when you get t'pen in your 'and to send me that big bill, won't ye?"

I didn't answer. As the last drop of fluid trickled into the vein the heifer extended her fore limbs, stared sightlessly ahead for a second, then stopped breathing. I watched her for a few moments and put my hand over her heart. "I'm afraid she's dead, Mr. Biggins."

He bent quickly. "Have ye killed 'er?"

"No, no, of course not. She was just ready to go."

The farmer rubbed his chin. "It wasn't much of a bloody stimulant, was it?"

I had no answer to that one and began to put my syringe away. I was conscious of an increasing desire to get off this farm as quickly as possible.

I was on the way to the car when Mr. Biggins caught at my arm.

"Well, what was t'matter with 'er?"

"I don't know."

"You don't know? Well, you've wasted ma money with that injection. Vets are supposed to know, aren't they?"

"Yes, Mr. Biggins, they are. But in this case I could only say that the animal was dying. You would need a postmortem examination to find out the cause of death."

The farmer began to pluck excitedly at his coat. "Well, this is a funny carry-on. I 'ave a dead beast here, and nobody knows what killed her. Could be anything, couldn't it?"

"Well . . . I suppose so."

"Could be anthrax!"

"Oh no, Mr. Biggins. Anthrax is very sudden, and you say this heifer was ill for over a week."

"Nay, nay, not right ill. Just a bit off it, then she went down like a shot at t'end. That was sudden enough!"

"Oh, but . . ."

"And Fred Bramley along t'road had a beast wi' anthrax last month, didn't he?"

[184]

"Yes, that's right. There was a positive case there—first around here for several years. But that was in a cow he found dead."

"Ah don't care!" Mr. Biggins stuck his jaw out. "The *Darrowby and Houlton Times* was on about it, and they said that all sudden deaths should be examined for anthrax because it was right dangerous and fatal to people. I want ma heifer examined!"

"Okay," I replied wearily. "If you say so. As it happens, I have my microscope with me."

"Microscope? That sounds a costly job. How much will that be?"

"That's all right, the Ministry pays me," I said and began to walk towards the house.

Mr. Biggins nodded with glum satisfaction, then raised his eyebrows. "Where you goin' now?"

"Into the house. I've got to use your phone to report to the Ministry. I can't do anything till I get permission. I'll pay for the call." I added the last few words because he was beginning to look worried.

He stood by me as I spoke to the Ministry clerk. He fidgeted impatiently when I asked him for his full name, the proper name of the farm, the breed of the heifer.

"Didn't know ah'd have to go through all this," he mumbled.

I went out and produced my postmortem knife from the car boot. It was a large and dangerous carving knife that I used only on dead animals.

Mr. Biggins's eyes widened at the sight of it. "By gaw, I don't like the look of that bloody great knife. What are you goin' to do with that?"

"Just take a bit of blood." I bent and made a nick at the root of the heifer's tail and smeared a film of blood onto a glass slide. I took this, along with the microscope, into the farmhouse kitchen.

"Now what do you want?" Mr. Biggins asked sourly.

I looked around. "I want the use of the sink, the fire and that table by the window."

The sink was full of dirty dishes which the farmer removed with groans of protest, while I fixed the blood film by drawing it through the flames in the hearth. Then I moved to the sink and poured methylene blue over the slide. In the process, a small blue pool formed in the white sink bottom, and the colouration stayed there after I had swilled the slide with cold water from the tap.

"Look at the bloody mess you've made!" Mr. Biggins exclaimed. "You've stained t'sink. The missus'll play 'ell when she gets home this afternoon."

I forced a smile. "Don't worry, that isn't a stain. It will come off quite easily." But I could see he didn't believe me.

I dried the slide off at the fire, rigged up the microscope on the table and peered through the eyepiece. As I expected, I found only the usual pattern of red and white corpuscles. Not an anthrax bacillus in sight.

"Well, there's nothing there," I said. "You can call the knacker man quite safely."

Mr. Biggins blew out his cheeks and made a long-suffering gesture with one hand. "All that bloody fuss for nothin'," he sighed.

As I drove away I felt, not for the first time, that you just couldn't win with Mr. Biggins, and a month later the conviction was strengthened when he came into the surgery one market day.

"One of me cows has wooden tongue," he announced. "I want some iodine to paint on."

Siegfried looked up from the day book where he was checking the visits. "Oh, you're a bit out of date, Mr. Biggins," he said, smiling. "We've got far better medicine than that now."

The farmer took up his usual stance, head down, glowering under his eyebrows. "I don't care about your new medicine. Ah want the stuff I've allus used."

"But Mr. Biggins." Siegfried was at his most reasonable. "Painting the tongue with iodine went out years ago. Since then we've used intravenous injections of sodium iodide, which was much better, but now even that has been replaced by sulphanila-mide."

"Big words, Mr. Farnon, big fancy words," grunted the farmer. "But ah know what's best for me cow, so are you goin' to give me the iodine or not?"

"No, I am not," Siegfried replied, the smile fading from his face. "I wouldn't be a competent veterinary surgeon if I prescribed something as totally outdated as that." He turned to me. "James, would you slip through to the stockroom and bring a pound packet of the sulphanilamide?"

Mr. Biggins was protesting as I hurried from the office. In the stockroom the sulphanilamide packets stood in rows, some pounds, others half-pounds, but there were plenty of them because at that time this drug bulked very large in our veterinary life. It was such a striking improvement on our old remedies. It was useful in many kinds of bacterial diseases, it was an excellent dusting powder for wounds and, of course, as Siegfried had said, it cleared up actinobacillosis, or wooden tongue, quite rapidly.

The packets were square and wrapped in white paper tied down with string. I grabbed one from the shelf and returned at a trot, listening to the two voices echoing along the passage.

The argument was still raging when I came back to the office, and I could see that Siegfried's patience was running out. He seized the packet from me and began to write the instructions on the label.

"You give three tablespoonsful in a pint of water to start with, then . . ."

"But ah tell you ah don't want . . ."

". . . you follow with one tablespoonful three times daily . . ."

". . . got no faith in them new things . . ."

". . . and after you've used the packet, let us know, and we'll give you another supply if necessary."

The farmer glared at my partner. "That stuff'll do no good."

"Mr. Biggins," Siegfried said with ominous calm. "It will cure your cow."

"It won't!"

"It will!"

"It won't!"

Siegfried brought his hand down on the desk with a thud. Clearly he had had enough. "Take this, and if it doesn't do the trick I won't charge you, all right?"

Mr. Biggins narrowed his eyes, but I could see that the idea of something for nothing had an irresistible appeal. Slowly he stretched out his hand and took the sulphanilamide.

"Splendid!" Siegfried jumped up and patted the farmer's shoulder. "Now, you get in touch with us when you've used it. I bet you anything your cow will soon be much better."

It would be about ten days after this interview that Siegfried and I were out together castrating colts, and on the way back to the surgery we had to pass through Mr. Biggins's village.

Siegfried slowed down when he saw the farmhouse. It was square-faced and massive, and the front garden showed only the sprouting heads of potato plants. Mr. Biggins did not believe in wasting money on ornamentation.

"Tell you what, James," my partner murmured. "We'll just drop in there. We haven't heard from our old friend about the sulphanilamide. Doesn't want to lose face, I suspect." He laughed softly. "We'll be able to rub it in a bit."

He turned the wheel and drove round to the yard at the back of the house. Outside the kitchen door Siegfried raised his hand to knock, then he gripped my arm. "Look at that, James!" he said in an urgent whisper.

He pointed to the kitchen window, and there on the sill was our square white packet, virgin and unopened, the string binding undisturbed.

My partner clenched his fist. "The cussed old blighter! He won't try it — out of sheer spite."

At that moment the farmer opened the door and Siegfried

greeted him cheerfully. "Ah, good morning to you, Mr. Biggins. We were just passing and thought we'd check on how your cow was progressing."

The eyes under the shaggy brows registered sudden alarm, but my partner held up a reassuring hand. "No charge, I give you my word. This is just for our own interest."

"But . . . but . . . I've got me slippers on. Was just havin' a cup o' tea. There's no need for ye to . . . "

But Siegfried was already striding towards the cow byre. The patient was easy to pick out. Her skin was stretched tightly over the jutting ribs and pelvic bones, saliva drooled from her lips and a long swelling bulged from under her jaw. She was a scarecrow among her sleek neighbours.

Siegfried moved quickly to her head, seized the nose and pulled it towards him. With his other hand he prised open the mouth and fingered the tongue.

"Feel that, James," he said softly.

I ran my hand over the knobbly hard surface which for centuries has given actinobacillosis its evocative name. "This is awful. It's a wonder she can eat at all." I sniffed at my fingers. "And there's iodine here."

Siegfried nodded. "Yes, he's been to the chemist despite what I said."

At that moment the byre door burst open and Mr. Biggins hurried in, panting slightly.

My partner looked at him sadly along the cow's back. "Well, it seems you were right. Our medicine hasn't done a bit of good. I can't understand it." He rubbed his chin. "And your poor cow is a mess, I'm afraid. Almost starving to death. I do apologise."

The farmer's face was a study. "Aye, well . . . that's right . . . she's done no good . . . I reckon she'll . . ."

Siegfried broke in. "Look here," he said. "I feel responsible for this. My medicine has failed, so it's up to me to get her right." He strode from between the cows. "I have an injection in the car which I think will do the trick. Excuse me for a moment."

[189]

"Now, then, wait a minute . . . I don't know . . ." But the farmer's words went unheeded as my colleague hurried out to the yard.

He was back very quickly, holding a bottle that I couldn't recognise. He held it up and began to fill a 20 c.c. syringe, watching the rising level intently and whistling tunelessly under his breath.

"Hold the tail, will you, James?" he said and poised the needle over the cow's rump. With his hand still held high, he looked across at Mr. Biggins. "This is an excellent injection, but it's a good job you've been using our medicine."

"Why's that?"

"Well, on its own it could have serious effects on the animal."

"You mean . . . could kill 'er?"

"Just possible," Siegfried murmured. "But you've nothing to worry about. She's had the sulphanilamide." He was about to plunge the needle in when the farmer gave tongue.

"Hey, hey, haud on. Don't do that!"

"What is it, Mr. Biggins? Something wrong?"

"Nay, nay, but there's maybe been a bit of a misunderstandin'." Conflicting emotions chased across the farmer's face. "Ye see, it's like this—ah don't think she's been gettin' enough of your stuff."

Siegfried lowered his arm. "You mean you've been underdosing? I wrote the instructions on the packet if you remember."

"That's right. But ah must have got a bit mixed up."

"Oh, that doesn't matter. As long as you put her back to full dosage, all will be well." Siegfried inserted the needle and, ignoring Mr. Biggins's yelp of alarm, he injected the full contents.

As he put the syringe back in its case, he sighed with satisfaction. "Well, I'm sure that will put everything right. But remember, you must start again with the full three tablespoonsful and continue till you've finished the packet. The cow is in such a state that I'm pretty sure you'll need a further supply, but you'll let us know about that, eh?"

As we drove away I stared at my colleague. "What the devil was that injection?"

"Oh, mixed vitamins. It'll help the poor thing's condition, but it had nothing to do with the wooden tongue. Just part of my plan." He smiled gleefully. "Now he's *got* to use the sulphanilamide. It will be interesting to see what happens."

It was indeed interesting. Within a week Mr. Biggins was back in the surgery, looking sheepish.

"Can I have some more o' that stuff?" he muttered.

"By all means." Siegfried extended his arm in an expansive gesture. "As much as you like." He leaned on the desk. "I suppose the cow is looking better?"

"Aye."

"Stopped slavering?"

"Aye."

"Putting on flesh, is she?"

"Aye, aye, she is." Mr. Biggins lowered his head as though he didn't want to answer any more questions. Siegfried gave him another packet.

Through the surgery window we watched him cross the street, and my partner thumped me on the shoulder. "Well, James. That was a little victory. At last we've managed to beat Mr. Biggins."

I laughed, too, because it was very sweet, but when I look back over the years, I realise it was the only time we did beat him.

Chapter
20

There is nothing very exciting about tuberculin testing, and I was quite pleased when George Forsyth, the insurance agent, came into the byre and started to make conversation.

I was doing the annual test on the little farm of the Hudson brothers. Clem, the elder, about forty years old, was painstakingly writing the numbers in the book, while Dick, a few years younger, was rubbing the inner surfaces of the ears to find the tattoo marks.

As I clipped, measured and injected, I listened to George's observations on the weather, the latest cricket scores and the price of pigs. He was leaning against a wall, taking leisurely pulls at a cigarette as though he had all the time in the world, but I had a fair idea he had come along for something more than idle talk.

After a few minutes he got round to the point.

"You know, Clem," he said, "you fellows should be properly insured."

Clem carefully rounded off a figure in the book. "What are ye talkin' about? We've got the car insured and we're covered for fire and lightnin'. That's enough, isn't it?"

"Enough!" George was shocked. "That's nothing. You should both have life policies, for a start."

"Nay, nay." Clem shook his head. "Don't believe in all that. In fact, I don't believe in insurance at all except what we've got to have."

Dick raised his head from the front of the cow. "And ah don't believe in it either. You're wastin' your time, George."

"Honestly," the agent said, "you two are living in the past. Don't you think it would be a good thing for your dependants to have a nice sum of money in the event of your deaths?"

"Not goin' to die for a long time yet," Clem grunted, moving along to the next cow.

"How the heck do you know that?"

"All the Hudsons is long-lived," Dick said. "They nearly have to shoot some of 'em. Our old dad's over eighty, and he's fightin' fit. He passed the farm over to us, but 'e could be workin' now if he wanted."

George tiptoed daintily to one side in his patent leather shoes as a cow raised her tail dangerously in his direction. "You don't seem to get the point, but I won't press the matter. However," he raised a finger, "you should certainly have sickness policies."

Both the brothers had a good laugh at this.

"Sickness?" Clem said, a pitying smile creasing his craggy features. "Neither of us 'ave ever ailed a thing in our lives. Never even had a cold. We 'aven't missed a day's work since we started on this place."

"But how do you know that's going to continue?" the agent replied weakly. "As you get older, you'll be more liable to illness."

"Oh, leave off, George." Dick pushed his way out from between two cows. "We've told you—we don't believe in insurance, and that's all about it. And we're not goin' to chuck our money away on any of your fancy policies."

George narrowed his eyes. This was a challenge, and I could see he was going to rise to it.

"I tell you what . . ." he began, but I had got to the end of the byre.

"Where do we go now?" I asked.

Clem pointed across the yard. "Few heifers in a box over there."

These were big, rough beasts, and I pressed back against the wall as they careered around in the straw. The brothers had made a few ineffectual throws with a rope halter when I noticed George's head appearing over the box door.

"I tell you what," he repeated, and I was reminded of the old couplet, "There's no guy got endurance/like the guy who sells insurance." "How about an accident policy? Both of you ought to have one."

Clem managed to snare one of the galloping animals and leaned back on the rope. "Accident? Fiddlesticks! We've never 'ad a accident."

"Aha! That's the very reason why you should start protecting yourselves. The fact that nothing has happened to you makes it more probable that something is waiting round the corner. It's simple mathematics."

"There's nowt simple about it," Dick said. "Just because we've never had a accident doesn't mean that . . ." His words were cut off as the haltered beast went violently into reverse and its bony rump thudded into his midriff, crushing him with brutal force against the rough stones of the wall.

He sank down in the straw, completely winded, and sat motionless, holding his middle.

"Look at that!" George cried. "Just what I've been talking about! Yours is a dangerous trade. Anything could happen."

"Aye, well, 'e's all right," Clem said doubtfully as his brother eased himself to his feet.

George's eyes had the fanatical gleam of an insurance man who suddenly finds fate on his side. "Yes, yes, maybe he is all right this time, but he might have had an internal injury, mightn't he? Could have been off work for ages, and then where would you be? You'd have to pay for extra labour, wouldn't you? And with a nice little policy from me, you'd have the money to do it."

The musical sound of the word "money" appeared to stir something in Clem. He gave the agent a sidelong glance. "How much?"

George became brisk and businesslike. "Now, then, I have just the thing for you here." He pulled a sheaf of policies from his inside pocket. "For a premium of ten pounds per annum, you would receive twenty pounds a week in the case of incapacitating injuries. There are other benefits, of course; look here."

Clem put on a pair of steel-rimmed spectacles and perused the document while Dick looked over his shoulder. I could hear mutterings.

"Twenty pun a week . . . lot o' money . . . not bad."

Twenty pounds was indeed a tidy sum in 1948 when the average weekly wage for a qualified veterinary assistant was around ten pounds.

Finally Clem looked up. "Reckon we might 'ave a go at that. Twenty pun a week would come in right handy."

"Splendid, splendid." George produced a silver pencil. "Just sign here, both of you. Thank you very much."

He paused for a moment. "And of course there's young Herbert who works for you."

"Aye, he's down t'fields," Dick said. "What about 'im?"

"Well, you ought to have him covered, too."

"But he's nobbut a lad."

"Okay." George spread his hands. "He goes in cheaper. Five pounds a year. Same benefits."

The brothers' resistance seemed to have crumbled. "Awright, s'pose we might as well. We'll do 'im, too."

George tripped off to his car, whistling merrily, and we got on with the test.

It was about three weeks later that I met Clem in Darrowby market place. He was sauntering along, looking in the shop windows, and he was wearing a smart dark suit, obviously not his working clothes. It was late afternoon when he would normally have been bringing in his cows for milking, and I wondered at his presence in the town until he turned round and I saw that his arm was in a sling.

"What on earth have you been doing, Clem?" I asked.

He looked down at the bulky white cast. "Broke me arm.

Slipped up on the cow-house floor. And would you believe it?" His eyes widened. "It was nubbut three days after I'd signed that insurance form. Ah'm gettin' twenty pun a week, and the doctor reckons it'll be another nine weeks afore I can start work. That'll be more than two hundred quid I'll have collected. All right, eh?"

"It certainly is. What a blessing you took George Forsyth's advice. But you'll be paying for somebody to help you?"

"Nay, nay, we're managin' grand as it is." He walked away, chuckling.

Clem's injury had healed by the time I had to visit the Hudson farm again to "cleanse" a cow. Clem brought me a bucket of hot water, and I was soaping my arms when Dick came in. I should say he hobbled in, because he was on crutches.

I stared at him, and an eerie sense of the workings of fate stirred in my mind. "Broken leg?"

"Aye," Dick replied laconically. "Did it as easy as owt. Tryin' to catch an awd ewe on top pasture and upskittled meself in a rabbit hole."

"You'll be out of action for a while, then?"

"Aye, plaster's got to stay on for fourteen weeks. It's a bloody nuisance, but all them twenty quids is very nice. Good job we signed that paper."

I didn't see him until he came into the surgery one market day to pay his veterinary bill. He had shed his cast but was still limping slightly.

"How is the leg, Dick?" I asked as I wrote in the receipt book.

He grimaced. "Nobbut middlin'. Aches like 'ell sometimes, but I think it's gettin' stronger."

"Ah, well." I handed him the receipted account. "You'll just have to take things a bit easier till you're back to normal."

"Can't do that," he said, shaking his head. "We're short-handed as it is. Young Herbert's had a accident."

"What!"

"Aye, stuck a hay fork into 'is foot and got blood poisonin'. He's well enough in 'imself, but Doctor says it'll be a long time afore he can walk about."

In fact, it was ten weeks before Herbert returned to work, but as Clem confided to me over a beer when I encountered him one night in the Drovers' Arms, the two hundred pounds they collected from the insurance company had been something of a consolation.

"Remarkable thing," I said. "George Forsyth must have been sent from heaven that morning. His company has been a tremendous help to you."

Clem showed no enthusiasm but stared gloomily into his glass. "But ah'll tell tha summat. They're funny fellers, them insurance men. Would ye believe it, after all that talkin' they don't want us any more."

"Really? How's that?"

"Well, we got a letter from them sayin', 'We do not wish to renew your insurance.' What d'you make of that?"

"That sometimes happens, Clem," I said. Privately, I wasn't surprised. For an outlay of twenty-five pounds, the Hudsons had received more than seven hundred pounds within a few months. I could imagine any company beating a hasty retreat.

"Any road," he continued, "we got another lot to take us on at t'end of the year. We've shifted all our business to them— farm, car and t'lot."

"And another accident policy, I suppose?"

Clem tipped up his glass and took a long swallow. "Oh, aye." Then he turned to me with an injured expression. "But they've made us pay an extra pound each."

It was some months later, shortly after the new company had shouldered the burden of the Hudsons' insurance, that Dick fell into the bowels of the tractor. He could have been seriously injured but sustained only a fracture of the thumb, which kept him off work for eight weeks.

He told me about it himself when he had recovered and I was

having a cup of tea in the farmhouse. "Another one hundred sixty pounds into the kitty," he said philosophically, pushing a plateful of homemade scones towards me.

I must have looked bemused because he laughed. "And that's not all, Mr. Herriot. I had a accident with the car."

"No!"

"Aye, ah did. Ran into t'side of young Bessie Trenholm's car and smashed me radiator and lights."

"Well, that's almost unbelievable. And another claim, eh?"

Dick gave me a wry smile. "Well, now, I'll tell ye. There's a bit of a story there. It was Bessie's fault, all right—she came out of her farm gate with no warnin'—but ah'd only insured my car for third party, and I thought if it came to an argument wi' only my word against hers, I'd have no chance because she's a bonny young lass, is Bessie. So I decided not to claim, though ah did mention it to the agent."

"So nothing doing this time?"

Dick's smile widened. "That's what ah thought, but the agent came to see me a few days after and told me they'd made a mistake at his office. They'd insured me car comprehensive."

"Good Lord! So you collected again?"

"Aye, another one hundred fifty pounds. Not bad." Dick cut a piece from a wedge of Wensleydale cheese, and his expression grew serious. "There's only one thing we're worried about. The agent acted a bit queer-like when 'e gave us the money. Didn't seem ower pleased. We're just hopin' this company isn't goin' to give us t'push like the last one."

"Yes," I said. "I understand. That would be unfortunate."

"It would 'an all." Dick nodded gravely. "Clem and me's big believers in insurance."

Chapter
21

November 3, 1961

I crawled into my bunk at 3 A.M., and it seemed that I had hardly fallen asleep before I was awakened by the ship leaping and bucking like a wild thing. I looked out of my window at a vast stretch of wind-tossed ocean.

Away in the distance, the lights of Klaipeda glimmered and faded. So the mate had been right; our captain was not to be deterred by a bit of bad weather.

For the rest of the night I remembered painfully the warnings I had heard about coming home against the wind. On the way to Klaipeda, the main motion had been a sideways rolling, which I had countered by jamming knees and elbows against the sides of the bunk, but this was a violent fore-and-aft movement, and it was ten times worse. Over and over again I slid from one end of the bunk to the other, and there wasn't a thing I could do about it. From my weird changes of position, I could divine that the ship's bows were high in the air one moment and pointing right down the next.

Outside, the gale howled, spray dashed against the windows and the cabin furniture and my worldly goods flew around the place unchecked. I let them get on with it. Tidying up, I felt, would be a fruitless and dangerous business.

Being thrown about constantly and listening to the medley of bangs and clatterings from all over the ship gave me small chance of sleep, and when dawn came I peered out at a dismal scene.

I discovered then the reason for one of the new sounds I had heard during the night. Whereas the ship had slid down the sides of the huge waves with the wind behind it, it now fell, keel first, into each green chasm, and when this happened, there was a jarring crash as though we had hit a rock. It was like a diver doing a belly flop, and the effect was alarming.

It seemed that after this terrible night my friends on the ship had decided that I would be prostrate and helpless this morning, because instead of the mess boy calling me at 8 A.M., Nielsen himself knocked and spoke through the door.

"You stay in bed, Mr. Herriot. I bring you a little breakfast."

"No thanks," I replied. "Come in."

He opened the door and looked startled when he saw me trying to shave with my back jammed against one wall and my foot against another.

"You okay?" he asked disbelievingly.

I seized upon a momentary pause in the ship's pitching to scrape another inch of soap from my face. "Yes, fine. What did you say about breakfast?"

"Well . . . we have kippers, fried eggs and some nice smoked sausage."

"Sounds great. I'll be there in a few minutes."

He gave me a final incredulous glance and left.

When I entered the mess room, only the mate was present. He was working among the assorted foodstuffs, and he raised his eyebrows and paused, fork halfway to his mouth, when he saw me start enthusiastically on my piled plate.

"Mr. Herriot," he said solemnly, "you are the first landsman I have known who is not sick after last night."

It made me feel good. As I have said, there is nothing clever about not being sick, but it was nice to know I had something special in the way of stomachs.

It is interesting to note that the only time I felt strange was

[200]

when I struggled up to the deck for some fresh air and stood for some time looking out on the crazily swinging sea. After a while, as I hung onto a rail, I began to experience a sort of dizziness. It was a visual thing, brought on somehow by watching the constant lifting and falling of the world about me, but it wasn't pleasant and I went back to my cabin.

In fact, I have stayed in my bunk most of the day. It is the only safe place. Since my sheep have gone I have nothing to do and, in any case, it is dangerous for an inexperienced sailor like me to move about. I have had one or two frights through being suddenly catapulted off my feet, and the danger of breaking a limb or splitting my head on a sharp projection is very real.

So it looks as though my life for the next few days is going to consist of lying on my back, reading paperback books and eating. This is all very fine, but I am used to an active existence, and I feel that a very bloated Herriot is going to roll back to Darrowby.

One hazard is that the faithful Nielsen now has me at his mercy. The galley is only a few yards away, and he keeps opening my door and sliding in a crate of lager or a tray with a mug of coffee and bread and jam.

Sometimes it is a more substantial offering, as when he marched into my cabin this afternoon, his body adjusting miraculously to the shifting slope of the floor. In one hand he held a plate and in the other a jug. On the plate rested a ring of mashed potatoes, into which he poured hot fat containing bacon and onions.

He laughed eagerly. "This is beeg food of the poor in Denmark. Is called Hot Love."

He watched with deep satisfaction as I consumed this strange dish. I relished every morsel, though dieticians would frown on it. The same dieticians would be horrified if they knew that this was merely an interlude between a lunch of huge beefy things that looked like hamburgers followed by a chocolate soup with unpronounceable rusks broken into it, and a dinner consisting of a creation of sauerkraut cooked in butter, milk and flour and mixed with potatoes. I say nothing of the usual array of cold dishes always at my disposal to allay any lingering hunger pangs. Yes, there is no doubt about it. I am going to get fat.

If I was on this ship long enough, I would probably finish up like Carl Rasmussen, the plump little mate. He is the champion eater of the ship. He ploughs impassively through the official meal, then starts on the cold stuff, of which he consumes a vast quantity before finishing with slice after slice of bread and dripping. The captain often looks at him with his gentle smile and pats his stomach wonderingly.

I am not going to say that he has the biggest appetite I have ever seen because I have come across some mighty troughers on the Dales farms, but he is undoubtedly in the top flight. I myself have a modest reputation in this field—Tristan often refers to me as "the big eater from Darrowby"—but I am not in Carl's class. He enthralls me.

Over the schnapps the captain told me that they had intended to go to Danzig on the way back, but the plan has been changed. We are going instead to the Polish port of Stettin. At least, those were their names when they were part of Germany, but they are now called Gdansk and Szczecin, although the ship's officers refer to them by their German names. We have to pick up 800 pigs to transport to Lübeck.

He hopes to arrive in Stettin (I think I'll stick to the old spelling) on Sunday and get the pigs to Lübeck by Monday, but everything depends on the weather, which is still foul. With this gale against us, we are managing to do only six knots.

As I scribble in my diary I keep sliding down to the cabin door, then I have to drag myself back to the other end and start again. It looks like another sleepless night.

[202]

Chapter
22

"I let my heart fall into careless hands." Little Rosie's voice piped in my ear as I guided my car over a stretch of rutted road. I had singing now to cheer the hours of driving.

I was on my way to dress a wound on a cow's back and it was nice to hear the singing. But it was beginning to dawn on me that something better still was happening. I was starting all over again with another child. When Jimmy went to school I missed his company in the car, but I did not realise that the whole thing was going to begin anew with Rosie.

The intense pleasure of showing them the farm animals and seeing their growing wonder at the things of the countryside, the childish chatter that never palled; the fun and the laughter that lightened my days—it all happened twice to me.

The singing had originated in the purchase of a radiogram. Music has always meant a lot to me and I owned a record player that gave me a lot of pleasure. Still, I felt I wanted something better, some means of reproducing more faithfully the sounds of my favourite orchestras, singers, instrumentalists.

Hi-fi outfits hadn't been heard of at that time, nor stereo, nor wrap-around sound, nor any of the other things that have revolutionised the world of listening. The best the music lover could do was to get a good radiogram.

After much agonising and reading of pamphlets and listening

to advice from many quarters, I narrowed my list down to three models and made my choice by having them brought round to Skeldale House and playing the opening of the "Beethoven Violin Concerto" on one after the other, again and again. I must have driven the two men from the electric shop nearly mad, but at the end there was no doubt left in my mind.

It had to be the Murphy, a handsome piece of furniture with a louvred front and graceful legs, and it bellowed out the full volume of the Philharmonia Orchestra without a trace of muzziness. I was enchanted with it, but there was one snag; it cost over ninety pounds, and that was an awful lot of money in 1950.

"Helen," I said when we had installed it in the sitting room, "we've got to look after this thing. The kids can put records on my old player, but we must keep them away from the Murphy."

Foolish words. The very next day as I came in the front door, the passage was echoing with *Yippee ay ooooh, yippee ay aaaay, ghost riders in the skyyy!* It was Bing Crosby's back-up choir, belting out the other side of the "Careless Hands" record, and the Murphy was giving it full value.

I peeped round the sitting-room door. "Ghost Riders" had come to an end, and with her chubby little hands Rosie removed the record, placed it in its cover and marched, pigtails swinging, to the record cabinet. She selected another disc and was halfway across the floor when I waylaid her.

"Which one is that?" I asked.

" 'The Little Gingerbread Man,' " she replied.

I looked at the label. It was, too, and how did she know, because I had a whole array of these children's records, and many of them looked exactly the same. The same colour, the same grouping of words, and Rosie, at the age of three, could not read.

She fitted the disc expertly on the turntable and set it going. I listened to "The Gingerbread Man" right through and watched as she picked out another record.

I looked over her shoulder. "What is it this time?"

" 'Tubby the Tuba.' "

And indeed it was. I had an hour to spare, and Rosie gave me a recital. We went through "Uncle Mac's Nursery Rhymes," "The Happy Prince," "Peter and the Wolf" and many of the immortal Bing, to whom I was and am devoted. I was intrigued to find that her favourite Crosby record was not "Please," or "How Deep Is the Ocean" or his other classics, but "Careless Hands." This one had something special for her.

At the end of the session, I decided that it was fruitless to try to keep Rosie and the Murphy apart. Whenever she was not out with me, she played with the radiogram. It was her toy.

It all turned out for the best, too, because she did my precious acquisition no harm, and when she came with me on my rounds, she sang the things she had played so often and which were word-perfect in her mind. And I really loved that singing. "Careless Hands" soon became my favourite, too.

There were three gates on the road to this farm, and we came bumping up to the first one now. The singing stopped abruptly. This was one of my daughter's big moments. When I drew up she jumped from the car, strutted proudly to the gate and opened it. She took this duty very seriously, and her small face was grave as I drove through. When she returned to take her place by my dog, Sam, on the passenger seat, I patted her knee.

"Thank you, sweetheart," I said. "You're such a big help to me all the time."

She didn't say anything but blushed and seemed to swell with importance. She knew I meant what I said, because opening gates is a chore.

We negotiated the other two gates in similar manner and drove into the farmyard. The farmer, Mr. Binns, had shut the cow up in a ramshackle pen with a passage that stretched from a dead end to the outside.

Looking into the pen, I saw with some apprehension that the animal was a Galloway—black and shaggy with a fringe of hair hanging over bad-tempered eyes. She lowered her head and switched her tail as she watched me.

[205]

"Couldn't you have got her tied up, Mr. Binns?" I asked.

The farmer shook his head. "Nay, I'm short o' room, and this 'un spends most of 'er time on the moors."

I could believe it. There was nothing domesticated about this animal. I looked down at my daughter. Usually I lifted her into hayracks or onto the tops of walls while I worked, but I didn't want her anywhere near the Galloway.

"It's no place for you in there, Rosie," I said. "Go and stand at the end of the passage, well out of the way."

We went into the pen, and the cow danced about and did her best to run up the wall. I was pleasantly surprised when the farmer managed to drop a halter over her head. He backed into a corner and held tightly to the shank.

I looked at him doubtfully. "Can you hold her?"

"I think so," Mr. Binns replied, a little breathlessly. "You'll find t'place at the end of her back, there."

It was a most unusual thing—a big discharging abscess near the root of the tail. And that tail was whipping perpetually from side to side—a sure sign of ill nature in a bovine.

Gently I passed my fingers over the swelling, and, like a natural reflex, the hind foot lashed out, catching me a glancing blow on the thigh. I had expected this, and I got on with my exploration.

"How long has she had this?"

The farmer dug his heels in and leaned back on the rope. "Oh, 'bout two months. It keeps bustin' and fillin' up over and over again. Every time I thought it'd be the last, but it looks like it's never goin' to get right. What's t'cause of it?"

"I don't know, Mr. Binns. She must have had a wound there at some time, and it's become infected. And, of course, being on the back, drainage is poor. There's a lot of dead tissue which I'll have to clear away before the thing heals."

I leaned from the pen. "Rosie, will you bring me my scissors, the cotton wool and that bottle of peroxide?"

The farmer watched wonderingly as the tiny figure trotted to

[206]

the car and came back with the three things. "By gaw, t'little lass knows 'er way around."

"Oh, yes," I said, smiling. "I'm not saying she knows where everything is in the car, but she's an expert on the things I use regularly."

Rosie handed me my requirements as I reached over the door. Then she retreated to her place at the end of the passage.

I began my work on the abscess. Since the tissue was necrotic, the cow couldn't feel anything as I snipped and swabbed, but that didn't stop the hind leg from pistoning out every few seconds. Some animals cannot tolerate any kind of interference, and this was one of them.

I finished at last with a nice wide, clean area onto which I trickled the hydrogen peroxide. I had a lot of faith in this old remedy as a penetrative antiseptic when there was a lot of pus about, and I watched contentedly as it bubbled on the skin surface. The cow, however, did not seem to enjoy the sensation because she made a sudden leap into the air, tore the rope from the farmer's hands, brushed me to one side and made for the door.

The door was closed, but it was a flimsy thing, and she went straight through it with a splintering crash. As the hairy black monster shot into the passage I desperately willed her to turn left, but to my horror she went right and, after a wild scraping of her feet on the cobbles, began to thunder down towards the dead end where my little daughter was standing.

It was one of the worst moments of my life. As I dashed towards the broken door, I heard a small voice say, "Mama." There was no scream of terror, just that one quiet word. When I left the pen, Rosie was standing with her back against the end wall of the passage and the cow was stationary, looking at her from a distance of two feet.

The animal turned when she heard my footsteps, then whipped round in a tight circle and galloped past me into the yard.

I was shaking when I lifted Rosie into my arms. She could easily have been killed, and a jumble of thoughts whirled in my brain. Why had she said, "Mama"? I had never heard her use the word before—she always called Helen "Mummy" or "Mum." Why had she been apparently unafraid? I didn't know the answers. All I felt was an overwhelming thankfulness. To this day I feel the same whenever I see that passage.

Driving away, I remembered that something very like this had happened when Jimmy was out with me. It was not so horrific because he had been playing in a passage with an open end leading into a field, and he was not trapped when the cow I was working on broke loose and hurtled towards him. I could see nothing, but I heard a piercing yell of *"Aaaagh!"* before I rounded the corner. To my intense relief, Jimmy was streaking across the field to where my car was standing and the cow was trotting away in another direction.

This reaction was typical because Jimmy was always the noisy one of the family. Under any form of stress he believed in making his feelings known in the form of loud cries. When Dr. Allinson came to give him his routine inoculations, he heralded the appearance of the syringe with yells of *"Ow! This is going to hurt! Ow! Ow!"* He had a kindred spirit in our good doctor, who bawled back at him, *"Aye. You're right, it is! Oooh! Aaah!"* But Jimmy really did scare our dentist because his propensity for noise appeared to carry on even under general anaesthesia. The long quavering wail he emitted as he went under the gas brought the poor man out in a sweat of anxiety.

Rosie solemnly opened the three gates on the way back, then she looked up at me expectantly. I knew what it was—she wanted to play one of her games. She loved being quizzed, just as Jimmy had loved to quiz me.

I took my cue and began. "Give me the names of six blue flowers."

She coloured quickly in satisfaction because, of course, she knew. "Field Scabious, Harebell, Forget-me-not, Bluebell, Speedwell, Meadow Cranesbill."

"Clever girl," I said. "Now, let's see—how about the names of six birds?"

Again the blush and the quick reply. "Magpie, Curlew, Thrush, Plover, Yellowhammer, Rook."

"Very good indeed. Now, name me six red flowers." And so it went on, day after day, with infinite variations. I only half realised at the time how lucky I was. I had a demanding, round-the-clock job, and yet I had the company of my children at the same time. So many men work so hard to keep the home going that they lose touch with the families who are at the heart of it, but it never happened to me.

Both Jimmy and Rosie, until they went to school, spent most of their time with me round the farms. With Rosie, as her school days approached, her attitude, always solicitous, became distinctly maternal. She really couldn't see how I was going to get by without her, and by the time she was five she was definitely worried.

"Daddy," she would say seriously, "how are you going to manage when I'm at school? All those gates to open and having to get everything out of the boot by yourself. It's going to be awful for you."

I used to try to reassure her, patting her head as she looked up at me in the car. "I know, Rosie, I know. I'm going to miss you, but I'll get along somehow."

Her response was always the same. A relieved smile, and then the comforting words, "But never mind, Daddy, I'll be with you every Saturday and Sunday. You'll be all right then."

I suppose it was a natural result of my children seeing veterinary practice from early childhood and witnessing my own pleasure in my work that they never thought of being anything else but veterinary surgeons.

There was no problem with Jimmy. He was a tough little fellow and well able to stand the buffets of our job, but somehow I couldn't bear the idea of my daughter being kicked and trodden on and knocked down and covered with muck. Practice was so much rougher in those days. There were no metal crushes to hold the big struggling beasts; there were still quite a number of farm horses around, and they were the ones that regularly put the vets in hospital with broken legs and ribs. Rosie made it very clear that she wanted country practice, and to me this seemed very much a life for a man. In short, I talked her out of it.

This really wasn't like me because I have never been a heavy father and have always believed that children should follow their inclinations. But as Rosie entered her teens, I dropped a long series of broad hints and perhaps played unfairly by showing her as many grisly, dirty jobs as possible. She finally decided to be a doctor on humans.

Now, when I see the high percentage of girls in the veterinary schools and observe the excellent work done by the two girl assistants in our own practice, I sometimes wonder if I did the right thing.

But Rosie is a happy and successful doctor, and, anyway, parents are never sure that they have done the right thing. They can only do what they think is right.

However, all that was far in the future as I drove home from Mr. Binns's with my three-year-old daughter by my side. She had started to sing again and was just finishing the first verse of her great favourite, *"Careless hands don't care when dreams slip through."*

Chapter
23

It was in 1950 that one of my heroes, George Bernard Shaw, broke his leg while pruning apple trees in his garden. By a coincidence I had been reading some of the prefaces that same week, revelling in the unique wit of the man and enjoying the feeling I always had with Shaw—that I was in contact with a mind whose horizons stretched far beyond those of the other literary figures of the day, and most other days.

I was shocked when I read about the calamity, and there was no doubt the national press shared my feelings. Banner headlines pushed grave affairs of state off the front pages, and for weeks bulletins were published for the benefit of an anxious public. It was right that this should be, and I agreed with all the phrases that rolled off the journalists' typewriters. "Literary genius . . ." "Inspired musical critic who sailed fearlessly against the tide of public opinion . . ." "Most revered playwright of our age . . ."

It was just about then that the Caslings' calf broke its leg, too, and I was called to set it. The Casling farm was one of a group of homesteads set high on the heathery Yorkshire moors. They were isolated places and often difficult to find. To reach some of them you had to descend into gloomy, garlic-smelling gills and climb up the other side; with others there was no proper road, just a clay path through the heather, and it came as a surprise to find farm buildings at the end of it.

Caslings' place didn't fall into either of these categories. It was perched on the moor top, with a fine disregard for the elements. The only concession was a clump of hardy trees that had been planted to the west of the farm to give shelter from the prevailing wind, and the way those trees bent uniformly towards the stones of house and barns was testimony to the fact that the wind hardly ever stopped blowing.

Mr. Casling and his two big sons slouched towards me as I got out of the car. The farmer was the sort of man you would expect to find in a place like this, his sixty-year-old face purpled and roughened by the weather, wide, bony shoulders pushing against the ragged material of his jacket. His sons, Alan and Harold, were in their thirties and resembled their father in almost every detail, even to the way they walked, hands deep in pockets, heads thrust forward, heavy boots trailing over the cobbles. Also, they didn't smile. They were good chaps, all of them, in fact, a nice family, but they weren't smilers.

"Now, Mr. Herriot." Mr. Casling peered at me under the frayed peak of his cap and came to the point without preamble. "Calf's in t'field."

"Oh, right," I said. "Could you bring me a bucket of water, please? Just about lukewarm."

At a nod from his father, Harold made wordlessly for the kitchen and returned within minutes with a much-dented receptacle.

I tested the water with a finger. "Just right. That's fine."

We set off through a gate with two stringy little sheepdogs slinking at our heels, and the wind met us with savage joy, swirling over the rolling bare miles of that high plateau, chill and threatening to the old and weak, fresh and sweet to the young and strong.

About a score of calves was running with their mothers on a long rectangle of green cut from the surrounding heather. It was easy to pick out my patient, although, when the herd took off at the sight of us, it was surprising how fast he could run with his dangling hind leg.

[212]

At a few barked commands from Mr. Casling, the dogs darted among the cattle, snapping at heels, baring their teeth at defiant horns till they had singled out cow and calf. They stood guard then till the young men rushed in and bore the little animal to the ground.

I felt the injured limb over with a tinge of regret. I was sure I could put him right, but I would have preferred a foreleg. Radius and ulna healed so beautifully. But in this case the crepitus was midway along the tibia, which was more tricky.

However, I was thankful it was not the femur. That would have been a problem, indeed.

My patient was expertly immobilised, held flat on the sparse turf by Harold at the head, Alan at the tail and their father in the middle. One of a country vet's difficulties is that he often has to do vital work on a patient that won't keep still, but those three pairs of huge hands held the shaggy creature as in a vice.

As I dipped my plaster bandages in the water and began to apply them to the fracture, I noticed that our heads were very close together. It was a very small calf—about a month old—and at times the three human faces were almost in contact. And yet nobody spoke.

Veterinary work passes blithely by when there is good conversation, and it is a positive delight when you are lucky enough to have one of those dry Yorkshire raconteurs among your helpers. At times I have had to lay down my scalpel and laugh my fill before I was able to continue. But here all was silence.

The wind whistled, and once I heard the plaintive cry of a curlew, but the group around that prostrate animal might have been Trappist monks. I began to feel embarrassed. It wasn't a difficult job; I didn't need a hundred percent concentration. With all my heart I wished somebody would say something.

Then, like a glorious flash of inspiration, I remembered the recent clamour in the newspapers. I could start things off, at least.

"Just like Bernard Shaw, eh?" I said with a light laugh.

[213]

The silence remained impenetrable, and for about half a minute it seemed that I was going to receive no reply.

Then Mr. Casling cleared his throat. " 'oo?" he enquired.

"Bernard Shaw, George Bernard Shaw, you know. He's broken his leg, too." I was trying not to gabble.

The silence descended again, and I had a strong feeling that I had better leave it that way. I got on with my job, dousing the white cast with water and smoothing it over while the plaster worked its way under my fingernails.

It was Harold who came in next. "Does 'e live about 'ere?"

"No . . . no . . . not really." I decided to put on one more layer of bandage, wishing fervently that I had never started this topic.

I was tipping the bandage from the tin when Alan chipped in. "Darrowby feller, is 'e?"

Things were becoming more difficult. "No," I replied airily. "I believe he spends most of his time in London."

"London!" The conversation, such as it was, had been carried on without any movement of the heads, but now the three faces jerked up towards me with undisguised astonishment and the three voices spoke as one.

After the initial shock had worn off the men looked down at the calf again, and I was hoping that the subject was dead when Mr. Casling muttered from the corner of his mouth. "He won't be in t'farmin' line, then?"

"Well, no . . . he writes plays." I didn't say anything about Shaw's intuitive recognition of Wagner as a great composer. I could see by the flitting side glances that I was in deep enough, already.

"We'll just give the plaster time to dry," I said. I sat back on the springy turf as the silence descended again.

After a few minutes I tapped a finger along the length of the white cast. It was as hard as stone. I got to my feet. "Right, you can let him go now."

The calf bounded up and trotted away with his mother as though nothing had happened to him. With the support of the plaster his lameness was vastly diminished, and I smiled. It was always a nice sight.

"I'll take it off in a month," I said, but there was no further talk as we made our way over the field towards the gate.

Still, I knew very well what the remarks would be over the farmhouse dinner table. "Queer lad, that vitnery. Kept on about some friend of his in London broke his leg."

"Aye. Kept on just like the man knows us."

"Aye. Queer lad."

And my last feeling as I drove away was not just that all fame is relative but that I would take care in future not to start talking about somebody who doesn't live about 'ere.

Chapter 24

November 4, 1961

The weather was, if anything, worse this morning, and I spent a night very like the one before. I noticed at mealtimes that the tablecloth was soaking wet. I kept quiet because I assumed that somebody had spilled something, but when it stayed wet all day, I had to mention it.

The captain smiled at my query. "Ah, yes, Mr. Herriot, I should have told you. We have dipped it in water. It does not slide about the table so much." He looked at me ruefully. "When the cloth is wet, you can bet the weather is really bad.

I saw his point. The sliding cloth, the slopping soup and, indeed, the constant restlessness of everything on the table had been a problem for some time.

I cannot rid myself of the feeling that we have struck a rock every time the ship falls from the summit of the waves, and apparently it is a standing joke among the crew, because after one of these shattering belly flops during lunch, the plates and cutlery flew all over the room, and Hansen, the engineer, jumped to his feet and peered out of the porthole.

"Deed you see that beeg stone?" he cried, staring at me with a terrified expression. It was a little jest for my benefit.

Again I have spent another disgracefully lazy day, stretched on my bunk, reading. I would have loved to do a few exercises on my hidden corner on deck, but I dare not take the chance. Even my trip for my daily shower is fraught with danger. It is a communal shower and, so far as I know, the only one on this tiny vessel. It is just a few yards away down the passage past the crew's quarters, but it seemed a long way as I reeled along, armed with towel and soap.

On my way, I could see several of the big, flaxen-haired seamen lying on their bunks, and I am sure I did not imagine the hollow groans issuing from the doorways. Can it be that even these supermen are seasick . . . ?

I really have nothing more to write about today, but tomorrow we should be in Stettin, and with a bit of luck I might get ashore and see something of interest.

November 5, 1961

My wedding anniversary. Strange to be spending it in Poland.

This morning when I awoke, the world was still, and the sea and sky were not wheeling beyond my cabin windows. I realised that we must be in Stettin and heaved myself up in my bunk. I saw that we were moored to a frost-covered quay. It was very foggy, but I could see several men with rods fishing from the quayside.

There was a Polish soldier on guard, but he was not festooned with artillery like the Russians. Also, he smiled when I called out to him. We were lying in a quiet backwater of the main river, the Oder, and there were willow trees and rushes at the water's edge. I judged from the wooden sheds with pens that this was probably a special place for the loading of livestock.

The usual mob of officials descended on us. Representatives from customs, immigration and farms. Among them was a handsome young Polish army officer who insisted not only on seeing the passports, but on interviewing each of their owners too.

I tentatively approached the captain as he dealt with the throng in his cabin.

"I'd like to go ashore into the town," I said.

[217]

His expression was slightly harassed, and I couldn't help feeling that he would be glad to get rid of this pest from Yorkshire. He looked at me thoughtfully for a moment.

"I am too busy to go with you, Mr. Herriot, and we must leave here at 11 A.M."

"Well, that gives me two hours," I replied. My natural curiosity and my almost desperate desire for some exercise lent weight to my appeal.

"All right." He raised a finger. "But you will not be late?"

"No, I promise you."

He nodded and returned to his business, while I showed my pass to the soldier and set off for the town. Oh, it was lovely to be able to stride out in the frosty air, to feel my limbs moving after the days of immobility and Nielsen's insidious skills. The fog had lifted, and I could see, about two miles away, the roofs and spires of a sizable town.

First I passed a military barracks with gymnastic equipment outside it, then allotments with a few women digging in them. My immediate impression as I approached the town was of the tremendous devastation left from the R.A.F. raids in wartime. Everywhere there were ruins and empty spaces. Vast buildings, some with ornate statuary over the doors, stood roofless, with gaping windows.

During the first mile of my walk, I saw hardly any evidence of effort to repair these ravages. It was not until I reached the town centre that I came on modern blocks of flats with shops on their ground floors. I took great care to impress every turning on my mind—if I got lost, I couldn't ask my way back.

Right inside the town, I was able to gain a general impression of the place and people. Obviously they observed Sunday as a holiday, because there was nobody working in the port area, and most of the shops were closed. Notable exceptions were two hairdressers' salons side by side, designated "Damski" and "Meski" above their respective doors. A lady was having a manicure in the front window of "Damski."

[218]

The population was arrayed in its Sunday best, and it seemed to me remarkable that the well-dressed man in Poland wore what amounted almost to a uniform. Black beret with a small stalk projecting from the top, dark gabardine macintosh and navy-blue suit. Also, every single one had a scarf crossed under his coat. The women were much smarter than in Klaipeda.

There were little kiosks on every corner, and people were strolling up to buy their newspapers and cigarettes. These places also sold draught beer and, having been on an exclusive diet of bottled lager for some time, I watched with envy as one fellow downed a frothing pint. If I had possessed any Polish money, it would have been nice to emulate him.

Stettin has 350,000 inhabitants, and I was struck by the greater air of comfort and civilisation, compared with Klaipeda. The people looked altogether smoother and more urbane, and the town had a cheerful atmosphere despite the ever-present ruins.

Funny little single-decker tramcars ran through the streets, always in pairs, one joined to the other, and there were a lot of private cars and taxis.

Shops displayed attractive dresses and materials, but a huge picture of Lenin reminded me that I was still behind the iron curtain.

Groups of youths, well dressed and laughing among themselves, were sauntering around, and I watched one family getting off a tram: Mum very chic in a light, fluffy hat and brightly coloured coat, Dad in the unvarying black beret and mac, and two teenage sons in identically the same outfit.

As I passed over the main river bridge, I could see innumerable barges moored along the banks. I walked past many churches but saw only two elderly women going into them.

I was amused when a little man in a soft hat, breeches and riding boots came and asked me the way to somewhere in an unintelligible gibberish. He, too, it seemed was a stranger, but not, I warrant, as much a stranger as I.

It was now a glorious cold, sunny day and I was revelling in the activity after my incarceration, but I kept referring to my son Jimmy's pocket watch and, when I saw I had been away an hour, I had to turn back.

I reached the ship before 11 A.M. and found the Polish officials still in the captain's cabin. They had given the free booze and cigarettes a severe hammering and were exuding bonhomie when I came in.

They seemed very glad to see me and shouted for me to sit down with them with merry cries of "Doktor, please, Doktor, please." I thought it was the schnapps that made them so welcoming, but later the captain said they had been anxious in case I got lost and kept asking him, "Has the Englishman returned yet?"

But, he said, there was no doubt they had wrought havoc among the bottles, all except the young Polish officer, who had been very correct and after one drink politely declined any more.

I went down to the hold and had a look at the pigs. We have them for only twenty-four hours and nobody seems particularly concerned about them, but pigs are funny things—they often fight among themselves, and it occurred to me that if 800 of them started a free-for-all, it would be a problem.

However, Polish pigs are perhaps more placid than ours because I found them all lying asleep, snuggling up to each other in perfect harmony. During the day I heard an occasional squeal from the hold and dashed down there in some anxiety, but it always turned out to be an isolated squabble or flash of irritation, with none of the bleeding scars or torn ears I had seen so often in Yorkshire. On the whole, peace has reigned.

We have taken aboard a great load of potatoes to feed them till we reach Lübeck.

The crew do not like carrying pigs because of the smell, and there is no doubt the ship has an entirely different aroma now. This does not percolate as far as the cabins or mess room, but I am told that in the summer it is pretty bad and shipboard life is dominated by the ever-present atmosphere of pig.

After lunch I spent a fascinating afternoon on the deck as the

[220]

ship made its way through the delta of the Oder, which spreads itself into a maze of huge lakes. This, I was told, is characteristic of the coastline in this region, right along through Estonia, Latvia and Lithuania. If ever a pilot were needed, it is here.

We sailed through the strangest and most desolate countryside I have ever seen—endless miles of flat marshlands with innumerable rush-lined inlets and pools, and occasional belts of trees. Clouds of wild ducks and geese provided the only signs of life, and the effect was inexpressibly wild and lonely despite the bright sunshine.

After about four hours the delta narrowed to a straight channel, and we came to the port of Swinemunde on the Baltic. This is a big naval base, and I saw a lot of Russian destroyers, torpedo boats and submarines.

At the entrance to the port we dropped the pilot and headed out to sea again. The gale had dropped, and the weather was now much better. It was very pleasant to stand out there in the stern, watching the land recede as the ship glided through calm water with hardly any rolling.

As far as my eye could reach, the coastline was thickly wooded, mainly with pine trees right down to the water's edge. There were some sandy beaches and cliffs, but no hills.

I stayed outside as we cruised along the East German coast, never out of sight of land, and maybe it was because my voyage was nearly over, but I didn't want to go below. I came inside only when the daylight was drowned in a magnificent sunset.

The ship's officers have been particularly charming today since it is my anniversary. They have shaken my hand warmly and bombarded me with lager. The captain asked anxiously if he should send a telegram to my wife but I explained that I had left a card with Rosie and I felt that a telegram might alarm Helen.

The cook, too, produced what I think must have been a banquet in my honour because it had a touch of England about it— a delectable soup of celery spinach and other vegetables, then roast pork with crackling, accompanied by roast ham, potatoes and red cabbage. Dessert was sago pudding, thickly sprinkled with cinnamon.

After dinner we had our usual and, sadly, my last session with the schnapps. The captain, red-eyed and tired after one and a half hours of sleep in the last twenty-four, still managed to be the perfect host.

November 6, 1961

The end of it all. From Lübeck to Hamburg by train, then by plane to Heathrow, London, before the last lap to Darrowby. I had much to think of on the way. I had been lucky enough to have a peep at mysterious places, a glimpse of a totally different world, but when I looked back on the last ten days, my warmest and most vivid memories were of the animals, the ship and the people aboard her.

The brave little *Iris Clausen* butting her way through the storms with the sheep safe inside her; the big, tough, yellow-haired crewmen, especially Raun and "Yoombo"; and of course, the ship's officers who had treated me so kindly. The captain who never seemed to lose his grace; Carl Rasmussen, the mate, tubby, balding and with the mighty appetite; Peter Hansen, the engineer, always ready with a joke; and, of course, my devoted Nielsen, who, I feel sure, has put half a stone of surplus flesh onto me.

I hope they have the same friendly memories of me. The captain, invariably courteous as he was, must have regarded me as an unmitigated nuisance at times, but Nielsen I know is going to miss me.

Chapter
25

"Was there no peace in a vet's life?" I wondered fretfully as I hurried my car along the road to Gilthorpe village. Eight o'clock on a Sunday evening and here I was, trailing off to visit a dog ten miles away which, according to Helen who had taken the message, had been ailing for more than a week.

I had worked all morning then spent an afternoon in the hills with the children and some of their friends, a long-standing weekly event during which we had managed to explore nearly every corner of the district over the years. Jimmy had set a brisk pace with his hardy young pals and I had had to carry Rosie on my shoulders up the steepest slopes. After tea there was the usual routine of baths, story reading and bed for the two of them, then I was ready to settle down with the Sunday papers and listen to the radio.

Yet here I was back on the treadmill, staring through the windscreen at the roads and the walls that I saw day in, day out. When I left Darrowby, the streets of the little town were empty in the gathering dusk and the houses had that tight-shut, comfortable look that raised images of armchairs and pipes and firesides, and now, as I saw the lights of the farms winking on the fell-sides, I could picture the stocksmen dozing contentedly with their feet up.

I had not passed a single car on the darkening road. There was nobody out but Herriot.

I was really sloshing around in my trough of self-pity when I drew up outside a row of greystone cottages at the far end of Gilthrope. Mrs. Cundall, Number Four, Chestnut Row, Helen had written on the slip of paper, and as I opened the gate and stepped through the tiny strip of garden, my mind was busy with half-formed ideas of what I was going to say.

My few years' experience in practice had taught me that it did no good at all to remonstrate with people for calling me out at unreasonable times. I knew perfectly well that my words never seemed to get through to them and that they would continue to do exactly as they had done before, but for all that I had to say something, if only to make me feel better.

No need to be rude or ill-mannered, just a firm statement of the position: that vets liked to relax on Sunday evenings just like other people; that we did not mind at all coming out for emergencies, but that we did object to having to visit animals that had been ill for a week.

I had my speech fairly well prepared when a little middle-aged woman opened the door.

"Good evening, Mrs. Cundall," I said, slightly tight-lipped.

"Oh, it's Mr. Herriot." She smiled shyly. "We've never met, but I've seen you walkin' round Darrowby on market days. Come inside."

The door opened straight into the little low-beamed living room, and my first glance took in the shabby furniture and some pictures framed in tarnished gilt when I noticed that the end of the room was partly curtained off.

Mrs. Cundall pulled the curtain aside. In a narrow bed a man was lying, a skeleton-thin man whose eyes looked up at me from hollows in a yellowed face.

"This is my husband, Ron," she said cheerfully, and the man smiled and raised a bony arm from the quilt in greeting.

"And here is your patient, Hermann," she went on, pointing to a little dachshund who sat by the side of the bed.

"Hermann?"

"Yes, we thought it was a good name for a German sausage dog." They both laughed.

"Of course," I said. "Excellent name. He looks like a Hermann."

The little animal gazed up at me, bright-eyed and welcoming. I bent down and stroked his head, and the pink tongue flickered over my fingers.

I ran my hand over the glossy skin. "He looks very healthy. What's the trouble?"

"Oh, he's fine in himself," Mrs. Cundall replied. "Eats well and everything, but over the last week he's been goin' funny on 'is legs. We weren't all that worried but tonight he sort of flopped down and couldn't get up again."

"I see. I noticed he didn't seem keen to rise when I patted his head." I put my hand under the little dog's body and gently lifted him onto his feet. "Come on, lad," I said. "Come on, Hermann, let's see you walk."

As I encouraged him he took a few hesitant steps, but his hind end swayed progressively, and he soon dropped into the sitting position again.

"It's his back, isn't it?" Mrs. Cundall said. "He's strong enough on 'is forelegs."

"That's ma trouble, too," Ron murmured in a soft husky voice, but he was smiling, and his wife laughed and patted the arm on the quilt.

I lifted the dog onto my knee. "Yes, the weakness is certainly in the back." I began to palpate the lumbar vertebrae, feeling my way along, watching for any sign of pain.

"Has he hurt 'imself?" Mrs. Cundall asked. "Has somebody hit 'im? We don't usually let him out alone, but sometimes he sneaks through the garden gate."

[225]

"There's always the possibility of an injury," I said. "But there are other causes." There were, indeed—a host of unpleasant possibilities. I did not like the look of this little dog at all. This syndrome was one of the things I hated to encounter in canine practice.

"Can you tell me what you really think?" she said. "I'd like to know."

"Well, an injury could cause haemorrhage or concussion or oedema—that's fluid—all affecting his spinal cord. He could even have a fractured vertebra, but I don't think so."

"And how about the other causes?"

"There's quite a lot. Tumours, bony growths, abscesses or discs can press on the cord."

"Discs?"

"Yes, little pads of cartilage and fibrous tissue between the vertebrae. In long-bodied dogs like Hermann, they sometimes protrude into the spinal canal. In fact, I think that is what is causing his symptoms."

Ron's husky voice came again from the bed. "And what's 'is prospects, Mr. Herriot?"

Oh, that was the question. Complete recovery or incurable paralysis. It could be anything. "Very difficult to say at this moment," I replied. "I'll give him an injection and some tablets, and we'll see how he goes over the next few days."

I injected an analgesic and some antibiotic, and counted out some salicylate tablets into a box. We had no steroids at that time. It was the best I could do.

"Now, then, Mr. Herriot." Mrs. Cundall smiled at me eagerly. "Ron has a bottle o' beer every night about this time. Would you like to join 'im?"

"Well . . . it's very kind of you, but I don't want to intrude . . ."

"Oh, you're not doing that. We're glad to see you."

She poured two glasses of brown ale, propped her husband up with pillows and sat down by the bed.

[226]

"We're from south Yorkshire, Mr. Herriot," she said.

I nodded. I had noticed the difference from the local accent.

"Aye, we came up here after Ron's accident, eight years ago."

"What was that?"

"I were a miner," Ron said. "Roof fell in on me. I got a broken back, crushed liver and a lot o' other internal injuries, but two of me mates were killed in the same fall, so ah'm lucky to be 'ere." He sipped his beer. "I've survived, but Doctor says I'll never walk no more."

"I'm terribly sorry."

"Nay, nay," the husky voice went on. "I count me blessings, and I've got a lot to be thankful for. Ah suffer very little, and I've got t'best wife in the world."

Mrs. Cundall laughed. "Oh, listen to 'im. But I'm right glad we came to Gilthorpe. We used to spend all our holidays in the Dales. We were great walkers, and it was lovely to get away from the smoke and the chimneys. The bedroom in our old house just looked out on a lot o' brick walls, but Ron has this big window right by 'im and he can see for miles."

"Yes, of course," I said. "This is a lovely situation." The village was perched on a high ridge on the fell-side, and that window would command a wide view of the green slopes running down to the river and climbing high to the wildness of the moor on the other side. This sight had beguiled me so often on my rounds, and the grassy paths climbing among the airy tops seemed to beckon to me. But they would beckon in vain to Ron Cundall.

"Gettin' Hermann was a good idea, too," he said. "Ah used to feel a bit lonely when t'missus went into Darrowby for shoppin', but the little feller's made all the difference. You're never alone when you've got a dog."

I smiled. "How right you are. What is his age now, by the way?"

"He's six," Ron replied. "Right in the prime o' life, aren't you, old lad?" He let his arm fall by the bedside, and his hand fondled the sleek ears.

[227]

"That seems to be his favourite place."

"Aye, it's a funny thing, but 'e allus sits there. T'missus is the one who has to take 'im for walks and feeds 'im, but he's very faithful to me. He has a basket over there but this is 'is place. I only have to reach down and he's there."

This was something that I had seen on many occasions with disabled people: that their pets stayed close by them as if conscious of their role of comforter and friend.

I finished my beer and got to my feet. Ron looked up at me. "Reckon I'll spin mine out a bit longer." He glanced at his half-full glass. "Ah used to shift about six pints some nights when I went out wi' the lads but you know, I enjoy this one bottle just as much. Strange how things turn out."

His wife bent over him, mock-scolding. "Yes, you've had to right your ways. You're a reformed character, aren't you?"

They both laughed as though it were a stock joke between them.

"Well, thank you for the drink, Mrs. Cundall. I'll look in to see Hermann on Tuesday." I moved towards the door.

As I left I waved to the man in the bed, and his wife put her hand on my arm. "We're very grateful to you for comin' out at this time on a Sunday night, Mr. Herriot. We felt awful about callin' you, but you understand it was only today that the little chap started going off his legs like that."

"Oh, of course, of course, please don't worry. I didn't mind in the least."

And as I drove through the darkness I knew that I didn't mind —now. My petty irritation had evaporated within two minutes of my entering that house, and I was left only with a feeling of humility. If that man back there had a lot to be thankful for, how about me? I had everything. I only wished I could dispel the foreboding I felt about his dog. There was a hint of doom about those symptoms of Hermann's, and yet I knew I just had to get him right. . . .

On Tuesday he looked much the same, possibly a little worse.

[228]

"I think I'd better take him back to the surgery for X-ray," I said to Mrs. Cundall. "He doesn't seem to be improving with the treatment."

In the car Hermann curled up happily on Rosie's knee, submitting with good grace to her petting.

I had no need to anaesthetise him or sedate him when I placed him on our newly acquired X-ray machine. Those hind quarters stayed still all by themselves—a lot too still for my liking.

I was no expert at interpreting X-ray pictures, but at least I could be sure there was no fracture of the vertebrae. Also, there was no sign of bony extoses, but I thought I could detect a narrowing of the space between a couple of the vertebrae, which would confirm my suspicions of a protrusion of a disc.

Laminectomy or fenestration had not even been heard of in those days, so I could do nothing more than continue with my treatment, and hope.

By the end of the week, hope had grown very dim. I had supplemented the salycilates with long-standing remedies like tincture of nux vomica and other ancient stimulant drugs, but when I saw Hermann on the Saturday he was unable to rise. I tweaked the toes of his hind limbs and was rewarded by a faint reflex movement, but with a sick certainty I knew that complete posterior paralysis was not far away.

A week later, I had the unhappy experience of seeing my prognosis confirmed in the most classical way. When I entered the door of the Cundalls' cottage, Hermann came to meet me, happy and welcoming in his front end but dragging his hind limbs helplessly behind him.

"Hello, Mr. Herriot." Mrs. Cundall gave me a wan smile and looked down at the little creature stretched frog-like on the carpet. "What d'you think of him now?"

I bent and tried the reflexes. Nothing. I shrugged my shoulders, unable to think of anything to say. I looked at the gaunt figure in the bed, the arm outstretched as always on the quilt.

"Good morning, Ron," I said as cheerfully as I could, but there was no reply. The face was averted, looking out of the window. I walked over to the bed. Ron's eyes were staring fixedly at the glorious panorama of moor and fell, at the pebbles of the river, white in the early sunshine, at the criss-cross of the grey walls against the green. His face was expressionless. It was as though he did not know I was there.

I went back to his wife. I don't think I have ever felt more miserable.

"Is he annoyed with me?" I whispered.

"No, no, no, it's this." She held out a newspaper. "It's upset him something awful."

I looked at the printed page. There was a large picture at the top, a picture of a dachshund exactly like Hermann. This dog, too, was paralysed, but its hind end was supported by a little four-wheeled bogie. In the picture it appeared to be sporting with its mistress. In fact, it looked quite happy and normal, except for those wheels.

Ron seemed to hear the rustle of the paper because his head came round quickly. "What d'ye think of that, Mr. Herriot? D'ye agree with it?"

"Well . . . I don't really know, Ron. I don't like the look of it, but I suppose the lady in the picture thought it was the only thing to do."

"Aye, maybe." The husky voice trembled. "But ah don't want Hermann to finish up like that." The arm dropped by the side of the bed and his fingers felt around on the carpet, but the little dog was still splayed out near the door. "It's 'opeless now, Mr. Herriot, isn't it?"

"Well, it was a black lookout from the beginning," I said. "These cases are so difficult. I'm very sorry."

"Nay, I'm not blamin' you," he said. "You've done what ye could, same as the vet for that dog in the picture did what 'e could. But it was no good, was it? What do we do now—put 'im down?"

"No, Ron, forget about that just now. Sometimes paralysis

cases just recover on their own after many weeks. We must carry on. At this moment I honestly cannot say there is no hope."

I paused, then turned to Mrs. Cundall. "One of the problems is the dog's natural functions. You'll have to carry him out into the garden for that. If you gently squeeze each side of his abdomen, you'll encourage him to pass water. I'm sure you'll soon learn how to do that."

"Oh, of course, of course," she replied. "I'll do anything. As long as there's some hope."

"There is, I assure you, there is."

But on the way back to the surgery, the thought hammered in my brain. That hope was very slight. Spontaneous recovery did sometimes occur, but Hermann's condition was extreme. I repressed a groan as I thought of the nightmarish atmosphere that had begun to surround my dealings with the Cundalls. The paralysed man and the paralysed dog. And why did that picture have to appear in the paper just at this very time? Every veterinary surgeon knows the feeling that fate has loaded the scales against him, and it weighed on me, despite the bright sunshine spreading into the car.

However, I kept going back every few days. Sometimes I took a couple of bottles of brown ale along in the evening and drank them with Ron. He and his wife were always cheerful, but the little dog never showed the slightest sign of improvement. He still had to pull his useless hind limbs after him when he came to greet me, and, though he always returned to his station by his master's bed, nuzzling up into Ron's hand, I was beginning to resign myself to the certainty that one day that arm would come down from the quilt and Hermann would not be there.

It was on one of these visits that I noticed an unpleasant smell as I entered the house. There was something familiar about it.

I sniffed, and the Cundalls looked at each other guiltily. There was a silence, and then Ron spoke.

"It's some medicine ah've been givin' Hermann. Stinks like 'ell, but it's supposed to be good for dogs."

"Oh, yes?"

"Aye, well . . ." His fingers twitched uncomfortably on the bedclothes. "It was Bill Noakes put me onto it. He's an old mate o' mine—we used to work down t'pit together—and he came to visit me last weekend. Keeps a few whippets, does Bill. Knows a lot about dogs, and 'e sent me this stuff along for Hermann."

Mrs. Cundall went to the cupboard and sheepishly presented me with a plain bottle. I removed the cork, and as the horrid stench rose up to me, my memory became suddenly clear. Asafoetida, a common constitutent of quack medicines before the war and still lingering on the shelves of occasional chemist shops and in the medicine chests of people who liked to doctor their own animals.

I had never prescribed the stuff myself, but it was supposed to be beneficial in horses with colic and dogs with digestive troubles. My own feeling had always been that its popularity had been due solely to the assumption that anything which stank as badly as that must have some magical properties, but one thing I knew for sure was that it could not possibly do anything for Hermann.

I replaced the cork. "So you're giving him this, eh?"

Ron nodded. "Aye, three times a day. He doesn't like it much, but Bill Noakes has great faith in it. Cured hundreds o' dogs with it, 'e says." The deep-sunk eyes looked at me with a silent appeal.

"Well, fine, Ron," I said. "You carry on. Let's hope it does the trick."

I knew the asafoetida couldn't do any harm, and since my treatment had proved useless I was in no position to turn haughty. But my main concern was that these two nice people had been given a glimmer of hope, and I wasn't going to blot it out.

Mrs. Cundall smiled and Ron's expression relaxed. "That's grand, Mr. Herriot," he said. "Ah'm glad ye don't mind. I can dose the little feller myself. It's summat for me to do."

It was about a week after the commencement of the new treatment that I called in at the Cundall's as I was passing through Gilthorpe.

[232]

"How are you today, Ron?" I asked.

"Champion, Mr. Herriot, champion." He always said that, but today there was a new eagerness in his face. He reached down and lifted his dog onto the bed. "Look 'ere."

He pinched the little paw between his fingers, and there was a faint but definite retraction of the leg. I almost fell over in my haste to grab at the other foot. The result was the same.

"My God, Ron," I gasped. "The reflexes are coming back."

He laughed his soft, husky laugh. "Bill Noakes's stuff's working, isn't it?"

A gush of emotions, mainly professional shame and wounded pride, welled in me, but it was only for a moment. "Yes, Ron," I replied. "It's working. No doubt about it."

He stared up at me. "Then Hermann's going to be all right?"

"Well, it's early days yet, but that's the way it looks to me."

It was several weeks more before the little dachshund was back to normal, and, of course, it was a fairly typical case of spontaneous recovery, with nothing whatever to do with the asafoetida or, indeed, with my own efforts. Even now, thirty years later, when I treat these puzzling back conditions with steroids, broad-spectrum antibiotics and sometimes colloidal calcium, I wonder how many of them would have recovered without my aid. Quite a number, I imagine.

Sadly, despite the modern drugs, we still have our failures, and I always regard a successful termination with profound relief.

But that feeling of relief has never been stronger than it was with Hermann, and I can recall vividly my final call at the cottage in Gilthorpe. As it happened, it was around the same time as my first visit—eight o'clock in the evening—and when Mrs. Cundall ushered me in, the little dog bounded joyously up to me before returning to his post by the bed.

"Well, that's a lovely sight," I said. "He can gallop like a racehorse now."

Ron dropped his hand down and stroked the sleek head. "Aye, isn't it grand? By heck, it's been a worryin' time."

[233]

"Well, I'll be going." I gave Hermann a farewell pat. "I just looked in on my way home to make sure all was well. I don't need to come anymore now."

"Nay, nay," Ron said. "Don't rush off. You've time to have a bottle o' beer with me before ye go."

I sat down by the bed, and Mrs. Cundall gave us our glasses before pulling up a chair for herself. It was exactly like that first night. I poured my beer and looked at the two of them. Their faces glowed with friendliness, and I marvelled because my part in Hermann's salvation had been anything but heroic.

In their eyes everything I had done must have seemed bumbling and ineffectual, and, in fact, they must be convinced that all would have been lost if Ron's old chum from the coal face had not stepped in and effortlessly put things right.

At best, they could only regard me as an amiable fathead, and all the explanations and protestations in the world would not alter that. But though my ego had been bruised, I did not really care. I was witnessing a happy ending instead of a tragedy, and that was more important than petty self-justification. I made a mental resolve never to say anything that might spoil their picture of this triumph.

I was about to take my first sip when Mrs. Cundall spoke up. "This is your last visit, Mr. Herriot, and all's ended well. I think we ought to drink some sort o' toast."

"I agree," I said. I looked around for an inspiration, and on a far shelf my eye caught a glimpse of the asafoetida bottle. The memory of its stench lanced briefly at my nose, defying me to put my humbled resolution to the test. "I have just the right toast," I said, raising my glass. "Here's to Bill Noakes."

Chapter
26

The bull with the bowler hat.

That was one of the irreverent terms for Artificial Insemination when it first arrived on the postwar scene. Of course, A.I. was a wonderful advance. Up till the official licencing of bulls, the farmers had used any available male bovine to get their cows in calf. A cow had to produce a calf before it would give milk and it was milk that was the goal of the dairy farmers, but, unfortunately, the progeny of these "scrub" bulls were often low-grade and weakly.

But A.I. was a great improvement on licencing. To use a high-class, pedigree, proven bull to inseminate large numbers of cows for farmers who could never afford to own such an animal was and is a splendid idea.

Over the years I have seen countless thousands of superior young heifers, bullocks and bulls populate the farms of Britain, and I have rejoiced.

I am speaking theoretically. My own practical experience of Artificial Insemination was brief and unhappy.

When the thing first began, most practitioners thought they would be rushing about, doing a lot of insemination on their own account, and Siegfried and I could hardly wait to get started. We purchased an artificial vagina, which was a tube of hard, vulcanised rubber about eighteen inches long with a lining of latex.

There was a little tap on the tube, and warm water was run into this to simulate the temperature of a genuine bovine vagina. On one end of the A.V. was a latex cone secured by rubber bands, and this cone terminated in a glass tube in which the semen was collected.

Apart from its use in insemination, this instrument provided an excellent means of testing the farmers' own bulls for fertility. It was in this context that I had my first experience.

Wally Hartley had bought a young Ayrshire bull from one of the big dairy farmers, and he wanted the animal's fertility tested by the new method. He rang me to ask if I would do the job and I was elated at the chance to try out our new acquisition.

At the farm I filled the liner with water just nicely at blood heat and fastened on the cone and glass tube. I was ready and eager for action.

The required cow in oestrus was in a large loose box off the yard, and the farmer led the bull towards it.

"He's nobbut a little 'un," Mr. Hartley said, "but I wouldn't trust 'im. He's a cheeky young bugger. Never served a cow yet, but keen as mustard."

I eyed the bull. Certainly he wasn't large, but he had mean eyes and the sharp, curving horns of the typical Ayrshire. Anyway, this job shouldn't be much trouble. I had never seen it done but had flipped through a pamphlet on the subject, and it seemed simple enough.

All you did was wait till the bull started to mount, then you directed the protruded penis into the A.V. Apparently then, the bull, with surprising gullibility, thrust happily into the water-filled cylinder and ejaculated into the tube. I had been told repeatedly that there was nothing to it.

I went into the box. "Let him in, Wally," I said, and the farmer opened the half-door.

The bull trotted inside, and the cow, fastened by a halter to a ring on the wall, submitted calmly as he sniffed around her. He seemed to like what he saw because he finally stationed himself behind her with eager anticipation.

This was the moment. Take up position on the right side of the bull, the pamphlet had said, and the rest would be easy.

With surprising speed the young animal threw his forelegs on the cow's rump and surged forward. I had to move quickly, and as the penis emerged from the sheath I grabbed it and poised the A.V. for action.

But I didn't get the chance. The bull dismounted immediately and swung round on me with an affronted glare. He looked me carefully up and down as though he didn't quite believe what he saw, and there was not an ounce of friendliness in his expression. Then he appeared to remember the rather pressing business on hand and turned his attention to the cow again.

He leaped up, I grabbed and once more he suspended his activities abruptly and brought his forefeet thudding to the ground. This time there was more than outraged dignity in his eyes; there was anger. He snorted, shook the needle-sharp horns in my direction and dragged a little straw along the floor with a hoof before fixing me with a long, appraising stare. He didn't have to speak; his message was unequivocal. Just try that once more, chum, and you've had it.

As his eyes lingered on me, everything seemed to become silent and motionless as though I were part of a picture—the cow standing patiently, the churned straw beneath the animals and, beyond them, the farmer out in the yard, leaning over the half-door, waiting for the next move.

I wasn't particularly looking forward to that next move. I felt a little breathless and my tongue pressed against the roof of my mouth.

At length the bull, with a final warning glance at me, decided to resume his business and reared up on the cow once more. I gulped, bent quickly and as his slim red organ shot forth, I grasped it and tried to bring the A.V. down on it.

[237]

This time the bull didn't mess about. He sprang away from the cow, put his head down and came at me like a bullet.

In that fleeting instant I realised what a fool I had been to stand with the animals between me and the door. Behind me was the dark corner of the box. I was trapped.

Fortunately, the A.V. was dangling from my right hand, and as the bull charged I was able to catch him an upward blow on the snout. If I had hit him on the top of the head, he would never have felt it, and one or both of those nasty horns would inevitably have started to explore my interior. But as it was, the hard rubber cylinder thumping against his nose brought him to a slithering halt, and while he was blinking and making up his mind about having a second go, I rained blows on him with a frenzy born of terror.

I have often wondered since that day if I am the only veterinary surgeon to have used an artificial vagina as a defensive weapon. It certainly was not built for the purpose because it soon began to disintegrate under my onslaught. First, the glass tube hurtled past the ear of the startled farmer who was watching, wide-eyed, from the doorway, then the cone spun away against the flank of the cow who had started to chew her cud placidly, oblivious of the drama being enacted by her side.

I alternated my swipes with thrusts and lunges worthy of a fencing master, but still I couldn't jockey my way out of that corner. However, although my puny cylinder couldn't hurt the bull, I obviously had him puzzled. His instinct told him that right about now he should be having a good time, and yet all he was getting were raps on the nose. While he weighed this incongruity, apart from a lot of weaving and prodding with his horns he made no sign of repeating his first headlong charge and seemed content to keep me penned in the few feet of space.

But I knew it was only a matter of time. He was out to get me, and I was wondering how it felt to receive a *cornada* when he took a step back and came in again full tilt, head down.

I met him with a back-handed slash and that was what saved

me, because the elastic holding the latex lining came off and the warm water from within fountained into the bull's eyes.

He stopped suddenly, and it was then I think he just decided to give up. In his experience of humans I was something new to him. I had taken intimate liberties with him in the pursuit of his lawful duty, I had belaboured him with a rubber instrument and finally squirted water in his face. He had plainly had enough of me.

During his pause for thought I dodged past him, threw open the door and escaped into the yard.

The farmer looked at me as I fought for breath. "By gaw, Mr. Herriot, it's a 'ell of a job, this A.I., isn't it?"

"Yes, Wally," I replied shakily. "It is, rather."

"Is it allus like that?"

"No, Wally, no. . . ." I looked sadly at my bedraggled A.V. "This is an exceptional case. I . . . I think we'd better get a specialist in to collect a sample from this bull."

The farmer rubbed his ear where the tube had clipped it in passing. "Awright, then, Mr. Herriot. You'll let me know when you're comin', I suppose. It'll be another bit of excitement to look forward to."

His words did nothing to ease the feeling of abject failure as I crept away from the farm. Vets were taking semen samples every day now with no trouble at all. What was the matter with me?

Back in the surgery I phoned the advisory service. Yes, they said, they would send out one of their sterility advisory officers. He would meet me on the farm at ten o'clock the next morning.

When I arrived there on the following day, the officer was already in the yard, and I thought there was something familiar about the back of the jaunty figure strolling over the cobbles and blowing out clouds of cigarette smoke. When he turned round I saw with a gush of relief that it was Tristan. I hadn't been looking forward to recounting my shameful performance to a stranger.

His broad grin was like a tonic. "Hello, Jim, how are things?"

"Fine," I replied. "Except for this semen collection. I know

[239]

you're doing it all the time, but I had a shambolic experience yesterday."

"Really?" He pulled deeply at his Woodbine. "Tell me about it. Mr. Hartley's just on his way in from the fields."

We stepped inside the loose box, the scene of the previous day's debacle, and I began my tale.

I hadn't got far before Tristan's jaw dropped. "You mean you just let the bull in here on his own, without any restraint?"

"That's right."

"You daft bugger, Jim. You're lucky to be here. In the first place, this job should always be done out in the open, and secondly, the bull should always be held by a pole or a halter through the nose ring. I like to have two or three blokes helping me." He shot me an incredulous glance as he lit another Woodbine. "Anyway, go on."

As I proceeded with my story, his expression began to change. His mouth twitched, his chin trembled and little giggles burst from him. "Are you trying to tell me that you grabbed him by his old man?"

"Well . . . yes."

"Oh, dear, oh, dear!" Tristan leaned back against the wall and laughed immoderately for a long time. When he had recovered, he regarded me pityingly. "Jim, old lad, you are supposed to put your hand only on the sheath to do the directing."

I gave a wry smile. "Oh, I know that now. I had another read at the pamphlet last night and realised I had made a lot of mistakes."

"Well, never mind," he said. "Carry on with your story. You're beginning to interest me."

The next few minutes had a devastating effect on my colleague. As I described the bull's attack on me, he slumped, shouting, against the door, and by the time I had finished, he was hanging limply with his arms dangling over the woodwork. Tears coursed down his cheeks and feeble little moans issued from his mouth.

"You were . . . you were in that corner, fighting the bull off with the A.V. Clouting him over the nut with all that stuff . . . flying around." He reached for his handkerchief. "For God's sake, don't tell me any more, Jim. You'll do me an injury." He wiped his eyes and straightened up, but I could see that the whole thing had taken it out of him.

He turned unsteadily as he heard the farmer's footsteps in the yard. "Ah, good morning, Mr. Hartley," he said. "We can get started now."

Tristan was very businesslike as he directed operations. Yesterday's cow was still in oestrus, and within minutes she was tied to a gatepost in the yard with a man on either side. "That's to stop her swinging round when the bull mounts," he explained to me.

He turned to the farmer and handed him the A.V. "Will you fill this with warm water, please, and screw the stopper on tightly?"

The farmer trotted into the house, and as he returned, another of his men led out the bull. This time my antagonist of yesterday was securely held by a halter through his ring.

Tristan had certainly got everything arranged in an orderly fashion.

The farmer had said that the bull was keen as mustard, and his words were verified when the young animal took one look at the cow and started towards her, a picture of urgent lust. Tristan scarcely had time to get the A.V. into his hand before the bull was clambering eagerly aboard his quarry.

I had to admit that my young colleague was lightning-fast as he stooped, seized the sheath and sent the penis plunging into the A.V. So that was how it was done, I thought wistfully. So very easy.

My feeling of shame was building up when the bull pushed out his tongue and emitted a long-drawn, deafening bellow of rage. And he had scarcely entered the A.V. when he withdrew with a backward leap and began to caper around on the end of his halter, filling the air with disapproving bawls.

"What the hell . . ." Tristan stared at the animal in bewilderment. Then he poked his finger into the A.V. "Good God!" he cried. "The water in here is steaming hot!"

"Aye," Wally Hartley nodded, accepting the compliment. "The kettle had just come to the boil when I went into t'house."

Tristan clutched his brow and groaned. "Oh, bugger it!" he muttered to me. "I always check the temperature, but what with talking . . . Boiling water! No wonder the poor sod got out quick."

Meanwhile the animal had stopped his noise and was circling the cow, sniffing her over and regarding her with a mixture of disbelief and respect. "What a woman!" was clearly the dominant thought in his mind.

"Anyway, let's have another try." Tristan made for the farmhouse. "I'll fill the thing myself this time."

Soon the stage was set once more—Tristan standing at the ready, and the bull, apparently undeterred by his recent experience, patently eager to join battle yet again. By his attitude now, he looked as though, come hell or high water, he was going to serve that cow.

My impression was confirmed when he made a sudden rush at her. Tristan, slightly pop-eyed, managed to jam the A.V. over the penis as it hurtled past him. But then something went wrong. The bull, wild with frustration and distracted by those two-legged fools around him, lost his footing. In the next instant two images flashed before me. The bull went down, still flying forward, somehow got on his back and slid clean under the cow. In the same moment, I could see the A.V., jerked from Tristan's grasp and soaring high into the air. Mr. Hartley and I followed the glass container, open-mouthed, as it described a graceful parabola toward certain doom. Then our mouths clapped shut in disbelief as it landed harmlessly on a pile of straw at the other end of the yard.

The bull scrambled to his feet, and Tristan strolled unhurriedly towards the straw. The glass tube was still attached to the cylinder, and my friend held it up at eye level.

"Ah, yes," he murmured. "A nice three c.c. sample."

[242]

The farmer came puffing up. "You've got what you wanted, 'ave you?"

"Yes indeed," Tristan replied airily. "Exactly what I wanted."

The farmer shook his head admiringly. "By 'ell, it's wondrous how the veterinary business has advanced, isn't it?"

Tristan shrugged his shoulders. "Have to keep up with the times, Mr. Hartley. New science means new methods. I'll get my microscope from the car and examine the sample."

It didn't take long, and soon afterwards we were all having a cup of tea in the kitchen.

My colleague put down his cup and reached for a scone. "That's a fine fertile bull you have there, Mr. Hartley."

"Eee, that's champion." The farmer rubbed his hands. "I paid a fair bit o' brass for 'im, and it's grand to know he's up to scratch." He looked across at the young man with undisguised admiration. "You've done a grand job. I couldn't do what you did in a hundred years."

As I sipped my tea the thought occurred to me that, despite the passage of time, things hadn't changed. Like the glass tube landing on soft straw, Tristan always landed on his feet.

Chapter
27

I winced as Jack Scott's slender frame crashed against the cow's ribs, but Jack himself didn't seem unduly troubled. His eyes popped a little and his cap slid over one ear, but he took a fresh grip on the tail, braced his boots once more against the cobbles and prepared himself for further action.

I was trying to irrigate the cow's uterus with Lugol's iodine. This was the common postwar treatment for infertility in cattle caused by endometritis, but it involved the insertion of the long, metal Nielsen catheter through the uterine cervix, and this animal didn't seem to appreciate it. Every time I attempted to work the catheter through the cervical folds, she swung round violently, and since the farmer weighed only about eight stones, he was whirled repeatedly against the neighbouring cow.

But this time I had the feeling I was winning. The tube was sliding nicely into the uterus, and if only she would stand still for a few seconds, the job would be over.

"Hang on, Jack," I gasped as I began to pump in the Lugol's. As soon as the cow felt the fluid trickling in, she veered over again, and the farmer's mouth fell open as he was squashed between the big creatures. And when a hoof descended on his toes, a soft groan escaped him.

"Lovely, that's it." I withdrew the catheter and stepped back, thinking at the same time that this had been a singularly uncooperative patient.

Jack, however, didn't seem to share my view. Hobbling on his bruised foot, he went up to the front of the cow and put his arms round her neck.

"Ah, you're a grand awd lass," he murmured, resting his cheek against the craggy jaw.

I looked at him wonderingly. It was always like this with Jack. He had a deep affection for every creature, human and animal, on his farm, and, with an occasional exception such as the cow I had just treated, the feeling seemed to be returned.

When he had concluded his embrace, he pushed his way out and hopped over the dung channel. His face wore its usual smile. It was not the ruddy face of the typical farmer; in fact it was always pale and haggard, as though its owner hadn't slept for a few nights, and the deep wrinkles on the cheeks and forehead made Jack look older than his forty years. But the smile was radiant, like an inner light.

"Ah've one or two other jobs for ye, Mr. Herriot," he said. "First, I want you to give a bullock a shot. He's got a bit of a cough."

We walked across the yard with Jack's sheepdog, Rip, gambolling around his master in delight. Often these farm dogs were slinking, furtive little creatures, but Rip behaved like a happy pet.

The farmer bent and patted him. "Hello, feller, are you comin', too?" As the dog went into further transports, a little boy and girl, the two youngest of the Scott family, trotted along with us.

"Dad, where are ye goin'?" "Dad, what are ye doin'?" They cried. There were usually children mixed up with the visits on this farm, getting in between the cows' legs, often hindering the work, but it never worried Jack.

The bullock was lying in deep straw in a loose box. He was a huge animal and obviously not very ill because he was placidly chewing his cud as we entered.

"There's nowt much wrong with 'im," Jack said. "Maybe just a bit o' cold. But I've heard 'im cough a few times, and I reckon he'd be better with an injection."

The temperature was slightly elevated, and I filled a syringe with a penicillin suspension, which the veterinary profession had recently acquired. I leaned over, gave the hairy rump the usual quick thump with my hand and plunged the needle in.

On any other farm, an animal of this size could have been something of a problem to inject, perhaps involving a chase round the box, but this one did not even rise to his feet. Nobody was restraining him in any way, but he continued to chew, merely looking round with mild interest as I drove the needle deep into his muscle.

"Champion. Good lad, good lad." Jack scratched the hairy poll for a few minutes before we left. "There's some lambs ah want you to look at," he said and led me into a Nissen hut. "I've never seen owt like them."

There were a number of ewes and lambs in the hut, but it was not difficult to see what the farmer meant. Several of the lambs were wobbling on their hind legs as they walked, and two could take only a few faltering steps before collapsing on their sides.

Jack turned to me. "What's the matter wi' them, Mr. Herriot?"

"They've got swayback," I replied.

"Swayback? What's that?"

"Well, it's a copper deficiency. Causes degeneration of the brain, which makes them weak on their hindquarters. That's the typical form, but sometimes they become paralysed or take fits. It's a funny disease."

"That's strange," the farmer said. "Them ewes have had copper licks to go at all the time."

"I'm afraid that's not enough. If you get many cases, you ought to inject the ewes with copper halfway through pregnancy to prevent it for next time."

He sighed. "Ah, well, now we know what it is, you'll be able to put these lambs right."

"Sorry, Jack," I replied. "There's no cure. Only prevention."

"Well, that's a beggar." The farmer tipped back his cap. "What's goin' to happen to this lot, then?"

"Well, the ones that are just wobbly have a good chance of making fat lambs, but I haven't much hope for those two." I pointed to the pair lying on their sides. "They are already partially paralysed. I honestly think the kindest thing would be . . ."

That was when the smile left Jack's face. It always did at the merest suggestion of putting an animal down. It is a country vet's duty to advise his clients when treatment is obviously unprofitable. He must always have the farmer's commercial interest in mind.

This system worked on most places, but not at Jack Scott's. Tell him to get rid of a cow that had lost a couple of quarters with mastitis, and the curtain would come down over that smiling face. He had various animals on the farm that could not possibly be making him any money, but they were his friends and he was happy to see them pottering about.

He dug his hands deep in his pockets and looked down at the prostrate lambs. "Are they sufferin', Mr. Herriot?"

"No, Jack, no. It doesn't seem to be a painful disease."

"Awright, I'll keep them two. If they can't suck, I'll feed 'em meself. Ah like to give things a chance."

He didn't have to tell me. He gave everything a chance. No farmer likes to have the extra work of lamb feeding, especially when the little creatures are abnormal, but I knew it was no use arguing with Jack. It was his way.

Out in the yard again, he leaned against the half-door of a loose box. "Any road, I'll have to remember to do them ewes with copper next time."

As he spoke, an enormous head poked over the door. This was

the bull box, and the great Shorthorn inside clearly wished to pay his respects.

He began to lick the back of Jack's neck, and as the rasping tongue repeatedly knocked his cap over his eyes, the farmer remonstrated gently. "Give over, George, ye daft thing. What d'you think you're doin'?" But he reached back and tickled the animal's chin at the same time.

The expression on George's face made him look more like a dog than a bull. Goofy-eyed and anxious to please, he licked and nuzzled faster than ever, despite the farmer's protests. On many farms a bull that size would be a potential killer, but George was just another of Jack's pets.

As lambing time was left behind and the summer wore on, I was glad to see that Jack's dedication had paid off. The two semi-paralysed lambs were surviving and doing well. They still flopped down after a few steps, but they were able to nibble the fast-growing grass and the demyelination of their brains had mercifully not progressed.

It was in October, when the trees around the Scott farm were bursting into a blaze of warm colour, that Jack hailed me as I drove past his gate.

"Will ye stop for a minute and see Rip?" His face was anxious.

"Why, is he ill?"

"Naw, naw, just lame, but I can't mek it out."

I didn't have to go far to find Rip—he was never far from his master—and I experienced a shock of surprise when I saw him because his right foreleg was trailing uselessly.

"What's happened to him?" I asked.

"He was roundin' up t'cows when one of 'em lashed out and got him on the chest. He's been gettin' lamer ever since. The funny thing is, ah can't find a thing wrong with his leg. It's a mystery."

Rip wagged vigorously as I felt my way up his leg from foot to shoulder. There was no pain in the limb, no wound or injury, but he winced as I passed my hand over his first rib. Diagnosis was not difficult.

"It's radial paralysis," I said.

"Radial . . . what's that?"

"The radial nerve passes over the first rib, and the kick must have damaged rib and nerve. This has put the extensor muscles out of action so that he can't bring his leg forward."

"Well, that's a rum 'un." The farmer passed a hand over the shaggy head and down the fine white markings of the cheeks. "Will he get better?"

"It's usually a long job," I replied. "Nervous tissue is slow to regenerate, and it could take weeks or months. Treatment doesn't seem to make much difference."

The farmer nodded. "Awright, we'll just have to wait. There's one thing"—and again the bright smile flooded his face—"he can still get round them cows, lame or not. It 'ud break 'is heart if he couldn't work. Loves 'is job, does Rip."

On the way back to the car, he nudged me and opened the door of a shed. In the corner, in a nest of straw, a cat was sitting with her family of tiny kittens. He lifted two out, holding one in each of his roughened hands. "Look at them little fellers, aren't they lovely!" He held them against his cheeks and laughed.

As I started the engine, I felt I ought to say something encouraging. "Don't worry too much about Rip, Jack. These cases usually recover in time."

But Rip did not recover. After several months his leg was as useless as ever, and the muscles had wasted greatly. The nerve must have been irreparably damaged, and it was an unhappy thought that this attractive little animal was going to be three-legged for the rest of his life.

Jack was undismayed and maintained stoutly that Rip was still a good working dog.

The real blow fell one Sunday morning as Siegfried and I were arranging the rounds in the office. I answered the door bell and found Jack on the step with his dog in his arms.

"What's wrong?" I asked. "Is he worse?"

"No, Mr. Herriot." The farmer's voice was husky. "It's summat different. He's been knocked down."

We examined the dog on the surgery table. "Fracture of the tibia," Siegfried said. "But there's no sign of internal damage. Do you know exactly what happened?"

Jack shook his head. "Nay, Mr. Farnon. He ran onto the village street and a car caught 'im. He dragged 'imself back into t'yard."

"Dragged?" Siegfried was puzzled.

"Aye, the broken leg's on the same side as t'other thing."

My partner blew out his cheeks. "Ah, yes, the radial paralysis. I remember you told me about it, James." He looked at me across the table, and I knew he was thinking the same thing as I was. A fracture and a paralysis on the same side was a forbidding combination.

"Right, let's get on," Siegfried murmured.

We set the leg in plaster, and I held open the door of Jack's old car as he laid Rip on the back seat.

The farmer smiled out at me through the window. "I'm takin' the family to church this mornin', and I'll say a little prayer for Rip while I'm there."

I watched until he drove round the corner of the street, and when I turned I found Siegfried at my elbow.

"I just hope that job goes right," he said thoughtfully. "Jack would take it hard if it didn't." He turned and carelessly dusted his old brass plate on its new place on the wall. "He's a truly remarkable chap. He says he's going to say a prayer for his dog, and there's nobody better qualified. Remember what Coleridge said? 'He prayeth best who loveth best all things both great and small.' "

"Yes," I said. "That's Jack, all right."

The farmer brought his dog into the surgery six weeks later for the removal of the plaster.

"Taking a cast off is a much longer job than putting it on," I said as I worked away with my little saw.

Jack laughed. "Aye, ah can see that. It's hard stuff to get through."

I have never liked this job, and it seemed a long time before I splayed open the white roll with my fingers and eased it away from the hair of the leg.

I felt at the site of the fracture and my spirits plummeted. Hardly any healing had taken place. There should have been a healthy callus by now but I could feel the loose ends of the broken bones moving against each other, almost like a hinge. We were no further forward.

I could hear Siegfried pottering among the bottles in the dispensary, and I called to him.

He palpated the limb. "Damn! One of those! And just when we didn't want it." He looked at the farmer. "We'll have to try again, Jack, but I don't like it."

We applied a fresh plaster, and the farmer grinned confidently. "Just wanted a bit more time, I reckon. He'll be right next time."

But it was not to be. Siegfried and I worked together to strip off the second cast, but the situation was practically unchanged. There was little or no healing tissue around the fracture.

We didn't know what to say. Even at the present time, after the most sophisticated bone-pinning procedures, we still find these cases where the bones just will not unite. They are as frustrating now as they were that afternoon when Rip lay on the surgery table.

I broke the long silence. "It's just the same, I'm afraid, Jack."

"You mean it 'asn't joined up?"

"That's right."

The farmer rubbed a finger along his upper lip. "Then 'e won't be able to take any weight on that leg?"

"I don't see how he possibly can."

"Aye . . . aye . . . well, we'll just have to see how he goes on, then."

[251]

"But Jack," Siegfried said gently. "He can't go on. There's no way a dog can get around with two useless legs on the same side."

The silence set in again, and I could see the familiar curtain coming down over the farmer's face. He knew what was in our minds, and he wasn't going to have it. In fact, I knew what he was going to say next.

"Is he sufferin'?"

"No, he isn't," Siegfried replied. "There's no pain in the fracture now and the paralysis is painless anyway, but he won't be able to walk, don't you see?"

But Jack was already gathering his dog into his arms. "Well, we'll give him a chance, any road," he said and walked from the room.

Siegfried leaned against the table and looked at me, wide-eyed. "Well, what do you make of that, James?"

"Same as you," I replied gloomily. "Poor old Jack. He always gives everything a chance, but he's got no hope this time."

But I was wrong. Several weeks later I was called to the Scott farm to see a sick calf and the first thing I saw was Rip bringing the cows in for milking. He was darting to and fro around the rear of the herd, guiding them through the gate from the field, and I watched him in amazement.

He still could not bear any appreciable weight on either of his right limbs, yet he was running happily. Don't ask me how he was doing it because I'll never know, but somehow he was supporting his body with his two strong left legs and the paws of the stricken limbs merely brushing the turf. Maybe he had perfected some balancing feat like a one-wheel bicycle rider but, as I say, I just don't know. The great thing was that he was still the old friendly Rip, his tail swishing when he saw me, his mouth panting with pleasure.

Jack didn't say anything about "I told you so," and I wouldn't have cared because it thrilled me to see the little animal doing the job he loved.

"This calf, Mr. Herriot," Jack began, then he pointed excitedly at a pigeon perched on the byre roof. "By gaw, that little feller looks better. I've been watching 'im for months. He went down to skin and bone, but he's fillin' out now."

I smiled to myself. Even the pigeons were under Jack's eye.

He dragged himself back to more practical things. "Aye, now, this calf. Never seen one like it. Goin' round and round as if it was daft."

Depression flowed over me. I had been hoping for something straightforward this time. My recent contacts with Jack's animals could be described as abortive treatment and wrong prognosis, and I did want to pull something out of the bag. This didn't sound good.

It was a bonny little calf about a month old. Dark roan—the Shorthorn farmer's favourite colour—and it was lying on its straw bed looking fairly normal, except that its head was inclined slightly to one side. Jack touched the hairy rump with his toe, and the calf rose to its feet.

That was where the normality ended because the little creature blundered away to the right, as if drawn by a magnet, until it walked into the wall. It picked itself up and recommenced its helpless progress, always to the right. It managed to complete two full circuits of the pen until it collapsed against the door.

Ah, well, so that was it. I was relieved and worried at the same time because I knew what the trouble was, and I was pretty sure I could cure it . . . but not quite sure.

The temperature was 106°F.

"This is a thing called listeriosis, Jack," I said.

He looked at me blankly.

"Circling disease is the other name, and you can see why. It's a brain disease, and the animal can't help going round and round like that."

The farmer looked glum. "Brain again, just like them lambs? God 'elp us, there must be summat in the air about here. Are all

[253]

me stock goin' to go off their heads?" He paused, bent over the calf and began to stroke it. "And there'll be nowt you can do for this, either, I suppose."

"I hope I can do something, Jack. This is a different thing altogether from the swayback lambs. It's an actual bug affecting the brain, and with a bit of luck I can put this calf right."

I felt like crossing my fingers. I was still not vastly experienced. I had seen only a few of these cases and in the prewar days they had been invariably fatal, but the causal organism was sensitive to antibiotics and the whole scene had changed. I had seen animals with listeriosis recover completely within a few days.

I shook up my bottle of penicillin-streptomycin suspension and injected 5 c.c.'s into the thigh. "I'll be back tomorrow," I said. "I hope to find the little thing improved by then."

Next day the temperature was down, but the symptoms had not abated. I repeated the injection and said I would call again.

I did call, again and again, because I was gripped by a kind of desperation, but after a week, though the temperature was normal and the appetite excellent, the calf was still circling.

"How d'you feel about t'job, then, Mr. Herriot?" the farmer asked.

Actually I felt like screaming and railing against fate. Was there a hoodoo on this place? Could I do nothing right?

I calmed down and took a deep breath. "I'm sorry, Jack, but we don't seem to be getting anywhere. The antibiotic has saved the calf's life, but there must be some brain damage. I can't see any hope of recovery now."

He didn't seem to have heard me. "It's a grand 'un, a heifer, too, and out of me best cow. She'll make a smashin' milker. Just look at the shape of 'er—and that grand colour. We've called her Bramble."

"Yes, but Jack . . ."

He patted me on the shoulder and led me out to the yard. "Well, thank ye, Mr. Herriot. Ah'm sure you've done all you can." Quite obviously he didn't want to pursue the matter further.

Before I left, I took a final glance over the door of the pen at that calf reeling in the straw. As I walked to the car, Rip gambolled at my feet, and the almost useless legs mocked me with further evidence of my veterinary skill. What kind of an animal doctor was I, anyway?

As I started the engine, I looked out through the open window and was about to speak when I saw the familiar blank look on Jack's face. He didn't want to hear any advice from me on what he should do with his calf. Clearly he had decided to give Bramble a chance.

It turned out that Jack's faith was rewarded and that my prognosis was wrong again, but I cannot blame myself because the sequence of events in Bramble's recovery is not contained in any textbook.

Over the next two years the brain symptoms gradually diminished. The improvement was so slow as to be almost imperceptible, but every time I was on Jack's farm I had a look into her pen and saw to my astonishment that the little animal was just a bit better. For many weeks she circled, then this subsided into an occasional staggering towards the right. This, in turn, faded over the months into an inclination of the head to one side, until one day I looked in and found that this, too, had disappeared and a fine, normal two-year-old heifer was strolling around unconcernedly in the straw. I didn't mind being wrong. I was delighted.

"Jack," I said. "How marvellous! I'd have bet anything that this was a hopeless case, and there she is, absolutely perfect."

The farmer gave me a slow smile with a hint of mischief in it. "Aye, ah'm right capped with her, Mr. Herriot, and she's goin' to be one of the best cows in the herd before she's finished. But . . ." He raised a finger and his smile broadened. "She's not perfect, tha knows."

"Not . . . what do you mean?"

"I mean there's just a little somethin'." He leaned towards me conspiratorially. "Keep watchin' her face."

I stared at the heifer, and the calm, bovine eyes looked back at me with mild interest. We inspected each other for a couple of minutes, then I turned to the farmer. "Well, I can't see a thing wrong with her."

"Hang on a bit," Jack said. "She doesn't allus do it."

"Do what?" I was mystified. "There's nothing at all . . . my God!"

The farmer laughed and thumped me on the back. "Did ye see it?"

I certainly had, and it was startling. Just for an instant Bramble's placid expression was transfigured by a faint twitch of the eyes and head to the right. There was something human about the gesture; in fact, I was reminded instantly of the film "vamps" of the twenties, when a girl would stand, hand on hip, and beckon seductively at her quarry. It was a come-hither look.

Jack was still laughing. "I reckon you've never seen owt like that afore, Mr. Herriot?"

"No, you're right. I haven't. What an extraordinary thing. How often does she do it?"

"Oh, every now and then. I suppose it'll go away in time like all t'other things?"

"I expect it will," I said. "But how very strange."

The farmer nodded. "Aye, there's summat right cheeky about it. I allus get the feelin' she's trying to ask me somethin'."

I laughed, too. "Yes, that's it, exactly. You'd think she was trying to communicate, but, of course, it's just the last trace of the condition she had. Anyway, the main thing is, she's a grand, bonny heifer."

"She is that," Jack said. "I'm glad we persevered with 'er." (It was nice of him to say "we.") "Ah've had 'er served, and she should be calvin' just right for Darrowby show."

"Well, that will be interesting. She's certainly a show animal."

[256]

And there was no doubt that Bramble had developed into a classical Dairy Shorthorn with all the delicacy and grace of that now-lost breed—the beautifully straight back, the neat tail-head and the makings of a fine udder. She was a picture.

She was even more of a picture a few months later as she stood in the centre of the show ring with the August sun glinting on her rich, dark coat. She had recently produced a calf, and her udder, tight and flat-based, with a small teat thrusting proudly from each corner, bulged between the back limbs.

She would take some beating, and it was a pleasant thought that the seemingly doomed little creature of two and a half years ago might be just about to win a championship trophy.

However, Bramble was in pretty hot company. The judge, Brigadier Rowan, had narrowed the field down to three after much cogitation, and the other two contestants, a red-and-white and a light roan, were beautiful animals. It would be a close thing.

Brigadier Rowan himself was a splendid sight. He was a distinguished soldier, a gentleman farmer and an unrivalled judge of dairy cattle in the district.

His dress and general bearing were fully in keeping with his position. That tall, lean figure would have been aristocratic and impressive enough without the beautifully cut check suit, yellow waistcoat, cravat and bowler hat. The fact that he was one of the few people I have ever seen wearing a monocle added the final touch.

The brigadier strolled up and down the little row of cattle, shoulders high, hands clasped behind his back, occasionally screwing the glass tighter into his eye as he bent to inspect a particular point. Clearly, he was having difficulty in deciding.

His normally pink face was bright red, not, I felt, from the sunshine, but from the long succession of brandies and sodas I had seen him consuming in the president's tent. He pursed his lips and approached Bramble, who stood patiently at the end of the row nearest to me with her head held by Jack Scott on a halter.

The brigadier leaned forward and peered into the animal's face

[257]

as though to examine the eyes. Something happened then. I was standing behind Bramble and could not see her face, but my suspicion is that she gave the little twitch which had startled me. In any case, something undoubtedly pierced the brigadier's patrician calm. His eyebrows shot up and the monocle dropped to the end of its cord, where it dangled for a few seconds before he retrieved it, gave it a thorough polish and returned it to his eye.

He again studied Bramble fixedly for quite a long time, and even after he had moved away, he glanced back at her once or twice. I could read his mind. Had he really seen that, or was it the brandy?

As he came slowly back down the row, he had the look of a man who was definitely going to make up his mind this time, even though he was confronted by three superb animals. He finished up in front of Bramble, and as he gave her a final appraising stare, he flinched suddenly, and I had a strong conviction that she had done her trick again.

The brigadier kept a grip on himself this time, but though the monocle remained in position, the man was obviously shaken. It seemed, however, to remove all doubts from his mind. He immediately placed Bramble first, the red-and-white second and the light roan third.

The brigadier, having made his decision, strode straight as a cadet, albeit a red-faced one, to the edge of the ring where he was greeted by a beaming Jack.

"A bonny lass, 'ant she, Brigadier? Almost human, ye might say."

"Quite," said the brigadier, adjusting his monocle. "Actually, she reminded me of someone I used to know . . . briefly."

Chapter
28

"Disaster! Disaster! Disaster!"

The voice at the other end was so shrill and panic-stricken that I almost dropped the telephone. "Who . . . who is that?"

"It's Mrs. Derrick! Oh, such a disaster!"

"Yes, Mrs. Derrick, what on earth has happened?"

"It's my goat, Mr. Herriot! It's really terrible!"

The Derricks were a young couple who had recently come to live in one of the villages near Darrowby. They were in their early thirties, and Ronald Derrick was a businessman who commuted daily to Brawton. His wife was extremely attractive and a pleasant young woman in every way, but she was slightly scatterbrained, and I had felt misgivings in the first place when she told me she had bought a goat.

I gripped the receiver tightly. "Has the goat had an accident?"

"No, no, it's not the goat I'm worried about. It's the tomatoes!"

"Tomatoes?"

"Yes, the wretched thing has eaten all my husband's tomatoes. I left the greenhouse door open by mistake."

A chill swept through me. Ronald Derrick loved his tomatoes dearly and since I, too, found them fascinating things, I had been very interested when he had shown me his plants.

Like many people coming to live in a country district, he and his wife had been seized with a passion for the country things, like growing all sorts of vegetables in the big garden behind the house and keeping livestock. They had a few hens, ponies for their children and, of course, the goat. But with Ronald, the tomatoes were his great joy.

There was a little greenhouse in the garden, and on my last visit there he had shown me the twelve plants with justifiable pride. It was early July, and the young fruits were still green and small but obviously thriving.

"Magnificent trusses," I remembered saying. "You are going to have a wonderful crop." I could recall the smile of gratification on his face as his wife continued on the phone.

"He counts them every morning, Mr. Herriot. In fact, before he left for the office today, he told me there were two hundred and ninety-three. Do please come. I'm afraid that when he gets home he'll kill the goat *and* me!" There was a pause. "I think I can see him through the window. Oh, yes, my God, here he is now!"

There was a thud in my ear as she crashed the receiver down, and I found I was shaking slightly. What was I supposed to do? Act as peacemaker? Prevent a murder? Anyway, Ronald Derrick was a gentle, good-humoured man who would certainly not resort to violence. But, by heck, he was going to be annoyed—and maybe the goat would be ill after that feast. I dashed out to the car.

I was at the scene of the catastrophe within ten minutes. The Derricks' home was a gracious old manor house with an open drive at one side leading to the garden. I roared down there, leaped from my car and the whole sad spectacle lay before me.

Mrs. Derrick, still very attractive despite the tears which trickled down her cheeks, was standing on a strip of lawn, twisting a sodden handkerchief in her fingers.

"Darling," she was saying, "I just went in for a moment to get the watering can. I can't think why I forgot to close the door."

Her husband did not answer, and I could see that his was a bereavement too deep for words. He was leaning against the open

[260]

doorway, gazing into the greenhouse. He was quite motionless, and plainly he had not moved since his arrival because he was like a business executive who had been frozen to the spot: dark-suited, bowler-hatted, briefcase dangling from one hand.

I stepped forward and looked over his shoulder, and the sight was even more bizarre than I had expected. The tastes and eating habits of goats are often unfathomable, but this one had, for some reason, consumed all the tomatoes and leaves and left the slender green stalks, naked and pathetic, still neatly tied to the canes that led up to the glass roof.

As a fellow tomato lover, I felt for him deeply, but there was nothing I could do. I patted him on the shoulder and murmured a few words of sympathy, but still he continued to stare at the row of stalks.

I could see the goat on its tether at the other end of the garden. That was another point—how had it got free to wreak this devastation? But I wasn't going to add more tension to the situation by bringing that up.

I went over and had a look at the animal. It was bright-eyed and cheerful and clearly didn't require my services in any way. In fact, as I watched it began to nibble at a cabbage with obvious relish. As I say, I was sad for the Derricks, but I could not but look with admiration at any creature whose appetite was not satisfied by the consumption of two hundred and ninety-three tomatoes.

A large part of the veterinary life seems to be made up of these little incidents. Trivial, perhaps, but rewarding. I recall a visit I made to test the herd of Rupe and Will Rowney. Rupe and Will just didn't get on. They were bachelor brothers who had run a dairy farm for many years together, but they didn't seem to be able to agree about anything.

Visits there could be embarrassing as the brothers argued continually and criticised each other's every move, but on this particular day I found they had forgotten to keep the cows in for me.

I stood to one side as they castigated each other.

"Ah told ye the postcard said today."

"Naw, ye didn't, ye said Tuesday. It was me as said today."

"Well, fetch the bloody card from t'house and let's 'ave another look at it."

"How can I? Ye burned it, ye daft bugger!"

I let the debate go on for a few minutes, then intervened tactfully.

"It's all right," I said. "There's no harm done. The cows are just there in the field. It shouldn't take long to get them in."

Rupe gave his brother a final glare and turned to me. "Nay, it won't take long, Mr. Herriot. The byre door's open. Ah'll soon call 'em in."

He inflated his lungs and began a series of shrill cries. "Come on, Spotty Nose, come on, Big Lugs, come on, Mucky Tail, come on, Fat Tits, come on, Fuzzy Top!"

Will, nettled at being upstaged, broke in with his own shout. "Come on, Long Legs! Come on, Slow Coach!"

Rupe froze him with a stare, then bent towards me. "Ye'll have to excuse me brother, Mr. Herriot," he said in a confidential whisper. "Ah've tried to tell 'im many a time, but he will call the cows them daft names."

Contrasts in people always intrigue me. I was called to see a bullock with a swollen foot. The owner was one of the new breed of young farmer who had been to agricultural college and was steeped in modern science. He was a nice lad, but like many of his kind, he gave me the uncomfortable feeling that he knew about as much as I did.

He showed me the animal.

"Bit of infection there," he said. "Bacteria must have gained entry through that abrasion. I should think he needs about twenty c.c.'s of long-acting procaine penicillin intramuscularly."

He was right, of course, and I duly injected the dose into the animal's rump.

It happened that my next call, just a mile along the road, was to a similar case, but this time the farmer was old Ted Buckle, one of the fast-disappearing old characters and a great favourite of mine.

"Now, then, Mr. Herriot," he said and led me into the fold yard. He pointed to the lame bullock standing in a corner. "There's a youth ower there wants a jab in t'arse."

Then there was Mr. Bogg whose tight-fistedness was a byword in a community where thrift was the norm. I had heard many tales of his parsimony, but I have a few experiences of my own that I cherish.

He owned a herd of good Ayrshire cows and ran a few turkeys and chickens on the side. He certainly would not be short of money.

His turkeys were frequently afflicted with blackhead, and he used to come to us for Stovarsol tablets which were the popular treatment at that time.

One afternoon he approached me in the surgery.

"Look," he said. "Ah keep comin' here for fifty or a hundred of them little tablets, and it's a flippin' nuisance. I'd rather buy a whole tinful—it 'ud save a lot of journeys."

"Yes, Mr. Bogg, you're right," I replied. "It would be a much better idea. I'll get you some now."

When I returned from the dispensary, I held up the tin. "This contains a thousand tablets, and as it happens, it's the only one we have in stock. It has been opened and a few have been taken out, but it is virtually a new tin."

"A few . . . taken out . . . ?" I could read the alarm in his eyes at the idea of paying for the full thousand when he was getting less than that.

"Oh, don't worry," I said. "There's maybe something like a dozen tablets short—no more."

My words clearly failed to reassure him, and as he left the surgery he looked gloomy and preoccupied.

He was back again that same evening. He rang the bell at about eight o'clock, and I faced him on the front doorstep.

"I've just come in to tell ye," he said. "I've been counting them tablets, and there's nine hundred and eighty-seven."

On another occasion I went to buy some eggs from Mr. Bogg. I got a dozen from him most weeks because his farm was on the outskirts of the town. When I returned home with this particular batch I found that there were only eleven eggs in the bag, so when I saw him a week later I mentioned the fact.

"Mr. Bogg," I said. "There were only eleven eggs in last week's lot."

"Aye, ah know," he replied, fixing me with a steady eye. "But one of 'em was a double-yolked 'un."

I have a dear memory, too, of the time—the only time—I did a farm round in shorts.

I had just got back from the family holiday in Scotland. The weather had been perfect, and after spending a fortnight in shirt and shorts, I rebelled at the idea of climbing into workaday clothes.

Looking from our bedroom window at the sun blazing from a clear sky, I made a sudden decision. I pulled on the shorts. And as I walked down the long garden to get my car, the air played round my legs, and I half-closed my eyes at the sensation of coolness and freedom. I was still on holiday, still striding the hills around Ullapool.

The conviction that I had done the right thing was strengthened when I got out at the first farm. The day was going to be really hot, and the whole green landscape shimmered in the morning haze. Yes, this was the right garb for country practice in the summer.

The place was a smallholding, and old Mrs. Meynell answered my knock. At first she did not reply to my cheerful greeting but stared in silent fascination at my exposed knees. After a few seconds I repeated my query.

"Is your husband in, Mrs. Meynell?"

"Nay . . . nay . . . " She still had difficulty in dragging her eyes away from my legs. "He's over t'field, mendin' a wall." At last she looked up at my face. "I'm sorry, Mr. Herriot, but when I peeped through the window, I thought it was a boy scout comin' to see us."

Slightly abashed, I opened the gate to the pasture and headed over the long stretch of green to where the farmer was resetting the stones on the wall.

He did not hear my approach, and I spoke to his back. "Good morning, Mr. Meynell, it's a lovely day."

The old man turned round, and his reaction was very like his wife's. He did not speak but directed a prolonged, unsmiling gaze at my knees until I began to feel uncomfortable.

At length, I broke the silence. "I believe you have a sick calf."

He nodded slowly, still staring downwards.

I cleared my throat. "Touch of scour, is it?"

"Aye . . . aye . . . that's right." There was no change in his attitude, and I felt we weren't getting anywhere.

"Well," I said. "Will we go and have a look at him?"

Without warning, the old man dropped into the sprint starting position, one knee on the turf, fingers outsplayed.

He looked up at me eagerly. "Come on, then, I'll race ye back to the house."

Chapter
29

Again I step forward in time from the postwar years. It was 1963, and John Crooks was visiting me once more. He lay back in his chair and laughed.

"You know, Jim, I often think about your Russian trip, and honestly, it doesn't sound as though you had a very comfortable time. Force nine gales, only just avoiding being thrown into jail, nearly savaged by a killer dog—not my idea of pleasure. In fact, I feel a bit guilty about sending you out there."

"Please don't feel like that, John," I said. "I loved it. Wouldn't have missed it for anything."

He sat up. "I've been thinking. You deserve a bit of luxury and relaxation after that, and I've got just the thing for you."

"What's that?"

"Well, I'll tell you." He leaned closer, his eyes eager. John's natural enthusiasm and eloquence had pushed him to the top in veterinary practice and like most people, I fell easily under his spell. "Last spring I had the most wonderful voyage to Istanbul with a cargo of Jersey cows. How would you like that?"

"Istanbul?" Immediately my mind was full of the mysterious East. Mosques, minarets, blue skies, tranquil seas, exotic perfumes, Scheherazade . . .

"Yes, Jim, and it was memorable. We sailed from Hull to

Jersey, picked up the cattle from there and came right round to Gibraltar. After that, it was just a beautiful Mediterranean cruise. The cows never ailed a thing, and all I did was eat lovely food, bask out on the deck and sleep in a super cabin. The sea hardly rippled, the sun shone all the time and I saw places I'd only dreamed about: the Greek Islands, the coast of Asia and, of course, Istanbul itself."

"Fascinating city, they say."

"It certainly is," John said. "And really, you have to see it for yourself. You can't describe it—it's magic."

"Did you have some spare time to look around?"

"Oh yes, the whole trip took seventeen days, and I had a full two days to explore. The cattle were unloaded as soon as we arrived, and after that my time was my own. The Export Company put me up in a five-star hotel, too—luxury room, gourmet food—I tell you, it was terrific. Talk about living like a sultan!"

"And you got paid for that?"

"Yes, and so will you."

"You really mean I can go?"

"Yes, Jim, of course you can." John smiled. "There's another load of Jerseys to go over there in August, and I'll book you in."

I rubbed my hands. "That's marvellous, but how about you? Don't you want another trip?"

"Oh, it would be very nice, but I can't leave the practice too often. It would have to be you or another of my friends."

It was the beginning of another little adventure. For the next few weeks as I drove on my rounds, the green hills and bracken-clad slopes that sped past my windows were intermingled with the heady scenes of my imaginings. New places have always intrigued me, and as I have said before, I have seafaring blood. I could smell the salty freshness of the wide ocean that had thrilled me on the voyage to Klaipeda; only this time it would be sunshine and a calm sea and one of the most exciting cities in the world at the end of it.

[267]

As John promised, I had a telephone call at the beginning of August from Mr. Costain, the representative of the Export Company.

"I'd like you to be here at two o'clock on Thursday, the eighth, at our offices," he said. "And then I'll take you out to Gatwick."

"Gatwick?"

"Yes, that's right. The plane takes off at around eight o'clock in the evening."

"Plane! I thought we were going by sea."

Mr. Costain laughed for quite a long time at this. "No, no, no —whatever gave you that idea?"

"John Crooks did."

"Ah, well, as it happened John did go by sea, and I suppose it was natural he would think the next trip would be the same. But you'll thoroughly enjoy the flight, and it means you get the whole thing over quickly. Less than four days."

"I see." I didn't want to get the whole thing over quickly. I had been looking forward to that leisurely seventeen days. But never mind, this could be fun, too.

"Right," I said. "I'll see you on the day."

The night before I left, I packed the same attaché case I had taken to Russia. Antibiotics, calcium, steroids, bandages and suture materials. I hoped I would not have to use anything in that case, particularly the humane killer lying in the corner.

August 8, 1963

On the train to London my enthusiasm grew steadily. It was a pity about the sea voyage, and I was sorry that it would not be worth keeping a daily diary on such a short trip. I would have to write it up later. But on the other hand, I liked flying, and it would be interesting to see the reaction of the animals. On the Klaipeda voyage I had learned a lot about the behaviour of animals aboard ship, and now I had the chance to observe the reaction of cows to being whisked into the air. I felt a faint twinge of alarm when

I remembered a story of how a veterinary surgeon had been in charge of some racehorses flying to America, and one of the animals had gone berserk and kicked a hole in the side of the aircraft. But I put away the disturbing image. Jersey cows would never do that.

Another happy thought was that I was able to take my camera and bring back a record of my adventure. That had been forbidden on the Russian trip.

Mr. Costain was pleasant and friendly. We took the train to Gatwick, and I had my first view of our aircraft standing a few hundred yards away out on the airfield. It looked very smart, its red, white and silver-grey paint glittering in the sunshine.

"Gosh, it's big!" I said.

Mr. Costain nodded. "Yes, it's a Globemaster, and to the best of my knowledge it is the biggest aircraft in the world at the present time."

I don't know whether he was right about this but it was easy to believe, because as we approached the Globemaster it seemed to get larger all the time. It also became less smart because on closer inspection the paint wasn't nearly as glossy and there was a faint air of delapidation about the whole mighty machine. The rubber was worn smooth and frayed in parts and, in fact, if you took a motor car out with tyres like that you would be fined and have your licence endorsed.

There were four propellor engines, and along one side the name *Heracles* sprawled in large red letters.

I climbed up the steps into the flight cabin, and here the impression of age and a long, hard life was stronger still. The black paintwork had been almost rubbed away from the bank of dials and levers in the cockpit, leaving the bare metal gleaming through, and the seats showed the outline of their contents bulging dangerously against their leather coverings. A curtain, when drawn aside, revealed a toilet of the most primitive type. This was, indeed, an elderly aeroplane.

I looked back wonderingly at the enormous empty belly stretching away to the tail and at that moment Mr. Costain poked his head in from the steps.

"Tremendous, isn't it?" he said. "It was used as a troop carrier and general transport during the war."

I nodded silently. That was quite a long time ago.

We walked back together to the airport terminal and had a cup of tea and a sandwich while keeping an eye open for the arrival of the cattle. I learned that we were taking forty pedigree cows and heifers, and as the time stretched round to half-past six, I wondered just how they were going to be loaded in time for an eight o'clock take-off.

At length two cattle wagons rumbled onto the airfield, and we hurried to meet them. I was pleased and relieved to find that two Jersey farmers were joining us on the flight, and I was introduced to them before the loading started. They were both dark-haired and spoke with a slow drawl, very different from my Yorkshire clients. Noel would be in his early thirties, smiling and with an ingenious air about him; Joe, probably ten years older, similarly amiable but, it seemed to me, a hard man at bottom. He was easy to like, but I couldn't imagine him suffering fools gladly.

It didn't take me long to realise that the two of them knew what they were doing. One of the Globemaster's crew, a little Dane called Karl, operated an electric hoist with tubular metal sides that descended from the underside of the aircraft, while Joe and Noel led the cattle up a ramp and jockeyed them into position until the hoist was full and they could be lifted up.

Above, in the cavernous interior, they arranged the animals in rows of six facing the front, with a metal tube clamped behind each row.

Those farmers were good stocksmen. There was no shouting, no brandishing of sticks, just a continual gentle nudging and pushing and soft words of encouragement. And, of course, they had the ideal subjects to handle. I have often said that I wished all cows were Jerseys, and I felt it again that day.

[270]

I do not think I have ever seen a more beautiful group of cattle —mostly heifers with a few young cows, and all of them fine-boned and graceful, with their lambent, kind eyes regarding us with mild interest as they took their places.

It was a steamy, hot London evening and as Joe and Noel toiled, the sweat streamed down their faces. But, like my Yorkshire farmers, hard work seemed to be something they took for granted. Sleeves rolled high on their sunburned arms, they kept at it without pausing.

More than half the animals had been loaded when the main members of the crew arrived. Captain Birch looked down at me from a gaunt six feet four as he shook hands, and the sombre face above the black, grey-flecked beard emanated authority. This was a man of formidable presence.

The co-pilot and navigator, Ed, and the engineer, Dave, were in their twenties and grinned cheerfully as they hoisted their bags into the flight cabin. The captain was English and dressed in a formal dark uniform, but these young men were American, and their clothing intrigued me. They wore white, loose-fitting jackets and trousers of a light-weight material which, with their peaked caps cocked at an angle, gave them a carefree appearance.

As I thought, there was no possibility of an eight o'clock take-off, and it was nearly eleven when the last heifer was loaded and clamped in safely. The forty cattle were quite a sight as they stood patiently in their rows, their feet deep in straw and an armful of hay in front of each of them. The long stretch of backs made a ripple of fawn gold under the interior lights of the aircraft. One snag was that the heat in the packed interior was almost overpowering, and I prayed that some ventilation would come into operation when we were airborne.

Mr. Costain prepared to leave. He had spent quite a long time in a financial negotiation, almost a wrangle with the captain, about the cost of the transportation, and I gathered that the captain either owned the aircraft personally or was a top director of the firm that did. They came to an agreement at last, and Mr. Costain shook my hand.

"Have a good trip, Mr. Herriot," he said. "You will be refuelling in Rome and reach Istanbul early tomorrow. I know you'll love that city. Goodbye."

The thought of this huge, heavily loaded aeroplane landing anywhere on those bald tyres gave me a moment of disquiet, but I put it out of my mind and sat down with Joe and Noel on one of the battered seats in the cabin.

We waited and waited for something to happen, but a seemingly interminable discussion was going on in the cockpit. The humans in the aircraft were quite clearly in two camps—the crew and the cattlemen—and the only attention we three got during this period was a piercing look from the captain and a stern admonition. "You'll look after these cattle, won't you? They are very valuable and they're my responsibility. You'll keep a constant eye on them, I hope."

"Of course," I replied. "That's what we're here for." I spoke confidently, but I had no idea how the animals would react when this monster began to roar its way into the sky. If they started to run amuck and break their legs there wasn't much I could do but use my humane killer, and I didn't think the captain would be overjoyed at that.

The two farmers and I talked in the dimly lit cabin during the long wait. They told me of their stock troubles and I described the veterinary life in Yorkshire, then, to our relief, around 1 A.M., the aircraft's engine began to cough into life. We actually started to taxi along to the end of the runway.

This was the moment I had been waiting for, and I turned in my seat and gazed over the forty sleek backs as the aircraft began to roll. The engines bellowed, the vast frame shook and juddered as the machine hurtled down the runway, then there was the wrench of lift-off and the sensation of climbing, climbing.

And all those cattle did was sway gently from side to side, their

[272]

eyes looking at me, calm and untroubled. Some even nibbled at their hay as we rose into the night sky.

Thank heaven, flying seemed to be second nature to them, and I was relaxing happily when I noticed a commotion in the cabin. The huge undercarriage had not retracted fully and Karl, Dave and Ed were pulling with all their strength on a loop attached to it. After a few moments of concentrated effort, the wheels came up with a clunk, and the crewmen returned to their places. They did this calmly, as though it were a regular procedure. I wondered idly how many other things didn't work on this aeroplane.

I was grateful for one thing—my worries about the heat had been groundless because as we climbed, the atmosphere became steadily colder.

It had been a long day for Noel, Joe and me. We had left home early that morning and we dozed fitfully on the uncomfortable seats in the semi-darkness, glancing at our charges from time to time. After a few hours, I was jerked to wakefulness. We were coming in to land, descending quickly over the lights of an airfield. I watched the cattle again as we bumped and rattled along the runway, but they took it all with the same aplomb as before.

When we halted, I looked out at a brightly lit sign—Munchen.

"Refuelling," Karl muttered. Mr. Costain said it would be Rome, and it was Munich. The nagging little thought returned that nothing about this trip since John Crooks first drew the scenario had turned out as expected.

Anyway, we had landed safely on those awful tyres and we took off, too, without disaster, although once more Karl and Dave had to haul with all their might until the undercarriage thumped into position.

By 5 A.M., the two farmers and I were weary and desperate to stretch our cramped limbs. Finally Joe beckoned to us to follow him, and we groped our way down by the side of the animals right to the tail of the aircraft, where a deep pile of hay was lying. He stretched out and Noel and I followed suit.

Again, this was different from my friend John's bed in his cabin on the Mediterranean, but it was heaven. I closed my eyes and floated away. The captain had adjured us to do our duty carefully, but I couldn't keep my eyes open anymore. And though I was thousands of feet up somewhere in the dark skies above Yugoslavia, I might have been back in Darrowby, because the scents and the sounds were the same. The fragrance of hay, the sweet bovine smell and the soft grunting, coughing and champing of many cattle. These were familiar things and they lulled me into slumber within minutes.

Bright sunshine was streaming into the aircraft when I opened my eyes again. I looked at my watch—seven o'clock. The two farmers were still nestled motionless in the hay, and I got to my feet and looked with a touch of anxiety along the rows of cattle. I need not have worried; they were as contented as if they had been in their byres in Jersey. Some were lying in the straw; others stood chewing their cud. It was a peaceful scene.

It was not peaceful, however, in the flight cabin and cockpit. In fact, as I gazed beyond the animals to the front of the aircraft, I could see evidence of intense activity. The crew members were leaping around, staring at the starboard window and operating controls which I couldn't see.

I pushed my way past the metal standings to the cabin and had a look for myself.

The starboard inner engine had been switched off, and its four propellor blades hung motionless as oil gushed from its interior, spiralling into the flawless blue of the sky, flowing in black tendrils over the wing and spattering against the window. Nobody bothered to say good morning to me. There was no panic but there was definitely consternation.

As I looked, I saw that there was something more alarming than an oil leak. Flames were licking around the engine cowling, and a long tongue of fire crept back towards the wing. I scarcely had time to digest the meaning of all this when the flames disappeared, apparently extinguished by the crew's efforts.

There was a general relaxation in the cockpit, and some wan smiles were exchanged.

I heard a whisper in my ear. "Some bloody aeroplane, this, Jim boy." Joe had joined me at the window and was looking with disbelief at the still, scarred engine. Behind him, Noel was wide-eyed but silent.

On our three engines we flew on through the cloudless sky, and below, a turquoise sea sparkled. Soon we began to lose height, and I looked down on a great city with domes and minarets abounding. This was indeed some bloody aeroplane, but it had got us to Istanbul.

Chapter
30

Mr. Garrett's words about parents needing nerves of steel have come back to me many times over the years. One notable occasion was the annual recital given by Miss Livingstone's piano class.

Miss Livingstone was a soft-voiced, charming lady in her fifties who started many of the local children in piano lessons, and once a year she held a concert in the Methodist Hall for her pupils to show their paces. They ranged from six-year-olds to teenagers, and the room was packed with their proud parents. Jimmy was nine at the time and had been practising without much enthusiasm for the big day.

Everybody knows everybody else in a small town like Darrowby, and as the place filled up and the chairs scraped into position, there was much nodding and smiling as people recognised each other. I found myself on the outside chair of the centre aisle, with Helen on my right, and just across the few feet of space I saw Jeff Ward, old Willie Richardson's cowman, sitting very upright, hands on knees.

He was dressed in his Sunday best, and the dark serge was stretched tightly across his muscular frame. His red, strong-boned face shone with intensive scrubbing, and his normally wayward thatch of hair was plastered down with brilliantine.

"Hello, Jeff," I said. "One of your youngsters performing today?"

He turned and grinned. "Now then, Mr. Herriot. Aye, it's our Margaret. She's been comin' on right well at t'piano, and I just hope she does herself justice this afternoon."

"Of course she will, Jeff. Miss Livingstone is an excellent teacher. She'll do fine."

He nodded and turned to the front as the concert commenced. The first few performers who mounted the platform were very small boys in shorts and socks or tiny girls in frilly dresses, and their feet dangled far above the pedals as they sat at the keyboard.

Miss Livingstone hovered nearby to prompt them, but their little mistakes were greeted with indulgent smiles from the assembly, and the conclusion of each piece was greeted with thunderous applause.

I noticed, however, that as the children grew bigger and the pieces became more difficult, a certain tension began to build up in the hall. The errors weren't so funny now, and when little Jenny Newcombe, the fruiterer's daughter, halted a couple of times, then bowed her head as though she were about to cry, the silence in the room was absolute and charged with anxiety. I could feel it myself. My nails were digging into my palms and my teeth were tightly clenched. When Jenny successfully restarted and I relaxed with all the others, the realisation burst upon me that we were not just a roomful of parents watching our children perform; we were a band of brothers and sisters, suffering together.

When little Margaret Ward climbed the few steps to the platform, her father stiffened perceptibly in his seat. From the corner of my eyes I could see Jeff's big, work-roughened fingers clutching tightly at his knees.

Margaret went on very nicely till she came to a rather complicated chord which jarred on the company with harsh dissonance. She knew she had got the notes wrong and tried again . . . and again . . . and again, each time jerking her head with the effort.

"No, C and E, dear," murmured Miss Livingstone, and Margaret crashed her fingers down once more, violently and wrongly.

"My God, she's not going to make it," I breathed to myself,

aware suddenly that my pulse was racing and that every muscle in my body was rigid.

I glanced round at Jeff. It was impossible for anybody with his complexion to turn pale, but his face had assumed a hideously mottled appearance and his legs were twitching convulsively. He seemed to sense that my gaze was on him, because he turned tortured eyes towards me and gave me the ghastly semblance of a smile. Just beyond him, his wife was leaning forward. Her mouth hung slightly open and her lips trembled.

As Margaret fought for the right notes, a total silence and immobility settled on the packed hall. It seemed an eternity before the little girl got it right and galloped away over the rest of the piece, and though everybody relaxed in their seats and applauded with relief as much as approval, I had the feeling that the episode had taken its toll of all of us.

I certainly didn't feel so good and watched in a half-trance as a succession of children went up and did their thing without incident. Then it was Jimmy's turn.

There was no doubt that most of the performers and parents were suffering from nerves, but this couldn't be applied to my son. He almost whistled as he trotted up the steps, and there was a hint of swagger in his walk up to the piano. This, he clearly thought, was going to be a dawdle.

In marked contrast, I went into a sort of rigor as soon as he appeared. My palms broke out in an instant sweat, and I found I was breathing only with difficulty. I told myself that this was utterly ridiculous, but it was no good. It was how I felt.

Jimmy's piece was called "The Miller's Dance," a title burned on my brain till the day I die. It was a rollicking little melody which, of course, I knew down to the last semi-quaver, and Jimmy started off in great style, throwing his hands about and tossing his head like Artur Rubinstein in full flow.

Around the middle of "The Miller's Dance," there is a pause in the quick tempo where the music goes from a brisk ta-rum-tum-tiddle-iddle-om-pom-pom to a lingering taa-rum, taa-rum, before

[278]

starting off again at top speed. It was a clever little ploy of the composer and gave a touch of variety to the whole thing.

Jimmy dashed up to this point with flailing arms till he slowed down at the familiar taa-rum, taa-rum, taa-rum. I waited for him to take off again, but nothing happened. He stopped and looked down fixedly at the keys for a few seconds, then he played the slow bit again and halted once more.

My heart gave a great thud. Come on, lad, you know the next part—I've heard you play it a hundred times. My voiceless plea was born of desperation, but Jimmy didn't seem troubled at all. He looked down with mild puzzlement and rubbed his chin a few times.

Miss Livingstone's gentle voice came over the quivering silence. "Perhaps you'd better start at the beginning again, Jimmy."

"Okay." My son's tone was perky as he plunged confidently into the melody again, and I closed my eyes as he approached the fateful bars. Ta-rum-tum-tiddle-iddle-om-pom-pom, taa-rum, taa-rum, taa-rum,—then nothing. This time he pursed his lips, put his hands on his knees and bent closely over the keyboard as though the strips of ivory were trying to hide something from him. He showed no sign of panic, only a faint curiosity.

In the almost palpable hush of that room, I was sure that the hammering of my heart must be audible. I could feel Helen's leg trembling against mine. I knew we couldn't take much more of this.

Miss Livingstone's voice was soft as a zephyr or I think I would have screamed. "Jimmy, dear, shall we try it once more from the beginning?"

"Yes, yes, right." Away he went again like a hurricane, all fire and fury. It was unbelievable that there could ever be a flaw in such virtuosity.

The whole room was in agony. By now the other parents had come to know "The Miller's Dance" almost as well as I did, and we waited together for the dread passage. Jimmy came up to it at breakneck speed. Ta-rum-tum-tiddle-iddle-om-pom-pom, then taa-rum, taa-rum, taa-rum . . . and silence.

Helen's knees were definitely knocking now, and I stole an anxious glance at her face. She was pale, but she didn't look ready to faint just yet.

As Jimmy sat motionless except for a thoughtful drumming of his fingers against the woodwork of the piano, I felt I was going to choke. I glared around me desperately, and I saw that Jeff Ward, across the aisle, was in a bad way. His face had gone all blotchy again, his jaw muscles stood out in taut ridges and a light sheen of perspiration covered his forehead.

Something had to break soon, and once more it was Miss Livingstone's voice which cut into the terrible atmosphere.

"All right, Jimmy, dear," she said. "Never mind. Perhaps you'd better go and sit down now."

My son rose from the stool and marched across the platform. He descended the steps and rejoined his fellow pupils in the first few rows.

I slumped back in my seat. Ah, well, that was it. The final indignity. The poor little lad had blown it. And though he didn't seem troubled, I was sure he must feel a sense of shame at being unable to get through his piece.

A wave of misery enveloped me, and though many of the other parents turned and directed sickly smiles of sympathy and friend-ship at Helen and me, it didn't help. I hardly heard the rest of the concert, which was a pity because as the bigger boys and girls began to perform, the musical standard rose to remarkable heights. Chopin nocturnes were followed by Mozart sonatas, and I had a dim impression of a tall lad rendering an impromptu by Schubert. It was a truly splendid show—by everybody but poor old Jimmy, the only one who hadn't managed to finish.

At the end, Miss Livingstone came to the front of the platform. "Well, thank you, ladies and gentlemen, for the kind reception you have given my pupils. I do hope you have enjoyed it as much as we have."

There was more clapping, and as the chairs started to push back, I rose to my feet, feeling slightly sick.

"Shall we go then, Helen?" I said, and my wife nodded back at me, her face a doleful mask.

But Miss Livingstone wasn't finished yet. "Just one thing more, ladies and gentlemen." She raised a hand. "There is a young man here who, I know, can do much better. I wouldn't be happy going home now without giving him another opportunity. Jimmy." She beckoned towards the second row. "Jimmy, I wonder . . . I wonder if you would like to have one more try."

As Helen and I exchanged horrified glances, there was an immediate response from the front. Our son's voice rang out, chirpy and confident. "Aye, aye, I'll have a go!"

I couldn't believe it. The martyrdom was surely not about to start all over again. But it was true. Everybody was sitting down, and a small, familiar figure was mounting the steps and striding to the piano.

From a great distance I heard Miss Livingstone again. "Jimmy will play 'The Miller's Dance.' " She didn't have to tell us—we all knew.

As though in the middle of a bad dream, I resumed my seat. A few seconds earlier, I had been conscious only of a great weariness, but now I was gripped by a fiercer tension than I had known all afternoon. As Jimmy poised his hands over the keys, a vibrant sense of strain lapped around the silent room.

The little lad started off as he always did, as though he hadn't a care in the world, and I began a series of long, shuddering breaths designed to carry me past the moment that was fast approaching. Because I knew he would stop again. And I knew just as surely that when he did, I would topple senseless to the floor.

I didn't dare look round at anybody. In fact, when he reached the crucial bars I closed my eyes tightly. But I could still hear the music—so very clearly. Ta-rum-tum-tiddle-iddle-om-pom-pom, taa-rum, taa-rum, taa-rum . . . There was a pause of unbearable length, then, tiddle-iddle-om-pom, tiddle-iddle-om-pom, Jimmy was blissfully on his way again.

He raced through the second half of the piece, but I kept my eyes closed as the relief flooded through me. I opened them only when he came to the finale, which I knew so well. Jimmy was making a real meal of it, head down, fingers thumping, and at the last crashing chord, he held up one hand in a flourish a foot above the keyboard before letting it fall by his side in the true manner of the concert pianist.

I doubt if the Methodist Hall has ever heard a noise like the great cheer which followed. The place erupted in a storm of clapping and shouting, and Jimmy was not the man to ignore such an accolade. All the other children had walked impassively from the stage at the end of their efforts, but not so my son.

To my astonishment, he strode from the stool to the front of the platform, placed one arm across his abdomen and the other behind his back, extended one foot and bowed to one side of the audience with the grace of an eighteenth-century courtier. He then reversed arms and pushed out the other foot before repeating his bow to the other side of the hall.

The cheering changed to a great roar of laughter which continued as he descended the steps, smiling demurely. Everybody was still giggling as we made our way out. In the doorway we bumped into Miss Mullion, who ran the little school our son attended. She was dabbing her eyes.

"Oh, dear," she said breathlessly. "You can always depend on Jimmy to provide the light relief."

I drove back to Skeldale House very slowly. I was still in a weak condition, and I felt it dangerous to exceed twenty-five miles an hour. The colour had returned to Helen's face, but there were lines of exhaustion round her mouth and eyes as she stared ahead through the windscreen.

Jimmy, in the back, was lying full-length along the seat, kicking his legs in the air and whistling some of the tunes that had been played that afternoon.

"Mum! Dad!" he exclaimed in the staccato manner so typical of him. "I like music."

I glanced at him in the driving mirror. "That's good, son, that's good. So do we."

Suddenly he rolled off the back seat and thrust his head between us. "Do you know why I like music so much?"

I shook my head.

"Because it's"—he groped rapturously for the phrase—"because it's so soothing."

Chapter
31

When Walt Barnett asked me to see his cat, I was surprised. He had employed other veterinary surgeons ever since Siegfried had mortally offended him by charging him ten pounds for castrating a horse, and that had been a long time ago. I was surprised, too, that a man like him should concern himself with the ailments of a cat.

A lot of people said Walt Barnett was the richest man in Darrowby—rolling in brass which he made from his many and diverse enterprises. He was mainly a scrap merchant, but he had a haulage business, too, and he was a dealer in second-hand cars, furniture, anything, in fact, that came his way. I knew he kept some livestock and horses around his big house outside the town, but there was money in these things, and money was the ruling passion of his life. There was no profit in cat keeping.

Another thing that puzzled me as I drove to his office was that owning a pet indicated some warmth of character, a vein of sentiment, however small. It just didn't fit into his nature.

I picked my way through the litter of the scrap yard to the wooden shed in the corner from which the empire was run. Walt Barnett was sitting behind a cheap desk and he was exactly as I remembered him, the massive body stretching the seams of the shiny, navy-blue suit, the cigarette dangling from his lips, even the brown trilby hat perched on the back of his head. Unchanged, too, was the beefy red face with its arrogant expression and hostile eyes.

"Over there," he said, glowering at me and poking a finger at a black and white cat sitting among the papers on the desk.

It was a typical greeting. I hadn't expected him to say, "Good morning," or anything like that, and he never smiled. I reached across the desk and tickled the animal's cheek, rewarded by a rich purring and an arching of the back against my hand. He was a big tom, long-haired and attractively marked, with a white breast and white paws, and though I have always had a predilection for tabbies, I took an immediate liking to this cat. He exuded friendliness.

"Nice cat," I said. "What's the trouble?"

"It's 'is leg. There's summat wrong with that 'un there. Must've cut 'isself."

I felt among the fluffy hair, and the little creature flinched as I reached a point halfway up the limb. I took out my scissors and clipped a clear area. I could see a transverse wound, quite deep, and discharging a thin, serous fluid. "Yes . . . this could be a cut. But there's something unusual about it. I can't see how he's done it. Does he go out in the yard much?"

The big man nodded. "Aye, wanders around a bit."

"Ah, well, he may have caught it on some sharp object. I'll give him a penicillin injection and leave you a tube of ointment to squeeze into the wound night and morning."

Some cats object strongly to hypodermics, and since their armoury includes claws as well as teeth, they can be difficult, but this one never moved. In fact, the purring increased in volume as I inserted the needle.

"He really is good-natured," I said. "What do you call him?"

"Fred." Walt Barnett looked at me expressionlessly. There didn't appear to be anything particularly apposite about the name, but the man's face discouraged further comment.

I produced the ointment from my bag and placed it on the desk. "Right, let me know if he doesn't improve."

[285]

I received no reply, neither acknowledgment nor goodbye, and I took my leave feeling the same prickle of resentment as when I had first encountered his boorishness.

But as I walked across the yard, I forgot my annoyance in my preoccupation with the case. There was something very peculiar about that wound. It didn't look like an accidental laceration. It was neat and deep, as though somebody had drawn a razor blade across the flesh. I listened as I had listened so often before to that little inner voice—the voice that said things were not as they seemed.

A touch on my arm brought me out of my musings. One of the men who had been working among the scrap was looking at me conspiratorially. "You've been in to see t'big boss?"

"Yes."

"Funny thing, t'awd bugger botherin' about a cat, eh?"

"I suppose so. How long has he had it?"

"Oh, about two years now. It was a stray. Ran into 'is office one day, and, knowin' him, I thought he'd 'ave booted it straight out, but 'e didn't. Adopted it, instead. Ah can't reckon it up. It sits there all day on 'is desk."

"He must like it," I said.

"Him? He doesn't like anythin' or anybody. He's a . . ."

A bellow from the office doorway cut him short.

"Hey, you! Get on with your bloody work!" Walt Barnett, huge and menacing, brandished a fist, and the man, after one terrified glance, scuttled away.

As I got into my car, the thought stayed with me that this was how Walt Barnett lived—surrounded by fear and hate. His ruthlessness was a byword in the town, and though no doubt it had made him rich, I didn't envy him.

I heard his voice on the phone two days later. "Get out 'ere sharpish and see that cat."

"Isn't the wound any better?"

"Naw, it's wuss, so don't be long."

Fred was in his usual place on the desk, and he purred as I went

[286]

up and stroked him, but the leg was certainly more painful. It was disappointing, but what really baffled me was that the wound was bigger instead of smaller. It was still the same narrow slit in the skin, but it had undoubtedly lengthened. It was as though it was trying to creep its way round the leg.

I had brought some extra instruments with me, and I passed a metal probe gently into the depths of the cut. I could feel something down there, something which caught the end of the probe and sprang away. I followed with long forceps and gripped the unknown object before it could escape. When I brought it to the surface and saw the narrow brown strand, all became suddenly clear.

"He's got an elastic band round his leg," I said. I snipped the thing through, withdrew it and dropped it on the desk. "There it is. He'll be all right now."

Walt Barnett jerked himself upright in his chair. "Elastic band! Why the 'ell didn't you find it fust time?"

He had me there. Why the hell hadn't I? In those days my eyesight was perfect, but on that first visit all I had seen was a little break in the skin.

"I'm sorry, Mr. Barnett," I said. "The elastic was embedded in the flesh, out of sight." It was true, but I didn't feel proud.

He puffed rapidly at the ever-present cigarette. "And 'ow did it get there?"

"Somebody put it on his leg, without a doubt."

"Put it on . . . wot for?"

"Oh, people do that to cats. I've heard of cases like this but never actually seen one. There are some cruel folk around."

"One o' them fellers in the yard, ah'll wager."

"Not necessarily. Fred goes out in the street, doesn't he?"

"Oh, aye, often."

"Well, it could have been anybody."

There was a long silence as the big man sat scowling, his eyes half-closed. I wondered if he was going over the list of his enemies. That would take some time.

"Anyway," I said. "The leg will heal very quickly now. That's the main thing."

Walt Barnett reached across the desk and slowly rubbed the cat's side with a sausagelike forefinger. I had seen him do this several times during my previous visit. It was an odd, unsmiling gesture, but probably the nearest he could get to a caress.

On my way back to the surgery I slumped low in the car seat, hardly daring to think of what would have happened if I hadn't found that elastic. Arrest of circulation, gangrene, loss of the foot or even death. I broke into a sweat at the thought.

Walt Barnett was on the phone three weeks later, and I felt a twinge of apprehension at the sound of the familiar voice. Maybe I wasn't out of the wood yet.

"Is his leg still troubling him?" I asked.

"Naw, that's 'ealed up. There's summat matter with 'is head."

"His head?"

"Aye, keeps cockin' it from side to side. Come and see 'im."

This sounded to me like canker, and, in fact, when I saw the cat sitting on the desk twisting his head around uneasily, I was sure that was it, but the ears were clean and painless.

This amiable cat seemed to like being examined, and the purring rose to a crescendo as I made a close inspection of his teeth, mouth, eyes and nostrils. Nothing. Yet something up there was causing a lot of discomfort.

I began to work my way through the black hair, and suddenly the purring was interrupted by a sharp "miaow" as my fingers came upon a painful spot on his neck.

"Something here," I murmured. I took out my scissors and began to clip. And as the hair fell away and the skin showed through, a wave of disbelief swept through me. I was looking down at a neat little transverse slit, the identical twin of the one I had seen before.

My God, surely not on the neck. I went into the wound with probe and forceps, and within seconds I had brought the familiar brown band to the surface. A quick snip and I pulled it clear.

[288]

"More elastic," I said dully.

"Round 'is neck!"

"Afraid so. Somebody really meant business this time."

He drew his enormous forefinger along the furry flank, and the cat rubbed delightedly against him. "Who's doin' this?"

I shrugged. "No way of telling. The police are always on the lookout for cruelty, but they would have to catch a person actually in the act."

I knew he was wondering when the next attempt would come, and so was I, but there were no more elastic bands for Fred. The neck healed rapidly, and I didn't see the cat for nearly a year till one morning Helen met me as I was coming in from my round.

"Mr. Barnett's just been on the phone, Jim. Would you please go at once? He thinks his cat has been poisoned."

Another attack on this nice little animal, and after all this time. It didn't make sense, and my mind was a jumble as I hurried into Walt Barnett's office.

I found a vastly different Fred this time. The cat was not in his old place on the desk but was crouched on the floor among a litter of newspapers. He did not look up, but as I went over to him, he retched and vomited a yellow fluid onto the paper. More vomit lay around among pools of diarrhea which had the same yellowish hue.

Walt Barnett, overflowing the chair behind the desk, spoke past the dangling cigarette. "He's poisoned, isn't 'e? Somebody's given 'im summat."

"It's possible. . . . " I watched the cat move slowly to a saucer of milk and sit over it in the same crouching attitude. He did not drink but sat looking down with a curious immobility. There was a sad familiarity in the little animal's appearance. This could be something worse even than poison.

"Well, it is, isn't it?" the big man went on. "Somebody's tried to kill 'im again."

"I'm not sure." As I took the cat's temperature, there was none of the purring or outgoing friendliness I had known before. He was sunk in a profound lethargy.

The temperature was 105°F. I palpated the abdomen, feeling the doughy consistency of the bowels, the lack of muscular tone.

"Well, if it's not that, what is it?"

"It's feline enteritis. I'm nearly certain."

He looked at me blankly.

"Some people call it cat distemper," I said. "There's an outbreak in Darrowby just now. I've seen several cases lately, and Fred's symptoms are typical."

The big man heaved his bulk from behind the desk, went over to the cat and rubbed his forefinger along the unheeding back. "Well, if it's that, can you cure 'im?"

"I'll do my best, Mr. Barnett, but the mortality rate is very high."

"You mean, most of 'em die?"

"I'm afraid so."

"How can that be? I thought you fellers had all them wonderful new medicines now."

"Yes, but this is a virus, and viruses are resistant to antibiotics."

"Awright, then." Wheezing, he drew himself upright and returned to his chair. "What are you goin' to do?"

"I'm going to start right now," I said. I injected electrolytic fluid to combat the dehydration. I gave antibiotics against the secondary bacteria and finished with a sedative to control the vomiting. But I knew that everything I had done was merely supportive. I had never had much luck with feline enteritis.

I visited Fred each morning, and the very sight of him made me unhappy. He was either hunched over the saucer or he was curled up on the desk in a little basket. He had no interest in the world around him.

He never moved when I gave him his injections. It was like pushing a needle into a lifeless animal, and on the fourth morning I could see that he was sinking rapidly.

"I'll call in tomorrow," I said, and Walt Barnett nodded without speaking. He had shown no emotion throughout the cat's illness.

Next day, when I entered the office, I found the usual scene —the huge figure in his chair, brown trilby on the back of his head and cigarette hanging from his lips, the cat in the basket on the desk.

Fred was very still and as I approached, I saw with a dull feeling of inevitability that he was not breathing. I put my stethoscope over his heart for a few moments, then looked up.

"I'm afraid he's dead, Mr. Barnett."

The big man did not change expression. He reached slowly across and rubbed his forefinger against the dark fur in that familiar gesture. Then he put his elbows on the desk and covered his face with his hands.

I did not know what to say; I watched helplessly as his shoulders began to shake and tears welled between the thick fingers. He stayed like that for some time, then he spoke.

"He was my friend," he said.

I still could find no words, and the silence was heavy in the room until he suddenly pulled his hands from his face.

He glared at me defiantly. "Aye, ah know what you're thinkin'. This is that big, tough bugger, Walt Barnett, cryin' his eyes out over a cat. What a joke! I reckon you'll have a bloody good laugh later on."

Evidently he was sure that what he considered a display of weakness would lower my opinion of him, and yet he was so wrong. I have liked him better ever since.

Chapter
32

August 9, 1963

There was a general chattering and lightening of spirits when we landed safely and taxied to a halt. With everybody else, I climbed out and looked around. We were standing on a wide, concreted airfield. Nearby there was a hangar; away on the other side a long stretch of coarse grass ran down to the sea, and over everything the beautiful hot sunshine washed in a comforting flood. The airport buildings were about a quarter of a mile away and far beyond in the shimmering heat haze I could make out the high buildings of the city. It was just eight o'clock. We would unload the cattle, and then there would be most of the day to explore Istanbul. I felt a tinge of excitement at the prospect.

The two farmers were soon ready for action, jackets off, sleeves rolled up. Noel grinned at me as he flexed his muscles after the long night of inactivity. "Where are the wagons?" he asked.

It was a good question. Where indeed were they? They should have been awaiting our arrival, but I scanned the airfield in vain. Karl went over to the buildings to make enquiries but returned looking despondent.

"Nobody knows," he said. "We wait."

So we waited as the sun beat on the concrete and the sweat trickled inside our shirts. It was over an hour later when the wagons rolled up.

Just then, the captain's tall form hovered over me. "Mr. Herriot." The grave eyes looked down, and he ran a finger over his beard. Again I felt the impact of a masterful personality. "Mr. Herriot, there are a few things I must do. I have to see about getting that engine repaired and there is the hotel accommodation to arrange. I am leaving now and I rely on you to supervise things here."

"Okay," I replied. "Don't worry. I'll see that the animals are all right."

He nodded slowly. "Good, good." Then he swept the two farmers with his unsmiling gaze. "And that goes for you chaps, too. I don't want any of you to leave this spot until the last cow has been taken away. You do understand me?"

We mumbled our assent. I don't suppose many people would have tried to argue with Captain Birch. Anyway, the mention of the hotel had lit a cheerful spark in me as I remembered John Crooks's description of his five-star opulence. I am not attracted by continual luxury, but I do like a little bit now and again. Especially now. I was hot and sweaty and very hungry. The sandwiches at Gatwick were only a hazy memory, and the thought of a bath and a good meal was idyllic. I wanted the unloading to be as quick as possible.

The farmers seemed to have the same idea because they already had the first batch of heifers on the hoist. Little Karl pulled a lever, there was a long, high-pitched whine, but nothing happened. He operated the lever again with the same result.

"The hoist, she is jammed," he said and began to fiddle about with switches and other parts of the mechanism. Finally he dealt the shining metal a vicious kick. He shrugged his shoulders and looked at us. "Is no good. I have to get electrician."

He ambled off to the airport buildings, and the three of us were left looking at each other in some dismay. It was getting hotter by the minute.

It was half-past ten before he returned with a man in white overalls who appeared determined to take the hoist to pieces. He muttered and exclaimed in Turkish all the time, and I just hoped he knew his business because he was taking an age to find the cause of the trouble. Finally, after an hour and a half, the hoist answered to the pull on the lever and began to move. But we had lost a lot of time.

Meanwhile, it was reassuring to see a party of mechanics working on the damaged engine. I hoped even more fervently that they knew their stuff.

As Noel and Joe leaped into action and commenced the unloading, a party of Turkish vets arrived to inspect the animals. They were a most impressive group—handsome, olive-skinned men in smart light-weight suits, much more prosperous-looking than the average British vet. Only one of them spoke English, but he did so almost without accent.

"Beautiful creatures, Mr. Herriot," he murmured as the first cattle were ushered up the ramp into the wagons. The other vets, too, clucked their appreciation, and I felt personally proud that Britain could still lead the world in this field. So many countries had to turn to our green pastures to find livestock to improve their own strains.

The head man explained that they were all government vets from the Turkish Ministry of Agriculture, and their job was to examine the animals for health and to ensure that all the ear numbers were correct. We both laughed heartily at this because it seemed that in Turkey an ear number is as world-shakingly important and sacrosanct as in England.

The unloading was a painfully slow business. The electrician hadn't done a perfect job because the hoist kept stopping in mid-air for tense periods while Karl tugged at the lever and swore, but it always restarted and the work went on.

Fortunately, the animals' wagons were shaded by the hangar because the sun was truly fierce. Also, they had water and some hay, so they were comfortable.

The same could not be said of the farmers and myself. I was dirty, sweaty, unshaven and starving, and I was only popping up and down from aircraft to ground, supervising things. How Joe and Noel felt, wrestling with the cattle, I could not imagine. And all the time Istanbul lay tantalisingly out of reach.

As the hours wore on and the sun blazed, there was no sign of the captain, but the two young Americans, Ed and Dave, wandered over frequently to inspect the repairs on the engine. Occasionally they stopped and chatted to me about their life and job, and I found them most likable men. They didn't seem to have a care in the world. They slouched around smilingly in their baggy suits, hands deep in their pockets. Those pockets, I was to find later, were filled with the currency of a dozen nations. Pesetas rubbed shoulders with drachmas, guilders, lira, dimes, kroner, shillings. They roamed the world in their old aircraft, free as birds, taking each day and new country as it came, and, though hardly more than boys, they must have seen almost everything. They have remained in my mind as true soldiers of fortune.

It was around four o'clock when the last heifer entered its wagon and the Turkish vets were completing their examination. Noel came up to me. His shirt was a wet rag clinging to his chest, and he wiped his streaming face with his forearm. "I tell you, Jim," he said. "Moi stomach thinks moi throat's cut."

"Mine too, Noel," I replied. "I'm ravenous. I've gone nearly round the clock since the sandwiches at Gatwick."

"Oi could murder a pint, too," Joe put in. "Can't remember when oi've had such a bloody thirst on."

It seemed that our troubles weren't over yet. The vets were taking their time over the inspection, but at any rate there did not seem to be any complaints. They were clearly satisfied with what they saw.

Unfortunately, this did not last. From our place under the Globemaster's wing where we were sheltering from the sun, we saw a sudden stillness fall on the group of men. They were looking in a cow's ear and consulting a sheaf of papers again and again and even from a distance I sensed the tension. There followed a consultation, and then a lot of waving of arms.

[295]

Finally the head vet shouted across, "Mr. Herriot, come here, please!"

With the farmers I walked over to the wagon.

"Mr. Herriot," the man went on, "we have found a wrong number." His dark complexion had paled, and his lips trembled. The expressions on the faces of the other men in the group were uniformly distraught.

I groaned inwardly. The unthinkable had happened.

One of the vets, upright and set-faced, waved me towards the offending cow with a dramatic gesture of his arm. I climbed into the wagon and looked in the ear. It was number fifteen. With the same theatrical flourish, the vet handed me the sheaf of papers. They contained the descriptions, ages and numbers of the animals, and, sure enough, no number fifteen.

I smiled weakly. I wasn't quite sure whether this was my responsibility or not. I had checked off all the numbers on our own sheet when we loaded at Gatwick, and I had thought they all tallied. Had I made some awful boob? It made it worse being so far from home.

I turned to Joe. "You brought the list from Jersey, didn't you?"

"Oi did," Joe replied with an edge of belligerence in his voice. "And it's correct. It's in moi bag."

"Slip over and get it, will you, Joe?" I said. "We'll see if we can sort this out."

The farmer strolled unhurriedly to the Globemaster, climbed inside and duly returned with the sheet.

Breathlessly I scanned the list. "There it is!" I said triumphantly. "Pedigree number, then number fifteen!" Relief flowed through me. We were saved.

The Turkish vet took Joe's list and retired for a further consultation. For a long time there was an incomprehensible chattering and much brandishing of arms, then apparently there was a unanimous decision. All the men nodded firmly, and some of them folded their arms. The head man stepped forward, taut-faced.

"Mr. Herriot, we have concluded that there is only one thing to do. You will understand that we have to follow our own list. There is no guarantee that this is the animal which we purchased originally, so with regret I have to tell you that you must take her back."

"Take her back!" This was a bombshell. "But that's impossible!" I cried. "This cow doesn't just come from England, she is from the Island of Jersey. I can't see any way of doing what you say."

"I am sorry," he said, "but nothing can change our decision. We cannot accept a wrong animal. How you do it is your concern, but you must take her back."

"But . . . but . . . "I quavered. "How do you know it's a wrong animal? The whole thing is probably a simple clerical error at your office."

He drew himself up to his full height. He was a well-fleshed six-footer, and he looked most impressive as he stared at me and held up his hand. "Mr. Herriot, I repeat, what I have said is irrevocable."

"I . . . I . . . well, you see . . . " I was beginning to gabble when I felt Joe's hand on my arm. He eased me gently to one side and stepped up in front of the head vet. He put his hands on his hips and pushed his craggy, sweat-streaked face close to the man's moustache. His steady eyes held the imperious stare of the Turk for several seconds before he spoke.

"Oi ain't takin' 'er baack, mate," he said in his slow drawl. "That's *moi* job, and oi ain't takin' 'er baack." The voice was soft, the words unhurried, but they held a wonderful note of finality, and the effect was dramatic. The big man's facade collapsed with startling suddenness. His whole face seemed to crumble, and he looked at Joe with an almost pathetic appeal. His mouth opened and I thought he was going to say something, but instead he turned slowly and rejoined his friends.

There was a murmured consultation, punctuated by shrugging

of shoulders and sorrowful glances in the farmer's direction, then the head man gave the signal for the wagons to move away. The battle was over.

"Bless you, Joe," I said. "I thought we'd had it that time."

We obeyed the captain's instructions and hung around till the cows had left the airfield. It pleased me to think they were heading for a good life. They were all going to top-class pedigree farms; in fact, they were animal VIP's.

I was also pleased when my Turkish colleagues came up and bade us goodbye in the most cordial manner. I had an uncomfortable feeling that the incident might have spoiled their day, but they were all smiles and appeared to have recovered magically.

I looked at my watch. Five o'clock. We had been out on that oven of an airfield for nine hours. It was actually seven o'clock Turkish time, so the precious day was fast slipping away. I felt at the stubble on my chin. The first thing was a shave and a wash.

With the farmers, I made my way over to the airport terminal, and in the men's room we stripped off, drank a lot of water and made our ablutions. I have a vivid memory of a little man who kept dabbing talc on my bare back all the time. I thought he was working for a tip, but all he wanted was one of my razor blades, which I gave him.

"That's better," Noel said as we came into the lounge. "If only we could get some grub. Oi'm famished."

I knew how he felt. My appetite now was wolfish, but surely food couldn't be far away.

This hope received a boost when we saw the towering form of Captain Birch striding towards us.

"I've been looking for you fellows," he said. "There are a few things I want to tell you. Come and sit down over here."

We arranged ourselves on padded chairs round a small table, and the sombre eyes looked us over for a few moments before he spoke.

"I don't know who is in charge of your party, but I'll address my remarks to you, Mr. Herriot."

"Right."

"Now, I'm sorry to tell you that all attempts to rectify the oil leak in the engine have failed."

"Oh."

"This means that we will have to fly the aircraft on three engines to our headquarters in Copenhagen for major repairs."

"I see."

"It also means that you chaps can't come with us."

"What!"

His expression softened. "I'm sorry to have to spring this on you, but the position is, frankly, that the aircraft is in an unsafe condition, and we are not allowed to carry passengers or any personnel but the crew."

"But . . . " I asked the obvious question. "How do we get home?"

"I've been thinking about that," the captain replied. "The obvious thing is to contact the Export Company in London by telephone—I have their number here—and I'm sure they will make arrangements for you to be flown to England."

"Well . . . thank you . . . I suppose that would be the thing to do." Another thought occurred to me. "You say the aircraft is unsafe?"

The majestic head nodded gravely. "That is so."

"In other words, you might never make Copenhagen."

"Quite. There is that possibility. Flying over the Alps under these circumstances is going to be a little tricky."

"But how about you? How about you and the crew?"

"Ah yes." He smiled, and suddenly he looked like a kind man. "It's good of you to ask, but this is our job. We have to go, don't you understand? It's our job."

I turned to the farmers. "Well, I suppose we'd better do as the captain says?"

They nodded silently. They looked shattered, and I felt the same. But I took the point about that strange aeroplane. If one engine had given up, how reliable were the other three?

"I'd better find a phone, then. Will I do it from here or from the hotel?"

The captain cleared his throat. "That's another thing I was going to mention. I haven't been able to find a hotel."

"Eh?"

"Afraid not," he said. "I've tried everywhere, but it's some kind of a public holiday here, and all the hotels are booked."

I had nothing to say to this. Everything was turning out great.

"But don't worry," he went on. "I am assured that if we go a few miles up the Bosporus, we'll find some little place which will put us up."

Some little place . . . The visions of five-starred splendour evaporated rapidly.

"Yes, of course."

The captain smiled again encouragingly. "I've got a minibus outside. We'll soon find somewhere."

Dave and Ed were already installed in the little vehicle, lounging comfortably in their silky suits.

"Hi," they said cheerfully. "Hi," said little Karl, grinning at us from the back seat. Such contretemps were no doubt part of their normal lives, and they were taking everything in their stride. I made a sudden resolve to do the same. Things were looking a bit sticky, but I was here in Istanbul and I was going to enjoy what little time I had.

I fished out my camera. I had taken some pictures of the flight and of the Globemaster during the unloading. Even if it was a fleeting thing, I would capture some memories of this city.

As the minibus shot through the streets, I snapped away like mad, and when I wasn't snapping, I was devouring the scene greedily. The knowledge that I was going to have only a short time in these surroundings made every new spectacle imprint itself on my mind.

As we sped through the teeming traffic on that gloriously sunny evening, exquisite mosques and minarets towered incongruously over modern tenements, then unexpectedly there would be a long stretch of waste ground with stubbly, scorched grass and garish billboards. Tremendous stone aqueducts, ancient and overgrown, appeared briefly in our windows and were gone before I could do more than catch them on my film. The massive ruins of the walls of old Constantinople, the crumbling fortresses on the shattered walls—I glimpsed them briefly, but even today among my photographs I can still look at the slightly blurred images beyond the smeared glass.

Among all these wonders eddied the Istanbul street scene—the vendors of coloured cordials, sweetmeats and peaches, the dark-skinned pedestrians in Kemal Ataturk's obligatory westernised clothes: the women in cotton dresses, the men in an outfit of shirt and slacks so unvarying that it looked like a uniform.

Soon we were running along the side of the Bosporus, surely one of the most beautiful and romantic waterways in the world —wide and blue, bounded by tree-lined hills where elegant houses and even palaces nestled. Families sunned themselves on chairs on the little beaches, while out on the water a great variety of craft lay at anchor. There were large modern ships, fishing smacks and some wonderful old wooden vessels.

I had fair opportunity to view the Bosporus because we kept stopping in our efforts to find accommodation. At last we were successful, and we climbed out of the minibus in front of a small building. It wasn't Claridges, nor was it a flea pit. It was an unpretentious little hotel up a side street.

The members of the staff were friendly and cheerful, but I had a strong impression that they couldn't care less whether we stayed there or not. I managed to communicate to the manager that I wanted to telephone London. Smilingly he assured me that I would have to go to the local post office for that and said there was a taxi nearby.

The taxi whirled me through the streets with the same reckless speed as our minibus driver. This is something I had noticed straightaway; all traffic seemed to proceed at about seventy miles an hour.

At the post office I explained my needs to a little fat lady, who nodded and smiled repeatedly. She knew enough English to assure me that all would be well.

She lifted a phone and made enquiries. Turning back to me, she beamed happily. "Long wait, maybe hour. You go back hotel, I send taxi."

When I got back to the hotel, all my colleagues had been installed in rooms. There seemed to be no reception desk, so I asked various members of the staff where I was to sleep. My queries were received with uncomprehending shrugs until I found the manager again. He seemed to take a certain amount of pleasure in telling me that there was no room for me, but my obvious dismay softened his heart, because he took me downstairs and showed me into a cell-like apartment in the basement where he left me. There was a single unmade bed with a rumpled pile of blankets on a chair in a corner. That was all, but I was thankful for it. The bathroom was a long, long way away.

But then all my senses were submerged by one thing—the smell of food. A rich, spicy aroma was beginning to pervade the little place, and I began to stumble towards its source. I suppose eating nothing for more than twenty-four hours is an unimportant detail to people who go on diets and visit health farms, but I have always believed in a regular hearty intake, and at that moment I was more ravenous than I have ever been in my life.

I found the dining room where the crew and the farmers were already at the table, and as I sat down with them, the glorious victuals began to arrive—great heaped-up plates of kebabs resting on beds of saffron rice and peppers, steaming bowls of mixed vegetables and an abundance of coarse Turkish bread. I love bread, and I bit into this stuff immediately. It was delicious, and Ed laughed as he saw my expression. "Good, isn't it?" he said. "It's got sunflower seeds in it."

Whether it had or it hadn't, it was some of the best bread I have ever tasted. But I couldn't wait to get at the serious eating, and I was poising my fork over the skewer laden with chunks of assorted meats when the taxi driver burst into the room.

"Mr. Herroot, come quick. Phone, phone!"

I could have wept. To have my food snatched from me before I had even started was too much. But this was important. I dropped my fork and hurried out. Once more I was swept at breakneck speed to the post office, where the fat lady, still all smiles, indicated the phone.

I tried a lot of, "Hello, hello," before I heard anything, and then it was a faint voice in the crackling distance. "Meester Harrioot, Meester Harrioot." I replied with a, "Yes, yes, Herriot speaking," but that was as far as I got. I don't want to bore anybody with a detailed account of my session with that phone. Sufficient to say that it lasted about three-quarters of an hour and was made up of long silences, hopeful clicks and crackles and every few minutes that tiny voice, "Meester Harrioot." My desperate outbursts were totally wasted.

Only once was there a shaft of light in the darkness, when a very English female voice said loudly as though from the same room, "Oh, God, I can't hear a thing!" That was evidently London, and I set up an almost tearful yammering in reply, but the silence came down again, and though I waited hopefully the voice never came back.

As I looked out at the gathering dusk in the street, the realisation grew on me that I was never going to get through.

I thanked the fat lady and left.

At the hotel I didn't know how much to pay the taxi driver, so I held out a handful of notes. A huge grin split his face as he selected a few, but before he could get them into his pocket a little man, apparently one of the staff, dashed down the steps and grabbed the money from him. He reduced the amount by about half which he handed back to me, then he shook his fist in the man's face and showered him with eloquent abuse before getting out of the car.

The driver's big grin never slipped, and he bade me good night with a courteous wave of the hand before leaving.

I thanked my benefactor, but as I passed into the hotel, my spirits were touching zero. I was stranded in Istanbul with no prospect of ever returning to hearth and home, my relaxing trip to the Orient had so far turned out to be a fairly steady-going fiasco, I was hungrier than I had ever been in my life and I had missed my supper.

On top of that, I wasn't looking forward to telling my two nice farmers that I had failed them. Not my fault, of course, but it had been left to me to organise something, and I was coming back empty-handed.

Joe and Noel were waiting for me in the dining room. I was touched that they were more concerned about my food than their immediate future.

Noel leaped to his feet. "We asked them to keep it warm for you, Jim," he cried and ran from the room.

Within minutes he was back with a tray with the entire meal, including the gorgeous bread.

They watched in silence as I devoured everything down to the last crumb, then they looked at me expectantly.

"I'm sorry, chaps," I said. "I had no joy there." I gave them details of my forty-five minutes in the post office.

When I had finished my story, they looked pretty glum. Joe stared down at his knees. "What the 'ell are we goin' to do, Jim?"

A few minutes ago I would have been compelled to say I had no idea, but maybe the food had stimulated my brain because suddenly everything became clear.

"I didn't bring much with me from home," I said. "But I did bring a cheque book. I'll go to the B.E.A. desk at the airport tomorrow and get three tickets to London. The Export Company will reimburse me later. It's obvious, isn't it? There was no need for all that phoning tonight."

The mood of our little company cheered magically, and we

were doing a bit of mutual backslapping when I saw the captain passing the doorway.

I ran out and told him about our plan.

"Yes," he said seriously. "That sounds like a good scheme." He paused and looked at his watch. "The only alternative would be to go to the British Consul, but it's after nine now—I don't suppose they'd be able to arrange anything at this time of night, and we're taking off at ten o'clock tomorrow morning. No, I think yours is the best idea."

When he had gone, we were gripped by a frothy elation.

"We got nothing to worry about, Jim, boy," said Joe. "So we might as well enjoy ourselves. Oi could still murder that pint, so let's go out on the town and enjoy ourselves.

Joe's pint was our immediate goal, and there is no doubt we were three country cousins because searching for a pub in a Muslim city is a fruitless venture, but, full of enthusiasm, we piled into a taxi.

The night life of Istanbul seemed to be just getting into its stride. The streets were crowded, and the traffic had, if possible, speeded up after dark. Our taxi catapulted between other hurtling vehicles, the driver exchanging a running fire of shouted insults with his colleagues. I was relieved when he deposited us in what we hoped was the city centre.

Immediately, in the warm darkness, I was reminded that we were in the Orient. I could see nothing now of the romantic buildings and ruins, only the lighted shop windows, but the air was filled with mysterious scents, and over everything hung the heavy aroma of Turkish tobacco.

My other overriding impression was the noise: an unbroken, strident chorus of automobile horns of every conceivable pitch, punctuated by the screeching of brakes and the roar of engines.

In our search for a pub, we gazed into the windows of many interesting shops. Some were selling rugs and other souvenirs of the area, and I was intrigued by the large number of bakers who

[305]

were turning out very sweet-looking cakes and confections and doing a brisk trade.

We stuck to one side of the street because it seemed like suicide to head into that boiling torrent of vehicles. There were, in fact, pedestrian crossings, but I noticed only one unfortunate little man trying to negotiate one. He was about halfway across when, to my horror, a car struck him and sent him flying high in a tangle of arms and legs. In Britain that motorist would have been heavily fined and received a dressing-down from the magistrates, but as I watched, a large, helmeted policeman loomed over the injured victim, who stood trembling in his inevitable shirt and slacks and rubbing his backside. The policeman shook his truncheon over the little man's head and bawled out a flood of vituperation, which was unintelligible to me except for one word which sounded very like "stupido" and vividly reflected his attitude in the matter. He never even looked at the driver of the car.

"Hey, look, Jim." Joe nudged me. "There's a lot of fellers goin' in there. How about it?"

Joe's quest for a pint was becoming an obsession, so I acquiesced and followed him through a doorway and up a long staircase. We came out on an open balcony which was really the flat roof of the shop beneath and, to the farmer's disgust, scores of shirt-sleeved men were sitting at tables, smoking and drinking coffee out of tiny cups.

We would have retreated then but a waiter was upon us, so we sat down and ordered the coffee. It was very thick and very sweet, and both Joe and Noel screwed up their faces, but I rather liked it. I also enjoyed just sitting there above the roar and smell of the city, taking in the atmosphere of the place. In my hurried visit to Istanbul this is one of my persisting memories and, rightly or wrongly, it appealed to me as a typical scene.

After the coffee we resumed our tour of the streets, with Joe becoming more depressed by the minute. Then he suddenly gave tongue. "Look in there, lads! That's a bit more like it!" He pointed through a window at a big, brightly lit room where a large number of men and women were sitting around, drinking from tall glasses. There wasn't a coffee cup in sight.

He did not hesitate but opened a swing door and bustled inside, with Noel and I following. We sat down at a vacant table, and Joe beckoned to a waiter.

"Drink! Drink!" he said, and when the man's face registered polite incomprehension, he made the unmistakable motion of raising a glass to his lips.

The waiter smiled immediately and brought a tray bearing three tumblers of bright-red liquid. I offered him money, but he shook his head, laughed and walked away.

"What the 'ell's this?" Joe grunted. He tried a sip and pulled a worse face than over the coffee. "It's bloody lemonade!" he spluttered.

I tried it myself. It wasn't lemonade. It was a bland, syrupy concoction, sickly sweet and obviously non-alcoholic. It was too sugary for me, but Noel, who, I suspected, wasn't much of a drinker, seemed to enjoy it.

"All right, this," he said, imbibing contentedly.

Joe looked at him in disgust. Like me, he could not tackle the stuff, whatever it was, and with an air of defeat he flopped back in his chair.

Within a few minutes, the same waiter came back with a dish of cakes and pastries and laid them before us. Again he refused any money and walked away, laughing and shaking his head.

Biting into one of the sticky cakes, I found it had the same characteristic as the coffee and the coloured drinks. It seemed to me that a sweet tooth would be a prerequisite for anybody living in Istanbul.

However, it was an interesting scene. The big room was crowded with beautifully dressed people—I noticed that most of the women wore white evening gowns—and they nibbled the cakes and drank from glasses like ours not only bright-red liquid but equally brilliant blue, green and yellow.

When I saw that several children were present, something

[307]

began to stir in the back of my mind. The children were playing among the tables, and some of the adults were moving from group to group as though they knew everybody.

"Hey, wait a minute," I said. "Do you know what I think?"

Joe gave me a sideways glance. "What?"

"I think this is a private party and we've gate-crashed it."

Both the farmers sat up suddenly as I went on. "Those kids down there and all the people seem to be friends. And remember that waiter who thought it was funny to be offered money?"

Just at that moment a handsome young couple appeared at the far end of the room, the man in a dark suit, the girl in a glittering, spangled bridal gown.

"My God!" I said. "It's a wedding reception!"

And it was, indeed. The newlyweds moved around among their guests, and when they reached us, I half expected to be thrown out, but, on the contrary, they seemed to regard our presence as a gracious courtesy visit. They bowed and shook hands with us and made us welcome with smiles and gestures. Before they moved on, the bride gave each of us a long silver thread. She did this with some ceremony, and I deduced that it was an honoured local custom, the thread having possibly been taken from her gown. In any case, I took it in this spirit, and I carried that thread in my wallet for many years thereafter until it gradually disintegrated.

We were still recovering from our surprise when two men in traditional Turkish dress appeared on a stage at the other end of the room. They were obviously entertainers and comedians to boot, because very soon the room was echoing with laughter. It was strange for the three of us sitting there to hear the totally unintelligible cross talk, followed by the roars of mirth, the little children jumping up and down and clapping their hands in delight.

They were versatile chaps, those two. When they had finished being funny, one of them produced a one-string fiddle and began to play, while the other sang in that peculiar wail which is associated only with Eastern countries.

I had no way of telling whether it was a love song, a happy song or a sad song, but as I listened to that strange ululation going on and on, I felt very far from home.

It was about then that my eyelids began to droop. I remembered that I had had only two hours' sleep the night before and that rather a lot had happened in a short time. I was very tired, and when I turned to look at my farmer friends, I saw that Joe was nodding and Noel was slumbering peacefully, his chin on his chest.

I stood up and suggested that we ought to leave. They didn't need much persuading.

Back in the hotel, I descended to my basement room and made up the bed from the pile of blankets on the chair. I would have fallen asleep immediately but from somewhere quite close at hand came the same wailing which I had heard at the wedding reception. At first I thought I was dreaming but then I realised there was a party going on in one of the hotel rooms. It was a noisy party, too, with screams of laughter, outbursts of music, thumping of dancing feet. It went on and on, and it must have been the middle of the night before the din subsided and I fell into an exhausted sleep.

Chapter
33

I stood, head bowed, leaning on my great guillotine which stood chest high. It occurred to me that my pose was exactly that of the executioner resting against his axe as I had seen in old pictures of the beheading of Sir Walter Raleigh and other unfortunates.

However, I wasn't wearing a hood; I was standing in a deep-strawed fold yard, not on a scaffold; and I was waiting for a bullock to be dehorned, not for a hapless victim to lay his head upon the block.

In the fifties, bovine horns quite suddenly went out of fashion. To veterinary surgeons and most farmers their passing was unlamented. Horns were at best a nuisance, at worst extremely dangerous. They worked their way under vets' coats and pulled off the buttons and tore out pockets. They could whip round and bash the hand, arm or even the head of a man injecting the neck and, of course, in the case of a really wild cow or bull, they could be instruments of death.

Horns were a menace, too, to other bovines. Some cows and bullocks were natural bullies, and one animal could impose a reign of terror on its more timid neighbours, driving them away viciously from food troughs in open yards and inflicting savage wounds on any that resisted. The farmers in Yorkshire used to call these injuries "hipes," and they ranged from massive haematomata over the ribs to deep lacerations of the udder. It was strange how a boss cow would always go for the udder and the results were often ruinous. Since the passing of horns you never heard the word "hipe" now.

There were farmers, notably pedigree breeders, who attached great importance to well-set horns and pointed out that a neat, "cocky" little horn looked well in the show ring and that their highly bred animals would be disfigured, but their voices were lost in the tumult for abolition.

One down-to-earth dairyman said to me at the time, "You don't get much milk out of a bloody horn," and that seemed to be the general attitude.

From my own point of view, the only thing I missed was that convenient handle to get hold of a cow. For many years I had smacked one hand down on the horn, then pushed the fingers of the other hand into the nose, but after the dehorning revolution there was nothing to grasp. Most cows were expert at tucking their noses down on the ground or round the other side where you couldn't get at them, but that was a small thing.

So, by and large, the disappearance of these dangerous and largely useless appendages was a great blessing but, oh dear, there was one tremendous snag. The horns didn't just go away by themselves. They had to be removed by the vets, and that removal wrote a gory and ham-fisted chapter in veterinary history that still hangs like a dark cloud in my memory.

I suppose Siegfried and I reacted just like the other members of our profession. As the situation arose and we looked out on a countryside apparently dominated by a waving forest of horns, we wondered how we would start. Was it to be general or local anaesthesia? Did we saw them off or chop them off?

In the beginning the chop school appeared to hold sway, because there were many advertisements in the *Veterinary Record* for villainous-looking guillotines. We ordered one of these, but we both experienced a sense of shock when we unpacked it. As I said, it was nearly as tall as a small man and its weight was frightening.

[311]

Siegfried, groaning slightly, hefted the thing by its long wooden handles till the huge, sliding blades were at eye level, then he lowered it quickly and leaned against the wall.

He took a long, shuddering breath. "Hell, you need to be a trained athlete just to lift that bloody thing!" He paused in thought. "There's no doubt we'll need something like that for the big beasts, but surely we can find something else for the little stirks." He raised a finger. "James, I believe I know the very thing."

"You do?"

"Yes. I saw some nice light hedge-clippers in Albert Kenning's window yesterday. I bet they'd do the job. Tell you what—let's go round and try them."

When Siegfried had one of his ideas, he didn't mess about. Within seconds we were hurrying, almost at a trot, through the market place to the ironmonger's.

I followed close on Siegfried's heels as he burst into the shop.

"Albert!" he shouted. "Those hedge-clippers! Let's have a look at them!"

They certainly looked all right—round, gleaming, wooden shafts terminating in small, curved blades which crossed each other scissors-wise.

"Mm, yes," I said. "Do you think they'll be strong enough to cut through a little horn?"

"Only one way to find out." Siegfried brandished his new weapon. "Fetch me one of those canes, Albert!"

The little man turned towards a bundle of thick bamboos that were on sale for tying up flowers and shrubs. "These?"

"That's right. Look sharp."

Albert selected a cane and brought it over.

"Now, hold it out towards me," Siegfried said. "No, no, no, upright. That's fine, fine."

Starting at the top, he began to clip off inch lengths of the bamboo at lightning speed. The fragments flew in all directions, and Albert had to duck several times as they flew past his ears. But he was more anxious about his hand as the blades worked rapidly downwards. Apprehensively, he kept lowering his grasp until Siegfried made his final slash an inch above his thumb. Holding the tiny stump at arm's length, he looked wide-eyed at my colleague.

But Siegfried wasn't finished yet. He continued to chop away at the air, obviously enjoying his work. "Let's have another one, Albert!"

Wordlessly, the little man produced a second cane, half closed his eyes and held it as far away from his body as possible.

My colleague recommenced his onslaught with such vigour that the woody cylinders whizzed round the shop like machine-gun bullets. A customer entering by the door backed away and took cover behind a stack of milking buckets.

Albert had gone pale by the time Siegfried demolished the second cane, finishing once more just above the little man's thumb.

"Grand little machine, this, James." Siegfried hesitated, tried a few more practice snips, then turned to the ironmonger. "Just one more, Albert."

"Really, Mr. Farnon, don't ye think . . . "

"C'mon, c'mon, we've got work to do. Don't hang about!"

This time the little man's jaw dropped, and the cane wobbled uncontrollably in his grasp. Siegfried, obviously determined to make the most of this last test, put everything into his effort, and his movements were almost too rapid to follow. There was a brief fusillade of clippings, then Albert was left breathless, clutching his small remnant.

"Splendid!" Siegfried cried happily. "We'll take it. How much?"

"Twelve an' six," gasped the ironmonger.

"And the canes?"

"Oh, er . . . another shillin'."

My colleague delved in his pocket and pulled out a handful of notes, coins and small veterinary instruments. "There's a quid among that lot, Albert. Help yourself."

Tremblingly, the little man extracted the pound from Siegfried's palm, then crunched over the carpet of bamboo clippings to get change.

Siegfried crammed the money into his pocket without looking and tucked his new purchase under his arm. "Goodbye, Albert, and thank you," he said, and we left.

As I passed the shop window at a brisk pace, I could see the ironmonger following us wonderingly with his eyes.

The hedge-clippers did indeed perform nobly for us with the smaller bovines, but there were so many other complications. For a long time we used general anaesthesia by means of the chloroform muzzle, and when the animal collapsed unconscious, we whipped the horns off quickly. But we found to our dismay that the haemorrhage was massive and terrifying. Red jets fountained several feet in the air, spraying everything and everybody for yards around. In those days you could always tell when a vet had been out dehorning because his collar and face were spattered with blood.

An ingenious tourniquet was devised by laying a length of binder twine longways to the inside of each horn, then encircling both horns with another piece of twine. By knotting the first two tightly over the encircling one, the arteries were effectively compressed and haemorrhage was nil.

But then, often the chopping blades severed the twine and we were in trouble again.

As time passed, two advances emerged. The first was that by removing the horn by sawing and taking about half an inch of skin with it, there was virtually no bleeding. The second was that local anaesthesia was infinitely easier and more effective. It was quite simple to inject a few c.c.'s of local under the temporal ridge and into the branch of the fifth cranial nerve, which supplies the horn.

There was nothing to it, and it gave a perfect nerve block. The animal couldn't feel a thing.

I have seen cows chewing their cud while I sawed away, and this merciful improvement in our method signalled the end of all the old things. The horrible choppers and guillotines and tourniquets disappeared almost overnight.

Nowadays, of course, a horn is rarely seen anywhere because calves are painlessly disbudded early in life, using this same nerve block.

But, as I say, the whole period of adult dehorning left a scar on my memory, and it was during the guillotine period that Andrew Bruce came to visit me.

For several years after the war, people were still renewing contact with each other. The war brought the normal lives of so many to a full stop that the ensuing period was a time of taking stock, of looking around and wondering what had happened to one's friends.

Andrew and I had not met since our schooldays, and I hardly recognised the dark-suited, bowler-hatted figure on the doorstep. It turned out that he was doing very nicely in a bank in Glasgow and was on a business trip down south when he saw the sign to Darrowby and decided to pay me a call. A lot of my schoolmates seemed to have gone into banking, and since I have always had to use my fingers for counting, I regarded these men with a certain amount of awe.

"I don't know how you do it, Andy," I said after lunch. "I wouldn't last a couple of days in your job."

He shrugged and smiled. "Oh, it's meat and drink to me. I loved maths at school, if you remember."

"Oh yes." I shivered. "That's right. You used to get prizes for dreadful things like trigonometry."

We chatted for a few minutes over our coffee, then I stood up. "I'm afraid I've got to go," I said. "I have to be on a farm by two-fifteen."

"Okay, Jim. . . . " He hesitated for a moment. "Do you think I could come with you? I've never seen a country vet at work, and I could easily drive to Birmingham this evening."

I smiled. So many people wanted to accompany me on my rounds. There seemed to be some fascination in the veterinary life. "Of course you can, Andy. But I don't think you'll find it very entertaining. All I have is an afternoon's dehorning."

"Really? Sounds interesting. I'd love to come, if you don't mind."

I found a spare pair of Wellingtons for him, and we got into the car. As we drove away I noticed him looking around him: at the boxes of bottles and instruments on the back seat, at my clothes which contrasted so sharply with his own natty outfit. At that time I had discarded the breeches and leggings that were almost a vet's uniform when I qualified and now wore brown corduroy trousers with a sort of canvas jacket made for me by a German prisoner and which I had cherished for years.

The corduroys were frayed and stiffened with mud and muck, and the jacket, too, despite the protective clothing I always wore, bore ample evidence of my trade.

I could see Andy's nostrils wrinkling as he took in the rich bouquet of manure, dog hairs and assorted chemicals that was the normal atmosphere in my car, but after a few minutes he appeared to forget everything as he gazed out of the window.

It was a golden afternoon in October, and beyond the stone walls, the fell-sides, ablaze with their mantle of dead bracken, rose serenely into a deep, unbroken blue. We passed under a long canopy of tinted leaves thrown over us by the roadside trees, then followed a stretch of white-pebbled river before turning along a narrow track that led up the hillside.

Andrew was silent as we climbed into the stark, airy solitude that is the soul of the Dales, but as the track levelled out on the summit, he put a hand on my arm.

"Just stop a minute, Jim, will you?" he said.

I pulled up and wound down the window. For a few moments

he looked out over the miles of heathery moorland and the rounded summits of the great hills slumbering in the sunshine, then he spoke quietly as though to himself.

"So this is where you work?"

"Yes, this is it, Andy."

He took a long breath, then another, as if greedy for more.

"You know," he said. "I've heard a lot about air like wine, but this is the first time I've realised what it means."

I nodded. I always felt I could never get enough of that air, sharp and cool and tinged only with the grass scent that lingers in the high country.

"Well, you're a lucky beggar, Jim," Andrew said with a touch of weariness. "You spend your life driving around in country like this, and I'm stuck in a damned office."

"I thought you liked your job."

He ran a hand through his hair. "Oh yes, I suppose playing around with figures is what I'm best at but, oh hell, I have to do it all inside. In fact," he said, becoming a little worked up, "when I start to think about it, I live and have my being in a bloody centrally heated box with no windows and electric light blasting down all day, and I share what passes for air with a whole crowd of other people." He slumped back in his seat. "Makes me wish I hadn't come out with you."

"I'm sorry, Andy."

He laughed ruefully. "Oh, I didn't really mean that, but, honestly, this is idyllic."

At the end of the moor the land dipped into a lush valley where the herd of Mr. Dunning grazed and grew fat on the abundant grass around the farm buildings. The Dunnings were not dairymen, as was usual in the Dales, but raised beef cattle. And they did so on a large scale, with more than two hundred animals under their care.

I had been there for the last few afternoons, dehorning, and I was glad that this was my last visit because the bullocks on which I had been operating were massive three-year-old shorthorns, and

I had had a rough time. Nowadays, with the housewife's prefer-
ence for smaller, leaner joints, most beef cattle are slaughtered at
around eighteen months, and the kind of huge creatures I had to
face at Mr. Dunning's are rarely seen any more.

As we drove into the farmyard, there were about twenty of
them milling around in a collecting pen.

"We'll run 'em into the fold yard one at a time as usual," Mr.
Dunning cried as he trotted towards me. He was a small, excitable
man, bursting with energy, and his voice seldom fell below a
piercing shout.

His sons, large young men with the classical Dales names of
Thomas, James and William followed more slowly.

I introduced Andy, and he gazed with interest at the enormous
boots, the work-worn clothes and the tangle of hair pushing from
under the caps. The farmers, in turn, seemed similarly intrigued
with my friend's pinstripes, gleaming white collar and tasteful tie.

Once the action commenced, Mr. Dunning launched into full
cry, poking at the beasts' rumps with his stick and emitting shrill
yelps of, "Haow, haow, cush-cush, get on there!"

Finally one of the bullocks trotted into the fold yard, and the
brothers guided it into a loose box. I handed the chloroform
muzzle in to them and leaned on my mighty guillotine, thinking
how much easier life had become over the past few days.

At the start of this session I had applied every tourniquet
myself, then buckled on the muzzle before putting the halter over
the top. But farmers are very adaptable people and the brothers
soon devised a better way.

On the second day, Thomas, the eldest, made a quiet suggestion. "We could put on them bands and the muzzle ourselves,
Mr. Herriot, while you wait outside t'box."

I leaped happily at the idea. That rough binder twine had to
be pulled very tight and my soft palms had been rubbed sore, but
the horny fingers of the Dunning boys would be impervious to
such a detail. Also, I would not be thrown around in the tying
process.

As I leaned there, feeling again like an executioner, I bethought myself of my friend.

"Andy," I said, "I think it would be a good idea if you climbed up there." I pointed to one of a long row of square wooden feeding troughs known as "tumblers" which stretched down the middle of the straw-covered yard. Above them, running the full length of the tumblers, a hayrack dangled on chains.

He smiled indulgently. "Oh, I'll be all right here." He rested a shoulder against a post opposite the box and lit a cigarette. "I don't want to miss anything and, anyway, it sounds very interesting in there."

It did indeed sound interesting behind the wooden doors of the box. It always did. Gruff outbursts of "Ow!" "Stand still, ya bugger!" "Gerroff me foot!" blended with tremendous crashes as the big beast hurled itself against the timbers.

At length came the inevitable volley of yells. *"Right! 'e's comin' out!"*

I tensed myself as the doors were thrown wide and the great animal, festooned with binder twine and wearing the muzzle like a wartime gas mask, catapulted outwards, with two of the brothers hanging grimly to the halter.

As the bullock felt the straw around its knees, it paused for a moment in its headlong rush and looked around till the eyes, glaring above the rim of the muzzle, focussed on the elegant form of my friend leaning against the post. Then it put its head down and charged.

Andy, confronted by fourteen hundredweights of hairy beef hurtling towards him, did not linger. He vaulted onto the tumbler, grabbed the slats of the hayrack and swung himself to safety as the horns sent the tumbler crashing away beneath his feet. I recalled that he had been very good on the wall bars in the school gymnasium, and it was apparent that he had lost none of his agility.

Cradled in the fragrant clover, he looked down at me as the rack swung gently to and fro on its chains.

"I'd stay up there if I were you," I said.

Andy nodded. I could see he didn't need much persuading. He had lost a little colour, and his eyebrows were arched high on his forehead.

All three of the Dunning brothers were needed to bring the bullock to a halt, and they stood there, leaning back on the rope and breathing heavily as they waited for me to make the next move.

This was the tricky bit. I leaned the guillotine against a tumbler and slowly approached the beast. Opening the front of the muzzle, I trickled chloroform onto the sponge. At this moment I never knew what was going to happen. Some animals turned sleepy almost immediately, while others, on inhaling the strange vapour, seemed to resent my presence and took a sudden dive at me. And in the deep straw it was difficult to get out of the way.

I was relieved to see that this was one of the former type. His charge at Andy and his subsequent struggles had made him breathless, and as he gulped deeply at the anaesthetic, his eyes glazed and he began to sway. He took a few stumbling steps, toppled onto his side and slipped into unconsciousness.

Now I had to move fast. I struggled through the straw, grabbed the guillotine and dropped the cutting jaws over a horn. I seized the shafts and began to pull. With small animals a single swift clip did the job, but the horns of these big bullocks were extraordinarily wide at the base, and I had to haul away with all my strength for several panting seconds till the knives crunched together. I repeated the process with the other horn, and it was just as tough to remove.

"Right," I gasped. "Get the muzzle off him." I was sweating and I had done only one beast, with about nineteen to go.

The brothers leaped into action, unbuckling the muzzle and running to usher another bullock from the pen where their father was already screaming and flailing around him with his stick.

With the loss of a little more perspiration I did the second and third, but the fourth defeated me. The horns were so vast that I had to open the shafts wider and wider until they were almost in a straight line. I groaned and strained, but it was obvious I would never be able to close them. Thomas, who had the build of a heavyweight wrestler, came up behind me.

"Move in a bit closer, Mr. Herriot," he said.

I grasped the shafts halfway up their length, while Thomas seized the extreme ends in his great hands. Even with our united effort nothing happened for a few seconds, then the horn came off with a crack. But unfortunately I was the man in the middle, and as the shafts came together, they thudded with piti-less force against my ribs. It was the same with the other horn. Thomas had to help again, and my ribs took another hammer-ing.

As the brothers trotted off for the next beast, I sank down on the straw and moaned softly, massaging my aching sides.

"Are you all right, Jim?" The voice came from above, and I looked up into Andy's anxious face. I had been vaguely aware of him all the time, rocking on his chains as he twisted around in the rack to see as much as possible.

I gave him a rueful smile. "Oh yes, Andy, I'm okay. Just a bit bruised."

"I don't doubt it. I wouldn't like that big bloke squeezing me in those choppers." My friend's head, protruding from the hay, was all I could see of him, but his eyes looked startled.

They looked still more startled when the next beast, at the first sniff of chloroform, launched himself forward and knocked me flat on my back. In fact, it was clear that little Mr. Dunning was upsetting the cattle with his constant shrieking and the poking with his stick.

Thomas thought so, too. "For God's sake, Dad," he said in his slow way. "Put that bloody stick away and shurrup." He spoke without anger because he was fond of his father, as indeed I was, because he was a nice little man at heart.

[321]

Mr. Dunning quieted down, but he could contain himself for only a brief spell. Very soon he was yelling again.

About halfway through, the dreaded accident happened. I chopped through the tourniquet on one of the horns.

"Quick! More twine!" I shouted, groping my way through the red fountains spurting high from the sleeping animal. I had to retie the tourniquet with the warm fluid spraying my face. There was no escape. As I pulled the last knot tight, I turned to Mr. Dunning.

"Could I have a bucket of warm water, some soap and a towel, please?" My eyes were almost closed, the lashes gummed with the fast-clotting blood.

The little man hurried to the house and was back soon with a steaming bucket into which I eagerly plunged my hands. A second later I was hopping round the fold yard, yelping with pain and shaking my scalded fingers.

"That bloody water's boiling hot!" I cried.

The brothers regarded me stolidly, but little Mr. Dunning was highly amused.

"Hee-hee, hee-hee, hee-hee." His high-pitched giggles went on and on. He hadn't seen anything so funny for a long time.

While he was recovering, William fetched some cold water and diluted the original sufficiently for me to give my hands and face a rough wash.

I went on with my work almost automatically and with increasing weariness. The driving of each bullock into the box, the bangings and oaths from behind the door, the final yell of *"He's comin' out!,"* then the straining and the chopping, and all the time in the back of my mind the question every veterinary surgeon of that era must have asked himself—"Why in heaven's name did I have to study five years at college just to do this?"

But at last I saw with relief that there was only one more to do. I had just about had enough. Thomas had done his nutcracker act on my ribs a few times more, and every muscle in my body seemed to be protesting. I watched thankfully as Mr. Dunning started to drive the beast into the yard.

This animal, however, was reacting differently to the little man's bawling and stick work. I remembered that the brothers had described the beast as being "bully-headed," and indeed there was a vibrant masculinity about this shape and expression which suggested that the bloodless castrators might not have done their work completely.

The shaggy head, instead of turning away from Mr. Dunning's importunities, kept pushing towards him. The little farmer poked at the nose with his stick but still it came on, and at that point Mr. Dunning evidently decided he would be better out of the way.

He walked off through the straw and the bullock walked after him. He broke into a trot and the bullock did the same. The trot became a stiff-legged gallop and the bullock followed suit.

At no time did the beast show any sign of charging the farmer, but Mr. Dunning didn't seem reassured. He kept on running and his face registered increasing alarm. His progress was impeded by the deep straw and it must have been like running in knee-high water but for all that, he cut out a very fair pace for a sixty-year-old.

Nobody interfered. Maybe we were all a bit irritated by his antics during the afternoon, but we stood back and laughed. I laughed so much that it hurt my bruised ribs as Mr. Dunning shot down one side of the row of tumblers, then up the other, with the big animal's nose a foot behind his neck. It might have been a Roman arena, with the mocking spectators and Andy away above rocking perilously in his cradle as he watched the chase.

It had to end sometime. After the second circuit Mr. Dunning's cap flew off, he made a few lunging strides, then fell flat on his face in the straw. The animal did nothing more than run over the top of him, then allowed itself to be caught as though the whole thing had been a tease.

[323]

The little farmer jumped to his feet, hurt only in his dignity, and glared at us as he retrieved his cap.

With the help of the brothers I dehorned the beast, and the afternoon's work was over.

We helped Andy down from the rack, and it took quite a while to brush the hayseeds from his smart serge. He watched impassively as I cleaned and dried my guillotine and with an effort heaved it into the boot. Then, with my own little brush, I washed the thick plastering of muck from my Wellingtons before putting on my shoes.

We got into the car and drove away into the darkening countryside. Andy lit another cigarette, and I could see him glancing at my sweaty, blood-flecked face and at my hand feeling the tenderness of my ribs under my jacket.

"Jim," he said at length. "It's funny how you can jump to conclusions. Maybe my own job isn't so bad after all."

Chapter
34

In the semi-darkness of the surgery passage I thought it was a hideous growth dangling from the side of the dog's face, but as he came closer, I saw that it was only a condensed milk can. Not that condensed milk cans are commonly found sprouting from dogs' cheeks, but I was relieved because I knew I was dealing with Brandy again.

I hoisted him onto the table. "Brandy, you've been at the dustbin again."

The big golden Labrador gave me an apologetic grin and did his best to lick my face. He couldn't manage it since his tongue was jammed inside the can, but he made up for it by a furious wagging of tail and rear end.

"Oh, Mr. Herriot, I am sorry to trouble you again." Mrs. Westby, his attractive young mistress, smiled ruefully. "He just won't keep out of that dustbin. Sometimes the children and I can get the cans off ourselves, but this one is stuck fast. His tongue is trapped under the lid."

"Yes . . . yes . . ." I eased my finger along the jagged edge of the metal. "It's a bit tricky, isn't it? We don't want to cut his mouth."

As I reached for a pair of forceps, I thought of the many other occasions when I had done something like this for Brandy. He was one of my patients, a huge, lolloping, slightly goofy animal, but this dustbin raiding was becoming an obsession.

He liked to fish out a can and lick out the tasty remnants, but his licking was carried out with such dedication that he burrowed deeper and deeper until he got stuck. Again and again he had been freed by his family or myself from fruit salad cans, corned beef cans, baked bean cans, soup cans. There didn't seem to be any kind of can he didn't like.

I gripped the edge of the lid with my forceps and gently bent it back along its length till I was able to lift it away from the tongue. An instant later, that tongue was slobbering all over my cheek as Brandy expressed his delight and thanks.

"Get back, you daft dog!" I said, laughing, as I held the panting face away from me.

"Yes, come down, Brandy." Mrs. Westby hauled him from the table and spoke sharply. "It's all very fine, making a fuss now, but you're becoming a nuisance with this business. It will have to stop."

The scolding had no effect on the lashing tail, and I saw that his mistress was smiling. You just couldn't help liking Brandy because he was a great ball of affection and tolerance, without an ounce of malice in him.

I had seen the Westby children—there were three girls and a boy—carrying him around by the legs, upside down, or pushing him in a pram, sometimes dressed in baby clothes. Those youngsters played all sorts of games with him, but he suffered them all with good humour. In fact, I am sure he enjoyed them.

Brandy had other idiosyncracies, apart from his fondness for dustbins.

I was attending the Westby cat at their home one afternoon when I noticed the dog acting strangely. Mrs. Westby was sitting, knitting in an armchair, while the oldest girl squatted on the hearth rug with me and held the cat's head.

It was when I was searching my pockets for my thermometer that I noticed Brandy slinking into the room. He wore a furtive air as he moved across the carpet and sat down with studied carelessness in front of his mistress. After a few moments he began to work his rear end gradually up the front of the chair towards her knees. Absently, she took a hand away from her knitting and pushed him down, but he immediately restarted his backward ascent. It was an extraordinary mode of progression, his hips moving in a very slow rumba rhythm as he elevated them inch by inch, and all the time the golden face was blank and innocent, as though nothing at all were happening.

Fascinated, I stopped hunting for my thermometer and watched. Mrs. Westby was absorbed in an intricate part of her knitting and didn't seem to notice that Brandy's bottom was now firmly parked on her shapely knees which were clad in blue jeans. The dog paused, as though acknowledging that phase one had been successfully completed, then ever so gently he began to consolidate his position, pushing his way up the front of the chair with his fore limbs, till at one time he was almost standing on his head.

It was at that moment, just when one final backward heave would have seen the great dog ensconced on her lap, that Mrs. Westby finished the tricky bit of knitting and looked up.

"Oh, really, Brandy, you are silly!" She put a hand on his rump and sent him slithering disconsolately to the carpet, where he lay and looked at her with liquid eyes.

"What was all that about?" I asked.

Mrs. Westby laughed. "Oh, it's these old blue jeans. When Brandy first came here as a tiny puppy, I spent hours nursing him on my knee, and I used to wear the jeans a lot then. Ever since, even though he's a grown dog, the very sight of the things makes him try to get on my knee."

"But he doesn't just jump up?"

"Oh, no," she said. "He's tried it and got ticked off. He knows perfectly well I can't have a huge Labrador in my lap."

"So now it's the stealthy approach, eh?"

She giggled. "That's right. When I'm preoccupied—knitting

or reading—sometimes he manages to get nearly all the way up, and if he's been playing in the mud he makes an awful mess, and I have to go and change. That's when he really does receive a scolding."

A patient like Brandy added colour to my daily round. When I was walking my own dog, I often saw him playing in the fields by the river. One particularly hot day many of the dogs were taking to the water, either to chase sticks or just to cool off, but whereas they glided in and swam off sedately, Brandy's approach was quite unique.

I watched as he ran up to the river bank, expecting him to pause before entering. But, instead, he launched himself outwards, legs splayed in a sort of swallow dive, and hung for a moment in the air rather like a flying fox before splashing thunderously into the depths. To me it was the action of a completely happy extrovert.

On the following day in those same fields I witnessed something even more extraordinary. There is a little children's playground in one corner—a few swings, a roundabout and a slide. Brandy was disporting himself on the slide.

For this activity he had assumed an uncharacteristic gravity of expression and stood calmly in the queue of children. When his turn came he mounted the steps, slid down the metal slope, all dignity and importance, then took a staid walk round to rejoin the queue.

The little boys and girls who were his companions seemed to take him for granted, but I found it difficult to tear myself away. I could have watched him all day.

I often smiled to myself when I thought of Brandy's antics, but I didn't smile when Mrs. Westby brought him into the surgery a few months later. His bounding ebullience had disappeared, and he dragged himself along the passage to the consulting room.

As I lifted him onto the table, I noticed that he had lost a lot of weight.

"Now, what is the trouble, Mrs. Westby?" I asked.

She looked at me worriedly. "He's been off-colour for a few

days now, listless and coughing and not eating very well, but this morning he seems quite ill, and you can see he's starting to pant."

"Yes . . . yes . . ." As I inserted the thermometer I watched the rapid rise and fall of the rib cage and noted the gaping mouth and anxious eyes. "He does look very sorry for himself."

Temperature was 104. I took out my stethoscope and auscultated his lungs. I have heard of an old Scottish doctor describing a seriously ill patient's chest as sounding like a "kist o' whustles," and that just about described Brandy's. Rales, wheezes, squeaks and bubblings—they were all there against a background of laboured respiration.

I put the stethoscope back in my pocket. "He's got pneumonia."

"Oh, dear." Mrs. Westby reached out and touched the heaving chest. "That's bad, isn't it?"

"Yes, I'm afraid so."

"But . . ." She gave me an appealing glance. "I understand it isn't so fatal since the new drugs came out."

I hesitated. "Yes, that's quite right. In humans and most animals the sulpha drugs, and now penicillin, have changed the picture completely, but dogs are still very difficult to cure."

Thirty years later it is still the same. Even with all the armoury of antibiotics that followed penicillin—streptomycin, the tetracyclines, the synthetics and the new non-antibiotic drugs and steroids—I still hate to see pneumonia in a dog.

"But you don't think it's hopeless?" Mrs. Westby asked.

"No, no, not at all. I'm just warning you that so many dogs don't respond to treatment when they should. But Brandy is young and strong. He must stand a fair chance. I wonder what started this off, anyway."

"Oh, I think I know, Mr. Herriot. He had a swim in the river about a week ago. I try to keep him out of the water in this cold weather, but if he sees a stick floating, he just takes a dive into the middle. You've seen him—it's one of the funny little things he does."

[329]

"Yes, I know. And was he shivery afterwards?"

"He was. I walked him straight home, but it was such a freezing-cold day. I could feel him trembling as I dried him down."

I nodded. "That would be the cause, all right. Anyway, let's start his treatment. I'm going to give him this injection of penicillin, and I'll call at your house tomorrow to repeat it. He's not well enough to come to the surgery."

"Very well, Mr. Herriot. And is there anything else?"

"Yes, there is. I want you to make him what we call a pneumonia jacket. Cut two holes in an old blanket for his forelegs and stitch him into it along his back. You can use an old sweater if you like, but he must have his chest warmly covered. Only let him out in the garden for necessities."

I called and repeated the injection on the following day. There wasn't much change. I injected him for four more days, and the realisation came to me sadly that Brandy was like so many of the others—he wasn't responding. The temperature did drop a little, but he ate hardly anything and grew gradually thinner. I put him on sulphapyridine tablets, but they didn't seem to make any difference.

As the days passed and he continued to cough and pant and to sink deeper into a blank-eyed lethargy, I was forced more and more to a conclusion which, a few weeks ago, would have seemed impossible—that this happy, bounding animal was going to die.

But Brandy didn't die. He survived. You couldn't put it any higher than that. His temperature came down and his appetite improved, and he climbed onto a plateau of twilight existence where he seemed content to stay.

"He isn't Brandy anymore," Mrs. Westby said one morning a few weeks later when I called in. Her eyes filled with tears as she spoke.

I shook my head. "No, I'm afraid he isn't. Are you giving him the halibut liver oil?"

"Yes, every day. But nothing seems to do him any good. Why is he like this, Mr. Herriot?"

[330]

"Well, he has recovered from a really virulent pneumonia, but it's left him with a chronic pleurisy, adhesions and probably other kinds of lung damage. It looks as though he's just stuck there." She dabbed at her eyes. "It breaks my heart to see him like this. He's only five, but he's like an old, old dog. He was so full of life, too." She sniffed and blew her nose. "When I think of how I used to scold him for getting into the dustbins and muddying up my jeans. How I wish he would do some of his funny old tricks now."

I thrust my hands deep into my pockets. "Never does anything like that now, eh?"

"No, no, just hangs about the house. Doesn't even want to go for a walk."

As I watched, Brandy rose from his place in the corner and pottered slowly over to the fire. He stood there for a moment, gaunt and dead-eyed, and he seemed to notice me for the first time because the end of his tail gave a brief twitch before he coughed, groaned and flopped down on the hearth rug.

Mrs. Westby was right. He was like a very old dog.

"Do you think he'll always be like this?" she asked.

I shrugged. "We can only hope."

But as I got into my car and drove away, I really didn't have much hope. I had seen calves with lung damage after bad pneumonias. They recovered but were called "bad doers" because they remained thin and listless for the rest of their lives. Doctors, too, had plenty of "chesty" people on their books; they were, more or less, in the same predicament.

Weeks and then months went by, and the only time I saw the Labrador was when Mrs. Westby was walking him on his lead. I always had the impression that he was reluctant to move, and his mistress had to stroll along very slowly so that he could keep up with her. The sight of him saddened me when I thought of the lolloping Brandy of old, but I told myself that at least I had saved his life. I could do no more for him now, and I made a determined effort to push him out of my mind.

In fact, I tried to forget Brandy and managed to do so fairly well until one afternoon in February. On the previous night I felt I had been through the fire. I had treated a colicky horse until 4 A.M. and was crawling into bed, comforted by the knowledge that the animal was settled down and free from pain, when I was called to a calving. I had managed to produce a large live calf from a small heifer, but the effort had drained the last of my strength, and when I got home, it was too late to return to bed.

Ploughing through the morning round, I was so tired that I felt disembodied, and at lunch Helen watched me anxiously as my head nodded over my food.

There were a few dogs in the waiting room at two o'clock, and I dealt with them mechanically, peering through half-closed eyelids.

By the time I reached my last patient, I was almost asleep on my feet. In fact, I had the feeling that I wasn't there at all.

"Next, please," I mumbled as I pushed open the waiting-room door and stood back, expecting the usual sight of a dog being led out to the passage.

But this time there was a big difference. There was a man in the doorway all right, and he had a little poodle with him, but the thing that made my eyes snap wide open was that the dog was walking upright on his hind limbs.

I knew I was half-asleep, but surely I wasn't seeing things. I stared down at the dog, but the picture hadn't changed. The little creature strutted through the doorway, chest out, head up, as erect as a soldier.

"Follow me, please," I said hoarsely and set off over the tiles to the consulting room. Halfway along, I just had to turn round to check the evidence of my eyes, and it was just the same—the poodle, still on his hind legs, marching along unconcernedly at his master's side.

The man must have seen the bewilderment in my face because he burst suddenly into a roar of laughter.

"Don't worry, Mr. Herriot," he said. "This little dog was circus-trained before I got him as a pet. I like to show off his little tricks. This one really startles people."

"You can say that again," I said breathlessly. "It nearly gave me heart failure."

The poodle wasn't ill; he just wanted his nails clipped. I smiled as I hoisted him onto the table and began to ply the clippers.

"I suppose he won't want his hind claws doing," I said. "He'll have worn them down himself." I was glad to find I had recovered sufficiently to attempt a little joke.

However, by the time I had finished, the old lassitude had taken over again, and I felt ready to fall down as I showed man and dog to the front door.

I watched the little animal trotting away down the street—in the orthodox manner this time—and it came to me suddenly that it had been a long time since I had seen a dog doing something unusual and amusing. Like the things Brandy used to do.

A wave of gentle memories flowed through me as I leaned wearily against the doorpost and closed my eyes. When I opened them, I saw Brandy coming round the corner of the street with Mrs. Westby. His nose was entirely obscured by a large, red tomato-soup can, and he strained madly at the leash and whipped his tail when he saw me.

It was certainly a hallucination this time. I was looking into the past. I really ought to go to bed immediately. But I was still rooted to the doorpost when the Labrador bounded up the steps, made an attempt, aborted by the soup can, to lick my face and contented himself with cocking a convivial leg against the bottom step.

I stared into Mrs. Westby's radiant face. "What . . . what . . . ?"

With her sparkling eyes and wide smile, she looked more attractive than ever. "Look, Mr. Herriot, look! He's better, he's better!"

In an instant I was wide awake. "And I . . . I suppose you'll want me to get that can off him?"

"Oh, yes, yes, please!"

It took all my strength to lift him onto the table. He was heavier now than before his illness. I reached for the familiar forceps and began to turn the jagged edges of the can outwards from the nose and mouth. Tomato soup must have been one of his favourites because he was really deeply embedded, and it took some time before I was able to slide the can from his face.

I fought off his slobbering attack. "He's back in the dustbins, I see."

"Yes, he is, quite regularly. I've pulled several cans off him myself. And he goes sliding with the children, too." She smiled happily.

Thoughtfully I took my stethoscope from the pocket of my white coat and listened to his lungs. They were wonderfully clear. A slight roughness here and there, but the old cacophony had gone.

I leaned on the table and looked at the great dog with a mixture of thankfulness and incredulity. He was as before, boisterous and full of the joy of living. His tongue lolled in a happy grin, and the sun glinted through the surgery window on his sleek golden coat.

"But Mr. Herriot," Mrs. Westby's eyes were wide, "how on earth has this happened? How has he got better?"

"*Vis medicatrix naturae,*" I replied in tones of deep respect.

"I beg your pardon?"

"The healing power of nature. Something no veterinary surgeon can compete with when it decides to act."

"I see. And you can never tell when this is going to happen?"

"No."

For a few seconds we were silent as we stroked the dog's head and ears and flanks.

"Oh, by the way," I said, "has he shown any renewed interest in the blue jeans?"

"Oh, my word, yes! They're in the washing machine at this very moment. Absolutely covered in mud. Isn't it marvellous!"

Chapter
35

August 10, 1963

My sleep in that Bosporus hotel seemed to last only a short time, because apparently within minutes I was roused by one of the hotel staff and looked up to see the sunshine flooding into my room from the street above.

I washed and shaved and hurried to the dining room. Noel and Joe had suffered from the noisy party and were looking heavy-eyed, but the captain and the rest of the crew had been sleeping at the back of the hotel and had heard practically nothing. This was a good thing, because they were the ones who had a tough day ahead of them.

After breakfast the minibus whisked us along the glittering Bosporus and through the city, where I had my second fleeting glimpse of its wonders. It was frustrating. I had hoped to explore the treasures of Istanbul at my leisure—the Blue Mosque, Saint Sophia and so many others, but maybe another day . . .

At the airport there was the bustle of early-morning departures with aircraft taking off and climbing into the sunny sky, but I found something ominous in the sight of our Globemaster stand-ing on its own, vast, shabby, with the scorch marks on its useless engine. Dave, Ed and Karl didn't seem to be worried as they went over to it, the little Dane whistling, the young Americans slouching, relaxed, hands as ever buried in the pockets of their white trousers.

I made straight for the B.E.A. desk, and it was a relief to see the fresh-faced Englishman in the familiar uniform.

"And what can I do for you, sir?" he asked, smiling.

I brandished my cheque book. "I want three tickets to London on the first flight, if possible."

"You want to pay by cheque?"

"Yes, please."

"I'm sorry, but we cannot accept personal cheques."

"What!"

"I'm afraid that is the rule, sir." He was still smiling.

"But . . . we're stuck here." I gave him a brief outline of our plight.

He shook his head sadly. "I do wish I could help, but I have to abide by the rules."

I kept at him for a few minutes longer, but it was no good. Then, when he wasn't looking, I tried one of the other B.E.A. officials further along, but I got the same answer.

My heart was beating fast as I returned to my friends who were waiting for me in the airport lounge. They were speaking to the captain. I was beginning to feel like an expert in the bringing of evil tidings, and I hardly knew what to say to them. In fact, they took the news surprisingly well, and if they thought I was a hopeless organiser they disguised their feelings.

We all looked at the captain.

"If I were you," he said, "I should go to the British Consul."

I turned to the farmers. "Have you ever had anything to do with consuls?"

They shook their heads dumbly.

"Neither have I. I don't know how they'd react in a situation like this. Would they be sure to fly us home?"

"Oh, yes." The captain gave me a faint, reassuring smile. "I'm pretty certain you'd have no trouble."

"Pretty certain, you say, but not absolutely?"

The big man stroked his beard. "Well, Mr. Herriot, like yourself, I have never had the need to approach them."

"When do you take off?"

"In about half an hour."

I had a nasty vision of the three of us trailing back into the city, being turned down by the Consul and coming back with hardly any money in our pockets to find the Globemaster gone.

"Look, Captain," I said. "The way I see it, your aircraft is our only link with home. If you got us to Copenhagen, would you be able to arrange a flight to London from there?"

He gave me a long, appraising stare. "Oh, of course. Copenhagen is our headquarters. But you would be very silly to take the chance."

"Well, I'm willing to take it. How about you chaps?"

The farmers both nodded immediately.

"Oi'm game," Joe said. "Oi want to get 'ome."

The captain looked down at him. "But you do realise there is a very real danger."

Joe grinned back. "Ah, you'll get us there, Caap'n. I ain't worried about that."

He was voicing my own thoughts. Captain Birch inspired confidence.

"All right, then, if you've made up your minds," the big man said. "But I'm afraid you'll have to sign a document which I must leave here in Istanbul. I'll go and draw it up now." He paused. "As I explained earlier, since the aircraft is in an unsafe condition you are, in effect, unauthorised personnel. Signing this document verifies that you are aware of this and that you relinquish all rights to compensation if the worst should happen." He swept us again with his serious gaze. "I must point out that if you lose your lives today, your dependents will receive nothing, no insurance, nothing."

I think we all gulped a bit at this, and there was a longish silence. For once it was Noel who broke it, and he echoed his friend. "You'll get us there, Caap'n."

The document was drawn up and we signed it, and with hindsight I know without any doubt that we behaved like complete idiots, because the danger was not imaginary. We could have been killed that day.

The captain's advice was right, of course. We should have gone to the British Consul. Over the years I have read frequently of football fans being flown home by the Consul after getting drunk and missing their charter planes, and when I think that we three were on legitimate business, it makes our decision all the more crazy. I, in particular, should have known better.

I suppose part of the reason was that we were not thinking straight. The three of us were tired out with lack of sleep and the series of niggling mishaps in strange surroundings. We were in the mood to clutch at straws.

In any case the thing was done now, and we walked over the hot concrete to the Globemaster. It seemed that a fair proportion of the population of Istanbul had heard about our aircraft and had turned out to spectate, because a large crowd of people watched us as we went. I had an uncomfortable feeling that they didn't expect us to get off the ground.

When we climbed into the aircraft, I saw that the interior had been swept clean and that a large door had been removed from one side of the fuselage to allow aeration after the cattle had gone.

Joe elected to sit up front in the flight cabin, while Noel and I strapped ourselves into two drop-down seats at the very back. We felt very insignificant sitting there in the tail, looking at the yawning emptiness in front of us.

We couldn't see what was happening, and it was a shock when the engines roared into life. With that big opening in the side the noise was intolerable, and we both instinctively pushed our fingers into our ears. Noel's face worked, and his mouth opened and closed soundlessly as he tried to talk to me. I knew we couldn't stand this for long, and I reached for my bag. I pulled out some cotton wool and stuffed it into the farmer's ears. I did the same for myself and there was no doubt it relieved the noise problem, but at the same time it gave me a strange, unreal feeling, as if I were in limbo.

From the jerkings and vibrations, I deduced that we were taxi-ing to the end of the runway prior to take-off. Then we stopped, and I knew we were in position.

The roar of the engines increased to a deep-throated bellow which penetrated the ear plugs and made my head spin. I looked at Noel, and he shaped his lips into, *"Taking off now?"* I nodded encouragingly. I don't know what his emotions were, but I felt utterly fatalistic about the whole thing. I am not brave but I have always felt like that about flying and though this was a very special case, my attitude was the same.

For a long time we sat there, listening to the roar and feeling the great aircraft shaking under and around us. This went on and on until I began to wonder if we had, in fact, left the ground. Noel's puzzled face and the spreading of his hands told me he was thinking the same thing. After another five minutes I decided we must be high in the air by now but I had to have a look to make sure. I unstrapped myself and crawled on hands and knees to the open side. I pushed my head out and looked down, and with a jolt of disappointment I saw the grey concrete of the runway a few feet below me.

I slithered back to my place and shook my head at Noel. What, I wondered, was going on? Could the captain not get up enough power, or was he just giving his three remaining engines a long test before making his attempt?

I think it must have been the latter, because suddenly we were under way. We couldn't see anything, but the surge forward was unmistakable. There were a tense few seconds as the vibration rose to a crescendo, then a calm that told us we were airborne. I felt the impact of the undercarriage thudding into place, and

I pictured Karl and his friends hauling it up over the last few inches. I leaned back in my seat. The first obstacle was behind us.

The feeling of relief seemed to affect Noel immediately because when I looked round he was sound asleep, slumped against the webbing strap. My natural curiosity was too much for me, and I returned to the gap in the fuselage to view the scene passing below.

I sat there, entranced, all day, the cotton-wool plugs dangling from my ears. It wasn't like flying in a modern jet where you can't see much else besides clouds. I watched an unfolding, ever-changing panorama of mountains and sea, islands, yellow beaches, arid plains, the tightly clustered houses of large cities and tiny villages. Occasionally I took pictures, leaning precariously against the strip of sacking that was the only thing between me and the dazzling blue water thousands of feet below.

In mid-afternoon I broke off to consume the contents of a white carton the captain had solemnly handed out to each of us in Istanbul. It contained a slab of unidentifiable meat, the inevitable sticky cake and, to my delight, some slices of that delicious bread and a wedge of cheese.

I also went up to the flight cabin for a few minutes to get some pictures of the stricken engine with its four propellor blades, dangling still and useless. It was a sad sight, but I was glad to see that the other three engines were buzzing away with heartening vigour.

When I returned to my post by the open side, the great rampart of the Alps was rising before us. This, I knew, was the crucial time. The Globemaster climbed higher, but when we reached the tumbled mass of peaks we still seemed to be very near to the summits. Beneath me I could see the loose boulders and scarred rock on the mountaintops quite plainly, but, like my friends, I had faith in that bearded man's ability to take us over, and he did.

It was growing dusk when we circled above Copenhagen, and

I had a glimpse of the little mermaid in the bay. Soon Joe was happy at last with a glass of real beer in his hand in the airport bar.

There isn't much more to tell. We had to wait till 2 A.M. for a flight to Heathrow, and I was sitting on a luggage barrow trying to read the Sunday *Times* at seven o'clock in the morning at King's Cross Station. I wasn't very successful, because the paper kept slipping from my fingers as my eyes closed involuntarily.

My last memory is of a friendly old gentleman in the compartment of the north-bound train trying to engage me in conversation, but to my shame I fell asleep in front of him and didn't wake up until York.

After I had slipped again into the routine of the practice, I looked back on my Istanbul trip as a memorable experience. A bit too concentrated, perhaps, and by no means the rest cure my friend John had pictured, but fascinating in its way. And, of course, I felt I had greatly exaggerated any possible danger on the flight home. From the comfort of my car as I drove round the familiar roads of the Yorkshire Dales, the whole thing had a touch of fantasy.

It all came back to me in stark truth when I heard, many months later, that, soon after the Istanbul flight, the Globemaster had plunged into the Mediterranean with the loss of all her crew. The news came to me indirectly, and I did my best to find out if it was true, but it was a long time afterwards and I had no success.

Ever since, I have thought often about those men: the captain, the two young Americans and Karl. During those few days I had come to admire them, and even now I still cling to the faint hope that that terrible news was wrong.

Chapter
36

What horrible little dogs!

It was a sentiment that rarely entered my mind because I could find something attractive in nearly all my canine patients.

I had to make an exception in the cases of Ruffles and Muffles Whithorn. Try as I might, I could find no lovable traits, only unpleasant ones—like their unvarying method of welcoming me into their home.

"Down! Down!" I yelped, as I always did. The two little animals—West Highland Whites—were standing on their hind limbs, clawing furiously at my trouser legs with their front paws, and I don't know whether I have unusually tender shins but the effect was agonising.

As I backed away on tiptoe like a ballet dancer going into reverse, the room resounded to Mr. and Mrs. Whithorn's delighted laughter. They found this unfailingly amusing.

"Aren't they little pets!" Mr. Whithorn gasped between paroxysms. "Don't they give you a lovely greeting, bless them!"

I wasn't so sure about that. Apart from excoriating my flesh through my grey flannels, the dogs were glaring up at me balefully, their mouths half-open, lips quivering, teeth chattering in a characteristic manner. It wasn't exactly a snarl, but it wasn't friendly, either.

"Come, my darlings." The man gathered the dogs into his arms and kissed them both fondly on the cheeks. He was still giggling. "You know, Mr. Herriot, isn't it priceless that they welcome you into our house so lovingly and then try to stop you from leaving?"

I didn't say anything but massaged my trousers in silence. The truth was that these animals invariably clawed me on my entry, then did their best to bite my ankles on the way out. In between, they molested me in whatever ways they could devise. The strange thing was that they were both old—Ruffles fourteen and Muffles twelve—and one might have experienced some mellowness in their characters, but it was not so.

"Well," I said, after reassuring myself that my wounds were superficial, "I understand Ruffles is lame."

"Yes." Mrs. Whithorn took the dog and placed him on the table where she had spread some newspapers. "It's his left front paw. Just started this morning. He's in agony, poor dear."

Gingerly I took hold of the foot, then whipped my hand away as the teeth snapped shut less than an inch from my fingers.

"Oh, my precious!" Mrs. Whithorn exclaimed. "It's so painful. Do be careful, Mr. Herriot, he's so nervous and I think you're hurting him."

I breathed deeply. This dog should have a tape muzzle applied right at the start, but I had previously caused shock and dismay in the Whithorns by suggesting such a thing, so I had to manage as best I could. Anyway, I wasn't a novice at the business. It would take a very smart biter to catch me.

I curled my forefinger round the leg and had another look, and I was able to see what I wanted in the fleeting instant before the next snap—a reddish swelling pouting from between the toes.

An interdigital cyst! How ridiculous that a vet should be making a house call for such a trivial ailment. But the Whithorns had always firmly refused to bring their dogs to the surgery. It frightened the darlings, they said.

I stood back from the table. "This is just a harmless cyst, but I agree that it is painful, so I'd advise you to bathe it in hot water until it bursts, and that will relieve the pain. Many dogs burst these things themselves by nibbling at them, but you can hasten the process."

I drew some antibiotic into a syringe. "Nobody knows exactly what causes an interdigital cyst. No specific causal organisms have been found, but I'll give him this shot in case of infection."

I achieved the injection by holding the little animal by the scruff of the neck; then Mrs. Whithorn lifted the other dog onto the table.

"You'd better give him a checkup while you're here," she said.

This usually happened, and I palpated the snarling bundle of white hair and went over him with stethoscope and thermometer. He had most of the afflictions that beset old dogs—arthritis, nephritis and other things, including a heart murmur difficult to hear among the bad-tempered rumblings echoing round his thorax.

My examination completed, I replenished his various medicaments and prepared to leave. This was when the exit phase of my visit started, and it was relished by Mr. and Mrs. Whithorn even more than the entry.

The ritual never changed. As their owners tittered gleefully the two little dogs stationed themselves in the doorway, effectively barring my way out. Their lips were drawn back from their teeth. They were the very picture of venom. To draw them away from their posts I feinted to the right, then made a rush for the door, but with my fingers on the handle I had to turn and fend off the hungry jaws snapping at my ankles, and as I skipped around on my heels, my previous dainty ballet steps were superseded by the coarser hoppings of a clog dance.

But I escaped. A final couple of quick pushes with my feet and I was out in the fresh air, crashing the door thankfully behind me.

I was regaining my breath when Doug Watson, the milkman, drew up in his blue van. He kept a few dairy cows on a smallholding on the edge of the town and augmented his income by operating a retail round among the citizens of Darrowby.

"Mornin', Mr. Herriot." He gestured towards the house. "You been in to see them dogs?"

"Yes."

"Proper little sods, aren't they?"

I laughed. "Not very sweet-tempered."

"By gaw, that's the truth. I've got to watch meself when I deliver t'milk. If that door happens to be open, they're straight out at me."

"I'll bet they are."

His eyes widened. "They go for me feet. Sometimes I feel a right bloody Charlie, jumpin' about like a daft thing in front of everybody."

I nodded. "I know exactly how you feel."

"You've got to keep movin' or you've 'ad it," he said. "Look 'ere." He pushed his leg out of the van and pointed to the heel of one of the Wellington boots he always wore on his rounds. I could see a neat puncture hole on either side. "One of 'em got me there, just t'other day. Went right through to me skin."

"Good heavens, which one did that?"

"Don't rightly know—what's their names, anyway?"

"Ruffles and Muffles," I replied.

"Bloody 'ell!" Doug looked at me wonderingly. His own dog was called Spot. He spent a few moments in thought, then raised a finger. "But ah'll tell tha summat, and maybe ye won't believe me. Them dogs used to be real nice little things."

"What!"

"I'm not jokin' nor jestin'. When they fust came here, they were as friendly as any dogs I've ever seen. It was afore your time, but it's true."

"Well, that's remarkable," I said. "I wonder what happened."

Doug shrugged his shoulders. "God knows, but each one of 'em turned nasty after a few months, and they've got wuss and wuss ever since."

[346]

Doug's words stayed with me until I got back to the surgery. I was puzzled. Westies, in my experience, were a particularly amiable breed. Siegfried was in the dispensary, writing directions on a bottle of colic mixture. I mentioned the situation to him.

"Yes," he said. "I've heard the same thing. I've been to the Whithorns' a couple of times, and I know why those dogs are so objectionable."

"Really? Why is it?"

"Their owners make them that way. They never correct them, and they slobber over them all the time."

"You could be right," I said. "I've always made a fuss of my own dogs, but all that kissing and cuddling is a bit sickening."

"Quite. Too much of that is bad for a dog. And another thing, those two animals are the bosses in that home. A dog likes to obey. It gives them security. Believe me, Ruffles and Muffles would be happy and good-tempered if they had been controlled right from the start."

"There's no doubt they rule the roost now."

"Absolutely," Siegfried said. "And really, they hate it. If only the Whithorns would take off the rose-tinted spectacles and treat them normally. But it's too late now, I'm afraid." He pocketed the colic mixture and left.

The months passed, I had a few more visits to the Whithorns' and went through the usual dancing routine; then, oddly, both the old dogs died within a few weeks of each other. And despite their tempestuous lives, they had peaceful ends. Ruffles was found dead in his basket one morning, and Muffles wandered down the garden for a sleep under the apple tree and never woke up.

That was merciful, anyway. They hadn't treated me very well, but I was glad they had been spared the things that upset me most in small-animal practice—the road accident, the lingering illness, the euthanasia.

It was like a chapter in my life closing, but shortly afterwards Mr. Whithorn rang me.

"Mr. Herriot," he said, "we have acquired another pair of

Westies, and I wonder if you would call and give them their distemper inoculations."

It was a delightful change to go into the room and be met by two tail-wagging puppies. They were twelve weeks old, and they looked up at me with benevolent eyes.

"They're beautiful," I said. "What have you called them?"

"Ruffles and Muffles," Mr. Whithorn replied.

"Same again, eh?"

"Yes, we wanted to keep the memory of our other darlings alive." He seized the puppies and showered kisses on them.

After the inoculations, it was a long time before I saw the little dogs again. They seemed to be singularly healthy. It must have been nearly a year later when I was called to the house to give them a checkup.

When I went into the sitting room, Ruffles and Muffles Mark Two were seated side by side on the sofa. There was an odd immobility in their attitude. As I approached they stared at me coldly, and as if responding to a signal they bared their teeth and growled softly but menacingly.

A chill ran through me. It couldn't be happening all over again. But as Mr. Whithorn lifted Ruffles onto the table and I took the auroscope from its box, I quickly realised that fate had made history repeat itself. The little animal stood there, regarding me with a bristling mistrust.

"Hold his head, will you, please?" I said. "I want to examine his ears first." I took the ear between finger and thumb and gently inserted the auroscope. I applied my eye to the instrument and was inspecting the external meatus when the dog exploded into action. I heard a vicious snarl, and as I jerked my head back, the draught of the crunching teeth fanned my face.

Mr. Whithorn leaned back and abandoned himself to mirth. "Oh, isn't he a little monkey! Ha-ha-ha, he just won't stand any nonsense." He rested his hands on the table for some time, shaking with merriment, then he wiped his eyes. "Dear, oh dear, what a character he is."

[348]

I stared at the man. The fact that he might easily have been confronted by a noseless veterinary surgeon did not seem to weigh with him. I looked, too, at his wife standing behind him. She was laughing just as merrily. What was the use of trying to instil reason into these people? They were utterly besotted. All I could do was get on with the job.

"Mr. Whithorn," I said tautly, "will you please hold him again, and this time take a tight grip with your hands on either side of his neck?"

He looked at me anxiously. "But I won't hurt the little pet?"

"No, no, of course not."

"All right." He placed his cheek against the dog's face and whispered lovingly, "Daddy promises to be gentle, my angel. Don't worry, sweetheart."

He grasped the loose skin of the neck as I directed, and I warily recommenced operations. Peering at the interior of the ear, listening to Mr. Whithorn's murmured endearments, I was tensed in readiness for another explosion. But when it came with a ferocious yap, I found I was in no danger because Ruffles had turned his attention elsewhere.

As I dropped the auroscope and jumped back, I saw that the dog had sunk his teeth into the ball of his master's thumb. And it wasn't an ordinary bite. He was hanging on, grinding deeply into the flesh.

Mr. Whithorn emitted a piercing yell of agony before shaking himself free.

"You rotten little bugger!" he screamed, dancing around the room, holding the stricken hand. He looked at the blood pouring from the two deep holes, then glared at Ruffles. *"Oh, you bloody little swine!"*

Siegfried's words came back to me as Mr. Whithorn recommenced bending and jumping like an Apache summoning rain, all the while looking in a new way at the dog. Maybe, I said silently to Siegfried, we have a start here.

Chapter
37

"Are ye all right, Mr. Herriot?"

Lionel Brough looked down at me solicitously as I crawled on hands and knees through the gap in the wire netting.

"Yes," I gasped. Lionel was very thin and he had slipped through the aperture like a snake, but I was having a little difficulty.

There were some unusual farms and smallholdings in our practice—converted railway wagons, henhouses and other artifices—but this one, I always thought, took the prize.

Lionel was one of a plentiful breed in those days, a roadman who kept livestock as a sideline and hobby. Some of them had four cows, others a few pigs, but Lionel had the lot.

He had housed his motley collection in a large hut by the side of his cottage. He appeared to have divided the hut into sections by using the first thing that came to hand. It was a labyrinth, a monumental piece of improvisation, with up-ended bed frames, sheets of plywood and corrugated iron, and stretches of wire netting separating the animals. There were no doors or passages anywhere.

I got to my feet, puffing slightly. "Where is this calf?"

"Not far to go now, Mr. Herriot." We passed his solitary cow, then little pigs nibbled at my heels as Lionel laboriously undid a series of knots tied with coarse string so that we could enter the next compartment.

Here, a couple of nanny goats regarded us impassively.

"Grand milkers, them two," the roadman grunted. "T'missus makes some smashin' cheese from 'em, and it's healthy milk, isn't it?"

"That's right, it is." At that time, when T.B. infection was still a constant threat, the milk from the comparatively immune goat was highly regarded. The far wall of their pen consisted of a mahogany dining table lying on its side, its legs projecting into the interior. I skirted it warily before climbing over. I had suffered some nasty blows from those castored knobs.

We were among the calves now, three of them, and it was easy to pick out my patient, a small black animal with a purulent discharge crusting his nostrils.

As I bent to take his temperature I had to push aside a couple of squawking hens, and a fat Muscovy duck waddled out of my way. These feathered creatures seemed to have the run of the place, jumping and fluttering from pen to pen and in and out of the building. From my position by the calf I could see an assortment of cats perched on window sills or on the tops of partitions. A sudden snarling from the end of the hut marked the beginning of a friendly fight among Lionel's three dogs. Beyond the doorway two sheep were visible, grazing contentedly in the field by the cottage.

I looked at the thermometer—103°, then I ausculated the chest with my stethoscope. "Just a touch of bronchitis, Lionel, but I'm glad you called me. He's quite rough in his lungs, and pneumonia could be just round the corner. As it is, a couple of injections will probably clear him up."

Lionel nodded in quiet satisfaction. He was a vague man, but kind, and all his animals were comfortable and well fed in their eccentric dwelling. Deep straw abounded, and the hayracks and troughs were well supplied.

[351]

I felt in my pockets. They were bulging with bottles and syringes. I had brought everything I might possibly need. On this establishment, it wasn't easy to slip back to the car as an afterthought.

After the injection I turned to the roadman. "I'll look in tomorrow morning. It's Sunday, so you won't be working, eh?"

"That's right. Thank ye, Mr. Herriot." He turned and began to lead me back through the obstacle course.

On the following day I found the calf greatly improved. "Temperature normal, Lionel," I said. "And he's on his feet now. That's a good sign."

The roadman nodded abstractedly, and I could see that his mind was elsewhere. "Aye, well, that's grand . . . ah'm right pleased." His eyes looked past me vacantly for a few moments, then he suddenly seemed to come back to the world.

"Mr. Herriot!" His voice took on an unaccustomed urgency. "There's summat I want to ask ye."

"Oh, yes?"

"Aye, I'll tell you what it is." He looked at me eagerly. "Ah fancy goin' in for pigs in a big way."

"You mean . . . keep a lot of pigs?"

"That's right. Just pigs and nowt else, and keep 'em in a proper place."

"But that would mean building a piggery."

He thumped a fist into his palm. "You've just said it. That's what I fancy. I've allus liked pigs, and I'd like to do the job proper. Ah could build the piggery out there in t'field."

I looked at him in surprise. "But Lionel, these things cost a lot. There's the question of . . ."

"Money? Oh, ah've got t'money. Remember, me awd uncle died a bit back? Lived with us for years. Well, 'e left me a little legacy. Not a fortune, tha knows, but I could branch out a bit now."

"Well, it's up to you, of course," I said. "But are you sure it's what you really want? You've always seemed to be happy with

[352]

your bit of stock here, and you're not a youngster—you'll be fifty-odd, won't you?"

"Aye, I'm fifty-six, but they say you're never too old to have a go at something new."

I smiled. "Oh, I'm a strong believer in that. I'm all for it—providing you're happy doing it."

He looked very thoughtful and scratched his cheek a few times. I suppose, like most happy men, he didn't realise the fact. "Get bye, duck!" he grunted with a flash of irritation and nudged the Muscovy with his toe as it tried to march between his legs. Still deep in thought, he bent and lifted a hen's egg from the straw in the corner and put it in his pocket.

"Nay, ah've thought it over for a bit now, and me mind's made up. I've got to have a go."

"Okay, Lionel," I said. "Have at it, and the best of luck."

With a speed unusual in the Dales, the piggery took shape in the field. Rows of concrete pens with a covered yard appeared, and within a few weeks, sows and a boar were installed in the pens and a solid bunch of porkers grunted among the straw in the yard.

To me, this modern structure looked out of place, with the ancient dry-stone walls encircling its green setting and the smooth bulk of the fell rising to the stark moorland above, but I hoped it would bring Lionel the satisfaction he craved.

He still carried on with his road work. He had to get up earlier in the morning to feed and clean out his pigs, but he was a fit man and seemed to be enjoying it.

His vet bills went up, of course, but there was nothing serious, and everything I treated went on well—an occasional sow with mastitis, a farrowing, a few piglets with joint ill. He accepted these things without complaint because the old adage, "Where there's stock there's trouble," was as familiar to him as to anybody else.

The only thing that bothered me a little was that, whereas, before, he spent a lot of time just leaning on his various partitions looking at his animals and smoking his pipe, he now had no time for that. He was always bustling about, pushing wheelbarrows, filling up troughs, mucking out, and it seemed to me that all this was foreign to his nature.

He certainly wasn't as relaxed as he had been. He was happy enough, caring for his fine new charges, but there was a tautness in his expression, a slight anxiety that had not been there before.

There was anxiety in his voice, too, when he rang up one evening. "Just got back from work, Mr. Herriot, and there's some young pigs here I don't like t'look of."

"What symptoms are they showing, Lionel?"

"Well, they haven't been doin' right for a bit. Not thrivin' like the others. But they've been eatin' and not really off it, like, so I haven't bothered you."

"But how about now?"

There was a pause. "They look different now. They're kind o' crambly on their back legs, and they're scourin' a bit . . . and there's one dead. Ah'm a bit worried."

I was worried, too. Instantly and profoundly. It sounded horribly like swine fever. In my early days those two words were burned into my soul, and yet, to the modern young vet, they don't mean a thing.

For around twenty years I was literally haunted by swine fever. Whenever I did a postmortem on a dead pig, I feared I might come across the dreaded button ulcers and haemorrhages. And what I feared still more was that I might fail to spot the disease and be responsible for its spread.

It wasn't as bad as foot-and-mouth in that respect, but the same principles held good. If I didn't recognise the symptoms, pigs might go from that farm to a market and be sold to places scattered over many miles. And every pig would carry its own load of infection and would spread the incurable disease among its healthy neighbours. Then the Ministry of Agriculture would be called in, and they would painstakingly trace the thing right back to Herriot, the man who had made the original unforgivable blunder.

[354]

It was a recurring nightmare, because, unlike foot-and-mouth, the disease was a common one, waiting round the corner all the time. I often used to think I would be blissfully happy if only there were no such thing as swine fever. In fact, when I look back at all the worry it caused me and my contemporaries, I feel that the present-day veterinarians should leap happily from their beds each morning and dance around the room crying out, "Hurrah, hurrah, there's no swine fever now!"

At the farm, Lionel led me to a pen at the far end of the yard.

"They're in there," he said gloomily.

I leaned over the wall, and a wave of misery flowed through me. There were about a dozen young pigs in the pen—around sixteen weeks old—and they were nearly all showing the same symptoms.

They were thin and had a scruffy, unthrifty look, the backs of their ears were a dark purple-red, they staggered slightly as they walked and a thin diarrhea ran down the limp-hanging tails. I took a few temperatures. They were around 106.

It was classical—straight out of the book—but I didn't tell Lionel right away. In fact, I wasn't allowed to until I had gone through all the ritual.

"Where did you get this lot?" I asked.

"Haverton market. They were a right-good level bunch when they came, but by gaw they've gone down." He pushed at a little corpse with his Wellington. "And now ah've got this dead 'un."

"Yes . . . well, I'll have to open him up and look inside him, Lionel." My voice sounded weary. I was starting again on the agonising merry-go-round. "I'll get my knife from the car."

I came back with the postmortem knife, rolled the dead pig on its back and slit open the abdomen. How often had I done this with just the same feeling of taut apprehension?

The region of the ileo-caecal valve was the textbook site, and I aimed for it first. But as I cut into the intestine and scraped the mucosa with my knife, I found only haemorrhages and small necrotic spots, some dark red, others yellowish.

Sometimes you found the real thing further along in the colon,

[355]

and for a long time I snipped my way along the coils of bowel with my scissors without finding anything definite.

Here I was again. I was sure this was swine fever, but I couldn't say so to the farmer. The Ministry insisted that theirs was the right of diagnosis, and until they issued confirmation I could say nothing.

There were the usual petechial haemorrhages in kidney and bladder, but not one typical ulcer.

I sat back on my heels. "Lionel, I'm very sorry, but I'll have to report this as a suspected case of swine fever."

"Oh, 'ell, that's bad, isn't it?"

"Yes . . . yes, it is. But we can't be positive until the Ministry confirms it. I'm going to take samples and send them off to the laboratory in Surrey."

"And can't you do owt to cure them?"

"No, I'm afraid not. It's a virus, you see. There's no cure."

"And how about t'others? Does it spread?"

I cringed at having to answer, but there was no point in playing the thing down. "Yes, it spreads like anything. You'll have to take every precaution. Keep a tray of disinfectant outside this pen, and dip your boots if you have to go in. In fact, I would go in as little as possible. Feed and water them over the top, and always attend to the healthy pigs first."

"And how about if me other pigs get it? How many are goin' to die?"

Another horrible question. The books say the mortality rate is eighty to a hundred percent. In my experience it had been a hundred percent.

I took a long breath. "Lionel, they could all die."

The roadman looked slowly over the rows of new concrete pens with their sows and litters, and the pigs rooting happily among the straw in the yard. I felt I had to say something, however lame.

"Anyway, it might not be what I fear. I'll send these samples off to the lab and let you know what they say. In the meantime, get these powders into them, either in their food or by dosing."

I stowed the loops of bowel in my car boot, then went round the piggery making notes of the different grades of pigs. Because another little purgatory lay ahead of me—the filling up of the forms. I have a blind spot where forms are concerned, and the swine fever form was a horrendous pink thing about two feet long, with closely packed questions on each side about how many sows and boars and unweaned pigs and weaned pigs and fattening pigs, and heaven help you if you got any of the numbers wrong.

That evening at Skeldale House I wrestled with this pink thing for a long time, then turned to the real horror—the packing of the sample of bowel. The Ministry provided a special little outfit for this purpose. At first sight it looked just like a flat square of corrugated cardboard, some pieces of grease-proof paper, several lengths of hairy string and a sheet of brown paper. However, on closer examination you found that the cardboard folded into a small square box. The instructions were very explicit. You didn't just bung a piece of bowel into the box; you had to lay a three-feet portion lengthwise on the grease-proof paper, then fold the ends of the paper inwards and tie the whole thing up in one of the pieces of string.

However, there was a catch here, because among the swine fever kit were two stridently printed red and black cards saying, "Pathological Specimen. Urgent." With spaces for the address of the infected premises and all kinds of things. These cards had holes in each end, and the string containing the bowel had to be threaded through these holes before the box was closed. The other card went on the outside.

I painstakingly went through the ritual, and as I finally fumbled the string through the holes in the outside card and tied the box in the brown paper, I fell back exhausted because this sort of thing took more out of me than calving cows.

It was then, just as I was staring with glazed eyes at the envelopes containing the form for Head Office and the one for

[357]

Divisional Office, the cardboard creation packed at last, that I saw the other card lying on the table. I had forgotten to include it with the contents.

"Damn and blast it to hell!" I yelled. "I always do that! I bloody well always do that!"

Helen must have thought I might have had some kind of seizure because she hurried through to the dispensary where I was working.

"Are you all right?" she asked anxiously.

I hung my head and nodded weakly. "Yes, sorry. It's just this damned swine fever."

"Well, all right, Jim." She looked at me doubtfully. "But try to keep your voice down. You'll wake the children."

In grim silence I dismantled the box, threaded in the card and reconstructed the outfit once more. I had done this so often, and, oh, how I hated it. I thought bitterly that if ever I wanted something to kill a quiet evening, I had only to do an S.F. report.

I took the thing to the station and sent it off, and in an attempt to ease my mind I turned to one of my veterinary bibles, Udall's *Practice of Veterinary Medicine.* Even among those hallowed pages I found little comfort. The great man's pronouncements only reconfirmed my suspicions. He was an American and he called it hog cholera, but everything he described reminded me of what I had seen on Lionel's place. He talked about injection of serum to protect the healthy pigs, but I had tried that, and it just didn't work. It would be more expense for Lionel, with nothing to show for it.

Within a few days I got the result. The Ministry was unable to confirm the presence of swine fever on these premises. On that day I also heard from the roadman.

"Them pigs is worse. Your powders have done no good, and I 'ave another dead 'un."

Again the dash out to the piggery and the postmortem examination, and this time, as I slit the intestine along its length, I really thought I had found something definite. Surely those ulcers were slightly raised and concentric. The Ministry must confirm it this time, and then, at least, we would know where we were.

I had another evening of form filling and another struggle with the cardboard box and the papers, but as I sent off the samples, I was very hopeful that my doubts would be resolved.

When the word came back that the Ministry was once more unable to confirm the disease, I could have cried.

I appealed to Siegfried. "What the hell are they playing at? Can you tell me how they ever do diagnose S.F. from these samples at the lab?"

"Oh, yes." My partner looked at me gravely. "They take the length of bowel from the paper and throw it against the ceiling. If it sticks there it's a positive, if it falls off it's negative."

I gave a hollow laugh. "I've heard that one before, and sometimes I feel like believing it."

"But don't be too hard on the Ministry boys," Siegfried said. "Remember, they have to be dead sure before they confirm, and they'd look damn silly if they were wrong. Lots of things can look like S.F. You find necrotic ulcers in worm infestations, for instance. It's not easy."

I groaned. "Oh, I know, I know. I'm not blaming them, really. It's just that poor old Lionel Brough is sitting on the edge of a precipice, and I can't do anything to help him."

"Yes, James, it's a hell of a situation. I've been there and I know."

Two days later Lionel rang to say he had another dead pig. This time I found more typical ulcers, and though I still had no idea what the Ministry would say, I knew exactly what I had to do. My brain seemed to have worked it out during the night hours because my decision was crystal clear.

"Lionel," I said, "you've got to slaughter every healthy pig on the place."

His eyes widened. "But there's hardly any of 'em ready for killin' yet. And there's in-pig sows and all sorts."

"Yes, I know, but if the disease had been confirmed, I would have advised you to get rid of them all. You are under restrictions, as you know, and you can't send any pigs to the market, but I can give you a licence for all the healthy pigs to go to the bacon factory."

"Aye, but . . ."

"I can understand how you feel, Lionel. It's tragic, but if once the disease gets among your other pigs, I won't be able to give you a licence then, and you'll just have to watch them die. This way I can save you about a couple of thousand pounds."

"But the bacon pigs . . . the porkers . . . ah'd get a lot more in two months from now."

"Yes, but you'd get something for them now and nothing if they get swine fever. And apart from the money, wouldn't you rather have your pigs humanely slaughtered than see them waste away like this sick lot?"

My words brought home to me the fundamental sadness of a country vet's work—that so many of our patients are ultimately destined for the butcher's hook, and no matter how attractive farm animals may be, all our activities have a commercial foundation.

"Well, ah don't know. It's a big thing." He looked again over the new piggery and the animals he had tended so carefully, then he turned and gave me a level stare. "And what if it isn't swine fever?"

He had me there. Under those steady eyes I could only give him an honest answer. "If it isn't, Lionel, I'll be costing you thousands instead of saving you thousands."

"Aye . . . aye . . . I see that. But you think it is?"

"As I told you before, I am not allowed to make an official diagnosis, but in my own mind I'm bloody sure it is."

He nodded quickly. "Right, Mr. Herriot. Start makin' out your licences. I've got a bit o' faith in you."

A "bit o' faith" was a tremendous compliment from a plain Yorkshireman, and I hoped fervently that it was not misplaced. I got out my blue forms and started to write.

It wasn't long before the new piggery was an empty, silent place. There remained only the pen of affected animals, and they died off rapidly. With all its terrors I was sure that swine fever was not a painful disease, and the one gleam of light in the little tragedy was that the diseased pigs quietly faded away and the others had a humane end. There was no real suffering.

Towards the end of the episode I heard from the Ministry that they had confirmed the disease. I showed the letter to Lionel, and he put his spectacles on and read it through carefully.

"You were right, then," he said. "So it were a good job we did what we did." He folded the paper and handed it back to me. "I got a nice bit from the factory for them pigs we sent in, and if we'd hung on I'd have got nowt. Ah'm grateful to ye."

So that was what I got from that simple roadman after he had seen his dream collapse and melt away—no moaning, no complaints, only gratitude.

Different people reacted in different ways when they were ravaged by this terrible thing, but thank heaven it is all in the past now. A Crystal Violet vaccine was introduced and this helped to control the disease, but finally the Ministry started a compulsory slaughter policy, as in foot-and-mouth, and that was the end of swine fever. It must be nearly thirty years since I had to witness these disasters and wrestle with the forms and boxes and grease-proof papers, but the memory still lingers.

In the meantime, I wondered what Lionel would do with his new buildings. When the last pig had gone, he meticulously cleaned out and disinfected the place, but he didn't say anything about his intentions. When the place had stood empty for four months, I concluded that he had had enough of large-scale farming, but I was wrong.

One evening when I had finished seeing a few dogs and cats, I found him sitting in a corner of the waiting room.

"Mr. Herriot," he said without preamble, "I want to start again."

"You mean, with pigs?"

[361]

"Aye, ah want to fill that place up again. Can't bear seein' it standin' empty."

I looked at him thoughtfully. "Are you absolutely sure? You took a nasty knock last time. I thought it might have put you off."

"Nay, nay—ah still have this feelin'. I want to be in pigs. There's just one thing, and that's what I've come to ask ye. Could there be any of them germs left from t'last do?"

It was the sort of question I don't like being asked. In theory, the infection should have died out on that place long ago, but I had heard some funny things about the swine fever virus surviving for long periods. But four months . . . the place had to be safe by now.

Anyway, it's not much help when a vet says he doesn't know. This man wanted an answer.

"I'm sure it would be safe to bring more pigs on now—if you've quite made up your mind."

"Right, right, ah'll get started again." He turned and left me as though he couldn't begin quickly enough.

And, indeed, it wasn't long before the piggery echoed once more to the grunts, snorts and squeals of a new colony. And it wasn't long, either, before trouble struck.

Lionel's voice on the phone was more agitated than I had ever heard it. "I've just got back from me work, and me pigs are in a 'ell of a state. Laid out all over t'place."

My heart gave one mighty wallop against my ribs. "What do you mean . . . laid out?"

"Well, it's like they were takin' fits."

"Fits!"

"Aye, they're on their sides, kickin' and slaverin', and when they get up they stagger around and fall down again."

"I'll be right out." The receiver rattled on its rest as I replaced it. I felt suddenly drained. I had advised this poor man that it was safe to restock, and there was no doubt swine fever could display nervous symptoms. I rushed for Udall and whipped through the pages. Yes, by God, there it was. "Motor irritation may be noted in the beginning in the form of circling, muscular twitchings and even convulsions."

I didn't see a thing as I threw my car at full speed along the narrow road. I never even noticed the trees speeding past the windows or the green fell rising beyond. I had only a horrid mental picture of what was waiting for me at the other end.

And it was worse than I expected. Much worse. The yard was littered with pigs of all sizes, from young stores to big pregnant sows. Some of them were reeling and toppling in the straw, but most were on their sides, foaming at the mouth, trembling and pedalling frantically with their feet at the empty air. Udall had talked about convulsions, and, dear God, I had never seen worse convulsions than these.

Pale-faced and wordless, Lionel led me round the pens. Suckling sows lay twitching as their litters fought at their udders for milk. The boar paced around his area like a blind thing, bumping into the walls, then sitting down, doglike, in a stupor. There was hardly a normal animal on the place.

The roadman turned to me with an attempt at a smile. "Well, we can't licence off the healthy 'uns this time. There aren't any."

I shook my head dumbly. I was utterly bewildered. I found my voice at last. "When did this start?"

"They were all right as ninepence this mornin', t'whole lot of 'em. Bawlin' for their grub like they allus do. Then when I came 'ome, they were like this."

"But dammit, Lionel," I said almost in a shout, "it's too sudden! It doesn't make sense!"

He nodded. "Aye, that's what t'plumber said when 'e saw them. Got a bit of a shock, did t'feller."

"Plumber?"

"Aye, the missus noticed at dinnertime that t'pigs had no water. She sent for Fred Buller, and 'e came out this afternoon. Said there was a blockage in the pipes somewhere. He's put it right now."

"Then they've been without water most of the day?"

"Ah reckon so. They must 'ave."

Oh, glory be, now I knew. I was still full of apprehension, but the weight of guilt was suddenly lifted from me. Whatever happened now, it wasn't my fault.

"So that's it!" I gasped.

Lionel looked at me questioningly. "What d'ye mean? The water? That 'ud only make 'em a bit thirsty."

"They're not thirsty, they've got salt poisoning."

"Salt poisoning? But they haven't 'ad no salt."

"Yes, they have. There's salt in nearly all pig meal." My mind was racing. What was the first thing to do? I grabbed his arm and hustled him into the yard. "Come on, let's get some of these pigs onto their feet."

"But they've allus had the same meal. What's happened today?" He looked mystified as we trotted through the straw.

I selected a big sow that was lying quiet between convulsions and started to push at her shoulder. "They've been without water. That's what happened. And that causes a higher concentration of salt in the brain. Gives them fits. Push, Lionel, push! We've got to get her over to that trough. There's plenty of water in there now."

I could see he thought I was raving but he helped me to raise the sow to her feet, and we supported her on either side as she tottered up to the long metal trough that bounded one side of the yard. She took a few gulps at the water, then collapsed.

Lionel took a few panting breaths. "She hasn't had much."

"No, and that's a good thing. Too much makes them worse. Let's try this other pig. She's lying very still."

"Makes 'em worse?" He began to help me to lift. "How the 'ell's that?"

"Never mind," I puffed. "It just does." I couldn't very well tell him that I didn't know myself, that I had never seen salt poisoning before and that I was only going by the book.

He groaned as we pushed the second pig towards the trough.

"God 'elp us. This is a bloody funny carry-on. I've never seen owt like this."

Neither have I, I thought. And I only hoped all those things I was taught at college were true.

We spent a busy hour, assisting the stricken animals to the water or carefully dosing them when they were unable to move. We did this by pushing a Wellington boot with the toe cut off into the mouths and pouring the water down the leg of the boot. A pig would certainly crunch the neck off a glass bottle.

The animals with the most powerful convulsions I injected with a sedative to control the spasms.

When we had finished, I looked round the piggery. All the animals had got some water into them and were lying within easy reach of the troughs. As I watched, several of them got up, took a few swallows, then lay down. That was just what I wanted.

"Well," I said wearily, "we can't do anymore."

He shrugged. "Right, come in and 'ave a cup o' tea."

As I followed him to the house, I could tell by the droop of his shoulders that he had lost hope. He had a defeated look, and I couldn't blame him. My words and actions must have seemed crazy to him. They did even to me.

When the bedside phone rang at seven o'clock in the morning, I reached for it with half-closed eyes, expecting the usual calving or milk fever, but it was Lionel.

"I'm just off to me work, Mr. Herriot, but I thowt you'd like to know about them pigs first."

I snapped wide awake. "Yes, I would. How are they?"

"They're awright."

"How do you mean, all right? Are they all alive?"

"Aye, every one."

"Are they ill in any way?"

"Nay, nay, every one of 'em shoutin' for their breakfast just like they were yesterday mornin'."

I fell back on the pillow, still grasping the phone, and my sigh of relief must have been audible at the other end because Lionel chuckled.

"Aye, that's how ah feel, too, Mr. Herriot. By gaw, it's a miracle. I thought ye'd gone round the bend yesterday with all that salt talk, but you were right, lad. Talk about savin' ma bacon —ye really did it, didn't ye?"

I laughed. "I suppose I did. In more ways than one."

Over my forty years in practice, I have seen only about half a dozen cases of salt poisoning or water deprivation or whatever you like to call it. I don't suppose it is all that common. But the one at Lionel's stays in my mind as the most exciting and the happiest.

I thought this unexpected triumph would settle the roadman down for good as a pig keeper, but I was wrong again. It was several weeks before I was on his place, and just as I was leaving, a young man rode up on a bicycle.

Lionel introduced him. "This is Billy Fothergill, Mr. Herriot." I shook hands with a smiling lad of about twenty-two.

"Billy's takin' over ma place next month."

"What?"

"It's right. Ah've sold 'im the pigs, and he's goin' to rent the building's from me. In fact, he's doin' all t'work now."

"Well, I'm surprised, Lionel," I said. "I thought you were doing what you wanted to do."

He looked at me quizzically. "So did I, for a bit. But ah'll tell ye, that salt job really gave me a shock. I thowt I was ruined, and that's a nasty feelin' at my time of life. Billy's been pigman for Sir Thomas Rowe for three years, and he's just got married. Feels like branchin' out for 'imself, like."

I looked at the young man. He wasn't tall, but the bullet head, muscular shoulders and slightly bowed legs gave the impression of great power. He looked as though he could run through a brick wall.

"Ah know it's for t'best," Lionel went on. "That piggery was all right, but it was allus just a bit on top o' me. Sort of a worry, like. I reckon Billy'll manage the job better than me."

I looked again at Billy's stubby features, at the brown skin, the unclouded eyes and the confident grin.

"Oh yes," I said. "He'll manage all right."

As the roadman walked back towards my car with me, I tapped his elbow. "But Lionel, aren't you going to miss your livestock? It was your great hobby, wasn't it?"

"By gaw, you're right. It was and it still is. Ah couldn't do without some stock to look after. I've filled up t'awd hut again. Come and have a look."

We walked over to the hut and opened the door, and it was like turning back the clock—a cow, three calves, two goats, two pigs and some assorted poultry, all sectioned off with outlandish partitions. I could see the bed frames and wire netting with loops of binder twine hanging from every corner. The only difference was that he had moved the dining table to a position immediately inside the door, and a grand-piano lid stood proudly by the side of the cow.

He pointed out the various animals and gave me a brief history of each, and as he spoke there was a contentment in his face that had been absent for some time.

"Only two pigs, eh, Lionel?" I said.

He nodded slowly. "Aye, it's enough."

I left him there and went over to the car, and as I opened the door I looked back across the field. From this angle I could shut out the garish new piggery so that I saw only the stone cottage with its sheltering trees and the old hut nearby. The roadman was leaning against the upended dining table, and as he gazed in at his mixed charges, the smoke from his pipe rose high against the back-cloth of the hills. The whole picture looked just right, and I smiled to myself.

That was Lionel's kind of farming.

Chapter
38

It was a Sunday morning in June, and I was washing my hands in the sink in Matt Clarke's kitchen. The sun was bright, with a brisk wind scouring the fell-sides, so that through the window I could see every cleft and gully lying sharp and clear on the green flanks as the cloud shadows drove across them.

I glanced back beyond the stone flags at the white head of Grandma Clarke bent over her knitting. The radio on the dresser was tuned to the morning service and, as I watched, the old lady looked up from her work and listened intently to some words of the sermon for a few moments before starting her needles clicking again.

In that brief time I had a profound impression of serenity and unquestioning faith that has remained with me to this day. It is a strange thing, but over the years whenever I have heard discussions and arguments on religion, on the varying beliefs and doctrines, on the sincerity or otherwise of some pious individuals, there still rises before me the seamed old face and calm eyes of Grandma Clarke. She knew and was secure. Goodness seemed to flow from her.

She was in her late eighties and always dressed in black with a little black neckband. She had come through the hard times of farming and could look back on a long life of toil, in the fields as well as in the home.

As I reached for the towel, the farmer led Rosie into the kitchen.

"Mr. Clarke's been showing me some baby chicks, Daddy," she said.

Grandma looked up again. "Is that your little lass, Mr. Herriot?"

"Yes, Mrs. Clarke," I replied. "This is Rosie."

"Aye, of course. I've seen her before, many a time." The old lady put down her knitting and rose stiffly from her chair. She shuffled over to a cupboard, brought out a gaily coloured tin and extracted a bar of chocolate.

"How old are ye now, Rosie?" she asked as she presented the chocolate.

"Thank you, I'm six," my daughter replied.

Grandma looked down at the smiling face, at the sturdy, tanned legs in their blue shorts and sandals. "Well, you're a grand little lass." For a moment she rested her work-roughened hand against the little girl's cheek, then she returned to her chair. They didn't make much of a fuss, those old Yorkshire folk, but to me the gesture was like a benediction.

The old lady picked up her knitting again. "And how's that lad o' yours? How's Jimmy?"

"Oh, he's fine thank you. Ten years old now. He's out with some of his pals this morning."

"Ten, eh? Ten and six . . . ten and six . . ." For a few seconds her thoughts seemed far away as she plied her needles, then she looked at me again. "Maybe ye don't know it, Mr. Herriot, but this is the best time of your life."

"Do you think so?"

"Aye, there's no doubt about it. When your children are young and growin' up around ye—that's when it's best. It's the same for everybody, only a lot o' folk don't know it and a lot find out when it's too late. It doesn't last long, you know."

"I believe I've always realised that, Mrs. Clarke, without thinking about it very much."

[369]

"Reckon you have, young man." She gave me a sideways smile. "You allus seem to have one or t'other of your bairns with you on your calls."

As I drove away from the farm, the old lady's words stayed in my mind. They are still in my mind, all these years later, when Helen and I are soon about to celebrate our Ruby Wedding of forty years of marriage. Life has been good to us and is still good to us. We are lucky—we have had so many good times—but I think we both agree that Grandma Clarke was right about the very best time of all.

When I got back to Skeldale House that summer morning, I found Siegfried replenishing the store of drugs in his car boot. His children, Alan and Janet, were helping him. Like me, he usually took his family around with him.

He banged down the lid of the boot. "Right, that's that for another few days." He glanced at me and smiled. "There are no more calls at the moment, James; let's have a walk down the back."

With the children running ahead of us, we went through the passage and out into the long garden behind the house. Here the sunshine was imprisoned between the high old walls, with the wind banished to the upper air and ruffling the top leaves of the apple trees.

When we reached the big lawn, Siegfried flopped on the turf and rested on his elbow. I sat down by his side.

My partner pulled a piece of grass and chewed it contemplatively.

"Pity about the acacia," he murmured.

I looked at him in surprise. It was many years since the beautiful tree, which had once soared from the middle of the lawn, had blown down in a gale.

"Yes, it is," I said. "It was magnificent." I paused for a moment. "Remember, I fell asleep against it the first day I came here to apply for a job? We first met right on this spot."

Siegfried laughed. "I do remember." He looked around him at the mellow brick and stone copings of the walls, at the rockery and rose bed, the children playing in the old henhouse at the far end. "My word, James, when you think about it, we've come through a few things together since then. A lot of water, as they say, has flown under the bridge."

We were both silent for a while, and my thoughts went back over the struggles and the laughter of those years. Almost unconsciously I lay back on the grass and closed my eyes, feeling the sun warm on my face, hearing the hum of the bees among the flowers, the croaking of the rooks in the great elms that overhung the yard.

My colleague's voice seemed to come from afar. "Hey, you're not going to do the same trick again, are you? Going to sleep in front of me?"

I sat up, blinking. "Gosh, I'm sorry, Siegfried, I nearly did. I was out at a farrowing at five o'clock this morning and it's just catching up with me."

"Ah, well," he said, smiling. "You won't need your book tonight."

I laughed. "No, I won't. Not tonight."

Neither Siegfried nor I suffered from insomnia, but on the rare occasions when sleep would not come we had recourse to our particular books. Mine was *The Brothers Karamazov*, a great novel, but to me, soporific in its names. Even at the beginning I felt those names lulling me. "Alexey Fyodorovich Karamazov was the third son of Fyodor Pavlovich Karamazov." Then, by the time I had encountered Grigory Kutuzov, Yefim Petrovich Polenov, Stepanida Bedryagina and a few others, I was floating away.

With Siegfried, it was a book on the physiology of the eye which he kept by his bedside. There was one passage that never failed to start him nodding. He showed it to me once: "The first ciliary muscle is inserted into the ciliary body and by its contraction pulls the ciliary body forward and so slackens the tension on the suspensory ligament, while the second ciliary muscle is a circular muscle embedded in the ciliary body and by its contraction drags the ciliary body towards the crystalline lens." He had never managed to get much further than that.

"No," I said, rubbing my eyes. "I won't need any encouragement tonight." I rolled onto my side. "By the way, I was at Matt Clarke's this morning." I told him what Grandma had said.

Siegfried selected a fresh piece of grass and resumed his chewing.

"Well, she's a wise old lady and she's seen it all. If she's right we'll have no regrets in the future, because we have both enjoyed our children and been with them from the beginning."

I was beginning to feel sleepy again when my partner startled me by sitting up abruptly.

"Do you know, James," he said, "I'm convinced that the same thing applies to our job. We're going through the best time there, too."

"Do you think so?"

"Sure of it. Look at all the new advances since the war—drugs and procedures we never dreamed of. We can look after our animals in a way that would have been impossible a few years ago, and the farmers realise this. You've seen them crowding into the surgery on market day to ask advice—they've gained a new respect for the profession and they know it pays to call in the vet now."

"That's true," I said. "We're certainly busier than we've ever been, with the Ministry work going full blast, too."

"Yes, everything is buzzing. In fact, James, I'd like to bet that these present years are the high noon of country practice."

I thought for a moment. "You could be right. But if we are on the top now, does it mean that our lives will decline later?"

"No, no, of course not. They'll be different, that's all. I sometimes think we've only touched the fringe of so many other things, like small-animal work." Siegfried brandished his gnawed piece of grass at me and his eyes shone with the enthusiasm that always uplifted me.

"I tell you, this, James. There are great days ahead!"